THE BRITISH
OF THE ABDUCTION
AND GRAIL ROMANCES

Flint Johnson

University Press of America,® Inc.
Lanham · New York · Oxford

Copyright © 2002 by
University Press of America,® Inc.
4720 Boston Way
Lanham, Maryland 20706
UPA Acquisitions Department (301) 459-3366

12 Hid's Copse Rd.
Cumnor Hill, Oxford OX2 9JJ

All rights reserved
Printed in the United States of America
British Library Cataloging in Publication Information Available

Library of Congress Cataloging-in-Publication Data

Johnson, Flint.
The British sources of the abduction and Grail romances /
Flint Johnson.
p. cm
Originally presented as author's thesis (Ph. D.)
Includes bibliographical references (p.) and index.
1. Chrâtien, de Troyes, 12th cent. Chevalier de la charrette.
2. Lancelot (Legendary character)—Romances—History and criticism. 3. Chrâtien, de Troyes, 12th cent. Perceval le Gallois.
4. Perceval (Legendary character)—Romances—History and criticism. 5. Arthurian romances—History and criticism. I. Title.

PQ1445.L5 J64 2002
841'.1—dc21   2002018999 CIP

ISBN 0-7618-2218-6 (paperback : alk. ppr.)

The paper used in this publication meets the minimum
requirements of American National Standard for Information
Sciences—Permanence of Paper for Printed Library Materials,
ANSI Z39.48—1984

Table of Contents

Illustrations   v

Abbreviations   vii

Foreword   ix

Preface   xi

Acknowledgements   xvii

Le Chevalier de la Charrette

I. The Early Arthurian Romances   1

II. Chrétien's Known Sources and Influences   11

III. The Characters and their Roles   35

IV. Literary Tools	47
V. Motifs and Details: Clues of Celtic Origins	57
VI. The Sixth Century in Chrétien	81
VII. Conclusion	91

Le Conte du Graal

VIII. Introduction to *Le Conte du Graal*	95
IX. Philip of Flanders	99
X. Theories Regarding the Grail's Origins	105
XI. The Characters and their Roles	131
XII. Literary Tools	143
XIII. Religion in fifth- and sixth-century Britain	165
XIV. Motifs and Details: Clues of Celtic Origins	179
XV. The Sixth Century in Chrétien	203
XVI. Conclusion	209
Appendices	219
Primary Sources	225
Secondary Sources	231
Index	245

Illustrations

Hypothetical development of the *Northern Memoranda*	15
The Angevin Kingdom, c. 1100	19
Development of *Lanzelet*	49
Traditional developments of the common abduction story	52
The Meigle Chariot	81
Revised developments of the common abduction story	91
Progressive Influences on the Grail Legend	123
Traditional developments of the common grail story	155
Revised developments of the common grail story	209

Abbreviations

A	*Antiquity*
ASE	*Anglo-Saxon England*
B	*Bulletin of the Board of Celtic Studies*
CMCS	*Cambrian (Cambridge) Medieval Celtic Studies*
EC	*Étude Celtiques*
EHR	*English Historical Review*
LlC	*Llên Cymru*
MLN	*Modern Language Notes*
MP	*Modern Philology*
NMS	*Nottingham Medieval Studies*
PMLA	*Publications of the Modern Language Association of America*
PBA	*Proceedings of the British Academy*
PSAS	*Proceedings of the Society of Antiquaries of Scotland*
S	*Speculum*
SC	*Studia Celtica*
THSC	*Transactions of the Honourable Society of the Cymmrodorion*
TYP	*Trioedd Ynys Prydein: The Welsh Triads*, Rachel Bromwich (ed. and trans.)
TCWAAS	*Transactions of the Cumberland and Westmoreland Antiquarian and Archaeological Society*
TDGNAHS	*Transactions of the Dumfriesshire and Galloway Natural History and Antiquarian Society*
WHR	*Welsh History Review*
ZCP	*Zeitschrift für Celtische Philologie*
ZDP	*Zeitschrift für Deutsche Philologie*

Foreword

Flint Johnson's study, originally presented as a doctoral thesis, sets out to explore the possibility that familiar Arthurian stories which have come down to us through Medieval romance may contain relics of lost Welsh literary sources from the fifth or sixth century. He bases his analysis on the most popular and influential works by the French author, Chrétien de Troyes, the tale of the abduction of Guenevere, (*Le Chevalier de la Charrette*) and the early Grail romance (*Le Conte du Graal*).

On the one hand, the debt which Chrétien owes to his Celtic sources has long occupied critics such as Jessie Weston and Roger Sherman Loomis; and on the other we recognize in Chrétien the springboard for later treatments from Wolfram von Eschenbach through to Wagner and beyond. But Johnson's approach is novel; by comparing the various extant versions of his chosen stories, and scraping away the progressive influences which have shaped them, he attempts to uncover signs of original lost versions which can themselves shed light on the British Heroic Age within which we must assume that they were composed.

Thus, for each text, Johnson starts by looking at the role played by Chrétien's celebrated patrons in their conception and creation, Marie de Champagne for *Le Chevalier de la Charrette* and Philip of Flanders for *Le Conte du Graal*. In both cases he concludes that Chrétien manipulated his material to suit the whims of these political figures. But beneath the layer of interpretation fitted to the demands and expectations of the twelfth century, and through comparison with other early versions, it is possible to find evidence for versions independent of Chrétien's manipulative hand. These lost versions, in Johnson's view, reveal their origins at a date before 900, and possibly as early as of Chrétien's manipulative hand. These lost versions, in Johnson's view, reveal their origins at a date before 900, and possibly as early as the fifth century. He suggests the existence of written, literary texts at an early date, and, through attempting their partial reconstruction, hopes to provide the basis for a more complete understanding of fifth- and sixth-century Britain. Extending this approach to other texts of the twelfth and thirteenth centuries will be difficult, since there are few where the circumstances of their compositions can be reconstructed in the way they can for these two works by Chrétien de Troyes. Nevertheless, Flint Johnson has opened our eyes to new possibilities; his study will doubtless provide the impetus for further work in a popular field.

Alison Rawles   December 2000

Preface

In about 1136, a Welshman named Geoffrey of Monmouth wrote an ambitious composite of British literature and pseudo-history known as *Historia Regum Britanniae*. It featured a famed British figure named Arthur, who had been hitherto obscure to the continent.

Arthur was an immediate hero of medieval western Europe. This popularity was fortuitously supported by the size of Henry II's realm, which extended from Scotland south through half of France. This allowed for the unimpeded spread of the Arthurian legend to France and from there to all of Europe.

Quickly other British heroes were associated with Arthur.[1] The French musician/poets known as *trouvères* and *troubadours* formulated courtly personalities for them. Finally, the romance poet Chrétien de Troyes helped create a new genre with his Arthurian romances. Here he combined a British plot with the concept of courtly love and a broad knowledge of ancient and contemporary literature. The subject matter introduced by Geoffrey of Monmouth and the manner of presentation brought to fruition by Chrétien de Troyes influenced and at times served as an inspiration for thousands of medieval and modern writers. Their influence continues to do so to the present.

However, the British sources of information for Geoffrey, Chrétien, and many of the early romance writers remain in doubt. Geoffrey undoubtedly drew on Welsh genealogical tracts and Bede (Piggott 1941, 269-86), but beyond this scholars must remain uncertain. With many early romance writers nothing but a British plot and characters' names have been distinguished.

The trends in Celtic scholarship would favor caution about selecting a specific source or sources for the romances. Every major British written source for this period has come under scrutiny in the past twenty years. In several major articles Professor Dumville has demonstrated that *Historia Brittonum* is a composite, pseudo-historical book that has only a limited use as an historical source.[2] Gildas' historical prelude to his denunciation of several contemporary British kings in *De Excidio Britanniae* (c. 535) is often vague and historically incorrect. It has long been known that Gildas designed his preface to introduce a religio-political theme he then follows throughout his *Denuncio*.[3] Kathleen Hughes' study of *Annales Cambriae* has demonstrated that the original document was compiled in St. David's from 795 on (1975, 234-5). She has also shown that from the years 613 to 795 it drew on Irish chronicles and the *Northern British Chronicle* (1975, 242).

Professor Jackson, Dr. Jarman, and Professor Dumville have advocated a more tentative stance to the poem *Y Gododdin* concerning its historicity and reliability as a literary source of the sixth century.[4] In addition, Sims-Williams has stressed that few of the literary materials may be dated earlier than pre 1150. Thus, much of the native Welsh material cannot be proven to be free of Geoffrey's influence, especially when it comes to Arthur (Sims-Williams 1991, 35-6).

This thesis is in part a response to their labors. The above-mentioned scholars have cumulatively demonstrated the seeming futility of reconstructing fifth-century British history with the limited resources available, and therefore have inferred the desire for more material with which to work. This is the service I am rendering here. Although I do not pretend to fully understand the fifth century, I have here presented a good case for accepting two new sources British sources for this period. Future research may open new avenues which are not currently visible, but I think it more useful to propose a new and possibly incorrect thesis than to never make the attempt.

It is my contention that other, ancient literary sources of information, did exist in Britain at one point and dealt in the main with fifth- and sixth-century figures.[5] These oral and literary records were the rudimentary beginnings of the King Arthur of the medieval literary world. This data was transferred to the continent at a later stage, most likely during the eleventh and twelfth centuries, and as tales or, less probably, sagas.[6]

Further, I believe four of the five extant Arthurian poems written by Chrétien are based on one or several of these sources of information from Britain. I do not include the poem *Cligés* in this suggestion for several reasons. *Cligés*, despite Chrétien's statement and the Celtic names, is an invention. It contains none of the basic Celtic elements of the other romances and is clearly an attempt by the poet to pull away from the source material he was using.[7]

I avoid introducing both *Erec* and *Yvain* as literary sources for the fifth century chiefly because these two poems have been given a one-dimensional label. They have been widely accepted by Celtic scholars as being sovereignty myths. Both of these poems also contain comparatively little material that is definitively Celtic and therefore would produce less conclusive evidence. No such consensus has been reached concerning *Le Chevalier de la Charrette* and *Le Conte du Graal*. It may, however, be possible to pursue the former two poems from an historical perspective at a later time.

I believe it is possible to reconstruct the latter two tales' British prototypes with the use of several parallel versions that were also dependent on British sources. Further, I believe one might date these prototypes safely in the ninth century and tentatively as early as the sixth century. The idea that the Arthurian romance writers of the late-eleventh and early-twelfth centuries were historians in any sense is not suggested. Certainly no sixth-century Celtic warrior crawled across a sword, as Lancelot does in *La Charrette*. I would, however, suggest that the persons who wrote of these two romances accessed a body of sources deriving from the fifth century, whether this was directly or at one remove.[8] This notion is not as unreasonable as it may at first seem. Many pieces of myth and legend have often been found to contain some facts within the context of a purely non-historical story. In Greek myth, a voyage to Africa and the beheading of a Libyan queen by Perseus is a record of a conquest and the suppression of a matriarchal system in Africa (Graves 1955, 244). The invasion of the Heraclids may be an oral remain of the historical Dorian conquest (Graves 1955, 573). Even mythical islands of various nations have been geographically located.[9]

Central to these tales is Chrétien, the first and most imitated court poet of the continent during the middle ages. It is through an understanding of him that a solid concept of the original version of the hero tales may be achieved.

It is with these premises that I begin. I write with the further belief that the *Northern Memoranda* proposed by Thurneysen and similar pseudo-historical British sources did exist.[10] These sources were accessible as late as the twelfth century as written manuscripts.[11]

My formula for determining whether scenes in Chrétien's poetry could be historical is analogy. This form of argument permits the greatest depth of understanding in the period, but has many likely pitfalls. I hope to minimize this problem by employing several sources of provenance from both before and after the Roman occupation in every instance. I will employ native knowledge of the Irish, Welsh, and Gaulish Celts, and Greek, Roman, archaeological, and textual sources to establish connections.[12] Wherever possible I will also compare Chrétien's poetry to what has been traditionally deduced as the common traits of the heroic age.

The method by which I choose to argue this point accommodates this alternate manner in which to look on the poems. Every scene and detail that is out of place will be compared to the regions that were British around 500. Without a full understanding of fifth- and early sixth-century British society, I will make use of the next best evidence; information about the Celts derived from Roman, Greek, and native sources for the pre-Roman and Medieval period. I will also employ British archaeological finds for the post-Roman period. This data will then be employed to form a likely composite picture of how certain aspects of post-Roman British civilization functioned.[13]

In addition to the above comparisons, I will use the various redactions of the two works to determine a *terminus post quem* for them. Following this, I will take the results of French scholars who have studied Chrétien to determine which scenes derive directly from continental sources and which are the result of his patrons. Those which are continental in origin generally may be forgotten forthwith; they represent later accretions to the tale, probably as the direct result of Chrétien himself. This group accounts for a surprisingly large amount of the poems.

Those elements that were directly influenced by his patrons Marie de Champagne or Philip de Flandres, on the other hand, are the most likely places to find hidden historical elements. In these scenes and details Chrétien has in some cases apparently been asked to edit and disguise an existing part of the plot that does not serve the patron's wishes. Chrétien would then replace the scene or detail with something especially palatable to his patrons. Knowing the motivations of both Marie and Philip, it is possible to identify and retrace these instances. I will then compare them to what can be discovered of sixth-century Britain using the meager resources at hand. It will be seen that among these elements there are a significant number that belong to the British culture before 900. A larger number of these elements can be placed there more easily than in the twelfth century.

Along with the development of this theme will be a concurrent evolution of the characters and their predictable roles in a reconstructable original. In the case of both poems I will identify and analyze all analogous material to determine a table of relative influences. The analysis of all the comparable material will also be employed to determine the probable role of each character in the prototype.

---

[1] This process may well have taken place and been completed before the twelfth century. Arthur is an extremely popular figure in Welsh legend and most probably had already attracted a number of originally independent figures to his literary court.

[2] See the bibliography for references to Professor Dumville's most important works on the subject. Dr. Charles Thomas-Edwards has disputed the degree to which *Historia Brittonum* may be trusted (1991), but not the composite nature of the book.

[3] See *Gildas: new approaches*, which largely assumes this reading of Gildas' *De Excidio Britanniae*.

[4] (Dumville 1988, 1-16; *Aneirin: Y Gododdin, Britain's Oldest Poem*, ed. Jarman 1990; *The Gododdin: The Oldest Scottish Poem*. ed. Jackson 1969).

[5] I will henceforth refer to this hypothetical Arthurian source as *Cadegr*. I do not pretend that this was one source, or was ever at one time collected into one compendium. It is simply a convenient term which I will use to designate the British Source Material which contains Arthurian references.

[6] The traditional definition, according to the *Oxford Dictionary*, is "Any of the narrative compositions in prose that were written in Iceland or Norway during the Middle Ages". This narrow definition has been expanded to include similar literature of other cultures. The "b" definition is "A narrative having the [real or supposed characteristics of the Icelandic sagas]; a story of heroic achievement or marvellous adventure." (Murray et al 1961, 364). It is this meaning which will be the intended one throughout this paper.

[7] There are many other tales in Arthuriana which are either unique or seem to be entirely the creation of the writer. Those stories that fall into the former category have no text with which to compare and are therefore uneconomical studies at this time. The strictly fictitious stories and those which are later versions of Arthurian subjects generally have few visible Celtic signs apart from the onomastic evidence and therefore offer little potential information.

[8] It is this author's belief that these would originally have been heroic age legends on their way to developing into epics as described in (Ker 1957, 13-15).

[9] (Sims-Williams 1991, 69, note 132). He lists Sumerian Dilmun and Polynesian Tuma.

[10] The theoretical work known as the *Northern Memoranda* is believed to be the base source from which *Historia Brittonum* and *Annales Cambriae* took their information. See Chapter II for a full discussion of the topic.

[11] It has been possible to date no poem before the ninth century, but Professor John T. Koch has offered some linguistic evidence that *Y Gododdin* may contain just such clues. See all the references to Professor Koch in the bibliography. The fact that the sources used by Chrétien were in part written has been established (Bromwich 1991b, 283). However, the chronological point from which these manuscripts originated is open to debate.

[12] I shall make comparisons to the Gaulish Celts whenever possible, but this source of data is limited.

[13] I do not pretend to be able to fully or partially reconstruct British society in this period. Again, I am making full use of the resources at hand with the understanding that any theory derived from these composite sources may be invalid. The reconstructions are the most reasonable which are possible based on the limited information on the period.

Acknowledgements

This thesis is not just the result of three years intensive study. It is the end product of many peoples' contributions, both indirectly and directly related to the Arthurian topic. My longtime sensei, Mr. Warren, has taught me the need for mental discipline, tempered with compassion. Mr. Schleh has shown me that being an infant at heart is a talent. He has also made me realize that there is nothing beyond my grasp, only beyond my imagination. Ms. Fuller and Ms. Moschovidou have supported me in ways beyond my abilities of expression.

There have also been many whose direct contributions to this book have been essential. I acknowledge gratefully the aid of Professor Caie, who accepted an unknown quantity as an advisee in an area outside his expertise. He did this only on the faith he had in my ability to learn. He has patiently read through the drafts and, slowly, painstakingly, taught me the nuances of academic writing. I hope I have not disappointed.

This book has had two illustrators. My sister, Kenna, who has drawn a more realistic version of what may have been a Pictish chariot, based on David Longley's drawing of a lost Pictish stone (page 84). And Amanda Pawlak, who was kind enough to create the cover.

To Dr. Rachel Bromwich I owe a special thanks. It was she who graciously contributed both her time and efforts into making sure a frightened third-year Ph.D. student had read the right material and understood the basic Celtic literary and historical concepts. Much of this volume would be in worse condition without her. It is quite possible that this volume would never have reached a finished status without her. However, I accept full responsibility for any misunderstandings I may have had with her pertaining to this topic.

I wish to record my thanks to Ms. Chowdhury, who has meticulously scrutinized much of this book in early draft. I also wish to express my gratitude to the Rector Dr. Richard Wilson and the Clerk of Senate Professor R. R. Whitehead. They helped overcome some administrative difficulties and Professor Whitehead additionally read some of the drafts of this thesis.

Finally, my doctoral examiners, Professor William Gillies and Dr. Alison Rawles have supplied me with the necessary criticisms and reading material to polish this, by far the largest research project I have ever written. Reviewing the changes they have suggested and the materials they have had me read over the past few months, I can see the present version of my argument would be in a far worse state without their guidance.

I would like to dedicate this book to my grandmother, Betty Beatty. I only wish she could have lived until this day. I hope my academic accomplishments have made her proud.

Chapter I: The Early Arthurian Romances

Nearly a century ago, Gaston Paris began the painstaking process of proving that Irish mythology had been a weighty influence in the French romances with his work on *Le Chevalier de la Charrette* (1883). Sir John Rhys[1] and Professor Roger Loomis[2] both expanded this focus to include all the medieval Arthurian romances. In addition, they used the Welsh tales to identify Celtic motifs as themes that were transmitted from an unRomanized Ireland to France through Britain and its bards.[3] The names and motifs of these works are so clearly British that the Welsh-Breton theory has become deeply rooted. Beginning with Professor O'Rahilly and followed by Dr. Proinsias Mac Cana and Dr. Bromwich, a trend toward thinking of the common Irish, British, and Arthurian themes as pan-Celtic motifs has gained ground.[4] However, there is still a latent tendency to see the Celtic themes in the continental romances as the result of a Breton/Welsh connection.

Since the early and middle part of this century, Rachel Bromwich has initiated a more thorough research method involving onomastic features of the Arthurian romances and Welsh story. She has shown that the legend of Arthur was transmitted to Europe both orally and by written means by analyzing how the names of established characters have altered in the comparable insular and continental tales. She has also demonstrated that this material came with a setting comparable to that in Welsh tales, with the names and personae of many of the characters.[5] Her position, that the Welsh literary traditions supplied the original stock to the continental Arthurian romances, now stands uncontested by all who study the Celtic side of the Arthurian phenomenon. The details about the method of transference to the continent and the name transformations of individual Arthurian characters, on the other hand, remain open to much debate.[6]

Celtic scholars have for the most part stood clear of Arthur, except as a literary character.[7] However, some of their studies during the past twenty-five years will have some bearing on the proposed topic as well. The work of Dr. Rachel Bromwich, Professor Patrick Sims-Williams, Dr. Brynley Roberts, and a host of others have improved the level of understanding of Middle Welsh literature concerning Arthur. The scholarly efforts of Dr. Kathleen Hughes, Dr. Peter Bartrum, Dr. Molly Miller, and Professor David Dumville have given Welsh scholarship a clearer perspective on the historical sources for the period.[8] Work on the heroic-age milieu by Professor Hector and Dr. Nora Chadwick has yet to be equaled.[9] The pertinent Middle Welsh literature has been thoroughly edited and discussed by Sir Ifor Williams, Professor Kenneth Jackson, Dr. Rachel Bromwich, and Dr. Marged Haycock.[10] An idea of post-Roman Britain's customs was given a solid framework upon which to build by Dr. Nora Chadwick. This was initiated through her work on the *Mabinogion* collection and the Irish stories, mainly the tales of the Ulster cycle.[11] The work of Dr. David Binchy and Professor Fergus Kelly on Old Irish law texts have also made vast contributions to the knowledge of Dark Age society.[12]

In material pertaining uniquely to the study of the Grail, Dr. Bromwich, Dr. Nora Chadwick, and Professor Charles Thomas have examined certain aspects of the extent of Christianity in Dark Age Britain.[13] The work chiefly of Dr. Graham Webster, Dr. Margaret Murray, and Dr. Clare Stancliffe have opened up a new understanding of the nature of the British beliefs as they were practiced in fifth-century Celtic Britain.[14] Glenys Goetinck has done the most comprehensive study of the romance *Peredur* (1975). From the turn of the last century French scholars of the stature of Viscount Villemarqué, Professor Gaston Paris, Professor Alfred Nutt, Sir John Rhys, Dr. Jessie Weston, Dr. Roy Owen, Dr. Arthur Brown, Professor William Roach, Dr. William Nitze, Professor Roger Loomis, Dr. Eugene Weinraub, and Professor Nora Lorre Goodrich have added their knowledge and understanding of the grail question to the growing critical literature.[15]

The intervening twenty-seven years since *Arthur's Britain* have produced a great deal of scholarship in archaeology, too. An increased number of digs and a more complete view of early medieval political geography and culture have greatly improved our understanding of the people of Celtic heritage and their settlement choices. Archaeologists such as Dr. Kenneth Dark have also become interested in the political boundaries of the Celtic nations following the Roman occupation (1994). The broad knowledge and interests of the archaeologists Professor O.G.S. Crawford, Professor Stuart Piggott, Dr. P.K. Johnstone, Dr. Lloyd Laing, Professor Charles Thomas, Professor Leslie Alcock, and many others have been integral in this process. The increased understanding of Pictish as a language and cultural group separate from the British, but similar, has helped fill in many voids. The accumulation of knowledge about warfare, social organization, and architecture since *Arthur's Britain* was written is based almost entirely upon the subsequent digs that have been conducted.

A great deal of knowledge has been acquired pertaining to sub-Roman Britain and the literary connections between the themes and motifs of the Arthurian romances and those of the British people. Yet there remains the tantalizing statement by Dr. Bromwich of something more substantial: "But there is little reason to believe that the authors of these [French] poems had any specific knowledge of the places in Arthurian Britain." (1991b, 277). How, then, did they come to have access to the precise details regarding Arthur, the names of his men, and the peculiar traits of these heroes? Certainly a bard could describe the terrain of a particular scene, but continental romances demonstrate a knowledge of the toponomy of many areas in Scotland, northwestern England, and Cornwall, and Wales. This implies a source of knowledge much more precise than a normal oral source. Certainly the antiquity of several elements of both poems implies a source more ancient than twelfth-century *latimari*.[16] Unquestionably, much of the Arthurian puzzle has yet to be solved. A tentative solution will be forthcoming; the romances' primary material derives from sources whose history stretched back several centuries before Chrétien de Troyes began writing.

The following pages are an attempt to show that this hypothesis is not only defensible, but that there is some evidence that the process may have occurred in Britain. To demonstrate the verifiability of such a claim, I shall begin by examining the sources and influences of the most influential Arthurian poet, Chrétien de Troyes. His hand can be seen in all the later material. The study will focus on the two of his stories that are least understood, *Le Chevalier de la Charrette* and *Le Conte du Graal*. An understanding of the influences upon Chrétien in the two poems will serve to demonstrate two points. First, his own limited role in several scenes and elements that were traditionally considered his creations. Second, his function as an inspiration on later writers who integrated similar episodes. A close examination of the motival and historical elements of the poem will serve to demonstrate most simply the antiquity of both stories by the twelfth century. This will include Celtic and continental literary materials and the influence of Marie de Champagne and Philip of Flanders. The chapter will provide some idea of his and his patrons' *sens*. Chrétien is a master of integrating hundreds of concepts, scenes, and other elements into a flowing text. His *sens* is occupied chiefly with molding all these sources with the ideals of Marie de Champagne and later Philip de Flanders.

Following this, I will devote one chapter to identifying the original roles of each of the major characters and then a discussion focusing on a search for Celtic patterns of the British heroic age.[17] This in turn will preface a look for potentially historical Celtic material that is not based on a specific motif. The process will in large part be duplicated in my examination of *Le Conte du Graal*, with a few minor alterations.

Chief of these exceptions will be two chapters. The first will be devoted to demonstrating the main grail theories. The purpose of this chapter will be to demonstrate the inability of any one of the theories to fully explain the grail. It will also demonstrate the mutual dependence of three grail theories to satisfactorily explain the grail and the ceremony surrounding it. It is a Celtic ceremony with a Christian and possibly Jewish disguise.

Second, I will examine the state of religion in Britain during the fifth and sixth centuries. This will bring out the prominence of Celtic cults through the year 500 and the prominence, particularly in the North, of the fertility god *Belatacudros*, or *Beli*. In turn, this will begin to explain his presence in the romances as *Pelles*.

In the case of both poems, this will be supported by a chapter devoted to a brief analysis of all the material directly related to the plot of the two poems. The purpose of this exercise will be threefold: First, it will serve to point out that the romances similar to these two Chrétien poems had derived from a common original by 1100. Second, those items unique to each redaction will point out a degree of independence from Chrétien. Finally, they will show a dependence on a common Celtic source, *Glas* in the case of *Le Chevalier de la* Charrette and *Dysgyl* for *Le Conte du Graal*.[18] As it seems reasonable that similar material on the same person would come ultimately from the same source, I will call this prototype *Cadegr*.

Thus, this chapter will demonstrate that several romances were independently based on a common Celtic source that predated 1100. Using this new information, I will follow Sir John Rhys[19] and Sir Ifor Williams (1944) in proposing that the romances are loosely based on stories from the British heroic period. The present author is hardly the first to conceive of such a notion.

> It follows that if one wished to make a comprehensive collection of the sagas about Arthur, one would have to take the romances into account, since things even of mythological interest have been lost in Welsh, and are now only to be found in the Anglo-Norman versions and those based on them. (Rhys 1891, 4)

Sifting through the material, this seems the only possible conclusion. However, I will take this assumption one step farther. There is some early British history in the continental romances; it only needs to be found and unraveled. Professor Graves achieved a similar end for Hellenic studies in his *The Greek Myths*, making a direct correspondence between myths and the historically known occurrences of the Greek heroic-age period.[20] The heroes of many Norse, Germanic, and Japanese stories have been given their place in history through the oral and written remains.[21] Closer to home, O'Rahilly accepted most legendary Irish kings as historical in *Early Irish History and Mythology*, it was one of the premises of his book (O' Rahilly 1946, v).

The legends surrounding Arthur are therefore one of the few such cycles for which this connection has not been made. The manufactured "King" Arthur of the continent has been proclaimed fiction, and none has ventured otherwise. Yet the facts are clear, and point in another direction. There are many comparisons between what the romances write on the one hand, and the sub-Roman British culture on the other. The tales are not, therefore, creations of medieval minds, but instead are products of legend and fact. These materials were later clouded by the Celtic motifs of the bards and the *sens* of continental writers and their patrons. However, what remains does contain hints of British traditional and legendary material.

The proposed study will be done on the abduction and grail stories separately. To begin with, a brief summary of the poem *Le Chevalier de la Charrette* should give the reader a source of reference from which I will draw throughout the first section of this volume.

Chrétien de Troyes' *Le Chevalier de la Charrette* begins in Arthur's court. The evil prince Meleagant rides into Camelot's hall alone and demands the master's queen as a boon. There is some apprehension by the king, so Meleagant appeases him by giving Guinièvre a chance for freedom. He will fight a champion for possession of her. Arthur accepts this arrangement, though the court is flabbergasted by the audacity of Meleagant's boon. This is followed by a scene in which Sir Kei manipulates the king and queen into allowing him to be the queen's champion; he promptly loses the battle and Guinièvre.

However, Kei has been followed by Gauvain and Lancelot, who now pursue Meleagant. Lancelot rides two horses to death in pursuit of her, and in time submits to riding in a criminal's cart in order to hear news of Guinièvre. In time they are both escorted to a nearby castle, the Cart Castle. That night they sleep in its hall. The two knights take different paths to Gorre the next day. Gauvain decides to cross to Gorre by a mysterious water bridge and Lancelot will take a perilous sword bridge route. Before attempting it, Lancelot defeats a knight at a ford, has an odd rendezvous with the lady of another castle,[22] lifts a tomb, crosses a perilous stony passage, defeats another knight,[23] and finally arrives in the Land of Gorre.[24] Here he finds Guinièvre. Here he participates in a liberation battle, crosses the Sword Bridge, and is welcomed by Bademagus, Meleagant's father.[25]

Lancelot defeats the antagonist in two duels soon thereafter, but Guinièvre saves Meleagant at Bademagus' request on condition that there be a decisive battle in a year's time. Lancelot departs and is soon captured by Meleagant's men and imprisoned in one of Meleagant's castles. Meanwhile Guinièvre and the now-returned Gauvain get word that Lancelot has returned to Camelot, and leave Gorre to join him. There Guinièvre learns he is not with Arthur. She organizes a tournament to locate him. Through a gentleman's promise, Lancelot is allowed to go to the tournament incognito and returns. Meleagant moves him to an isolated tower. At this point, Chrétien breaks off and Godefroi de Leigni completes the narrative. The story's scope necessarily diminishes somewhat. Lancelot is eventually released from prison by the sister of Meleagant who nurses him back to health just in time for Lancelot to defeat and behead Meleagant, thus ending the story.[26]

[1] See the Bibliography for a complete list.

[2] Ibid.

[3] Loomis attempted to forge a closer relationship to the theoretical Irish sources by forwarding meager linguistic evidence that Gauvain, Lancelot, Lot, Gareth, and Arthur were all derivations of Celtic gods. It was probably to the overall benefit of the theory that he later, and often, discounted his earlier arguments.

[4] See the Bibliography for a complete list.

[5] The lore was most definitely transmitted by word of mouth, at least in part.

[6] Dr. Bromwich provides a convenient summary in "First Transmission from England to France", (1991b).

[7] I exclude here Professor Jackson, Professor Jones, Professor Alcock, Professor Barber, Dr. Bromwich, and Dr. Kirby, who have all supported his historicity, and Dr. Padel and Professor Dumville, who have denied it.

[8] It would be foolish to attempt a comprehensive reference here, but see the Bibliography for most of the relevant texts. In addition, Hughes, *The Church in Early Irish Society*, (1966), *Celtic Britain in the Early Middle Ages: studies in Welsh and Scottish sources*, (1980), and *Church and society in Ireland, A. D. 400-1200*, (1987). Also, Dumville's *The Anglo-Saxon Chronicle a collaborative edition* (1983), *Ireland in Early Mediaeval Europe studies in memory of Kathleen Hughes*, (1982), and *St. Patrick, A. D. 493-1993*, (1993) are all fundamental texts on the subject.

[9] In particular *The Heroic Age* (1912) and *The Development of Oral Literature* (1932-40).

[10] See the Bibliography under the cited persons for a complete listing of their contributions.

[11] (Chadwick 1958). Though the arguments are at times nearly opaque, more recent work on the topic has only found ways in which to confirm the views presented here.

[12] See the Bibliography for a complete list.

[13] Ibid.

[14] Ibid.

[15] These are only the most prominent scholars. The grail question is such an intriguing topic that it has invited a rather large number of publications. For a large base of ideas on the subject see the bibliography at the end of this paper with regard to the above mentioned authors.

[16] Welsh *Lladmerydd*; the contribution by Dr. Bullock-Davies (1966, 5) that there was a professional group of poets in the Marches of Wales has added weight to this statement.

[17] For the purposes of this paper I will take the conservative stance that the first and most prolific British Heroic Age was finished before 650 and the second stretched from roughly 1100-1300. Having said that, it must be stressed that the latter heroic age lacks many of the characteristics of the typical heroic age, and is not and would not be properly classified as an heroic age in the sense of the societies portrayed in *Iliad*, *Volsungasaga*, and *Mahabharata*. Professor Ker took the interesting view that an heroic age's ideals are ended only when romance takes the place of epic (Ker 1896, 6). However, this does not mean that an heroic age ends only when this occurs. As he himself says:

> The form of society in an heroic age is aristocratic and magnificent. At the same time, this aristocracy differs from that of later and more specialised forms of civilisation. It does not take an insuperable difference between gentle and simple. There is not the extreme division of labour that produces the contempt of the lord for the villain. The nobles have not yet discovered for themselves any form of occupation or mode of thought in virtue of which they are widely severed from the commons, ... (Ker 1896, 7).

According to this thought, the Celtic and German heroic ages would have ended when feudalism began. This is also feasible, and would eliminate the period 1100-1300 from the discussion altogether.

[18] From this point forward, *Glas* will be the designation for the common source of the Guinevere abductions and *Dysgyl* for the grail legend. These sources would have been in existence by the early twelfth century. I will have more to say about the nature of these sources in the following chapters.

[19] Rhys; a reflection most cogently argued in *Studies in the Arthurian Legend* (1891).

[20] The Greek heroic age is traditionally dated to 1300-1100 B.C.E.

[21] In a forthcoming book by the author. *Arthur: Historicity and Location.*

[22] For further reference, this is the Castle of the Four Axemen.

[23] This knight is associated with a bull. The full relevance of this will be made clear in the final chapters of this book.

[24] *The Vulgate Version of the Arthurian Romances* says it is that of his grandfather. The mysterious appearance here of a bull will be explained in conjunction with the Belacutros cult in my discussion of the characters in *Le Conte du Graal.*

[25] The name Bademagus has many hypothetical precursors, I simply use this form for convenience and recognizability.

[26] She is called Jandrée in other romances, and from this point on in the paper.

Chapter II: Chrétien's Known Sources and Influences

In the 1170s a Frenchman with extraordinary literary abilities wrote a romance for his patroness -- Marie de Champagne. It was not the first work he had done in this milieu, but it is the most celebrated. The tales he told, beginning with *Erec et Enide* and followed by *Yvain* and *Le Conte du Graal*, soon became the basic model of all Arthurian tales. His progressive development of Gauvain and Kei were molded in his poems to the stereotypical figures that are recognized today. The timelessness, the grail adventure, even the modest, often weak-minded Arthur of the romances has his origins in Chrétien's works. Creating the Arthurian setting as modern society understands it, however, was only one of the ways in which he was an inventor. His poems were the first of courtly love ever introduced into the literature of the North of France. This innovation alone places him in a unique position in medieval literature.

His known sources and influences are therefore of high importance if one is to hope to have any understanding of the origins of the Arthurian legend. Chrétien himself insists on using the terms *sens* and *matière*, so his intended meanings for these two words would appear to be crucial to an understanding of his sources and influences.

The terms *sens* and *matière* appear nearly always in Chrétien's Prologues. The medieval prologue had a universal purpose in the Middle Ages. This purpose had derived from the monasteries of western Europe. The monks had a genuine respect for the classical writers. This respect was so deep that it was thought by them that the wisdom of the Greeks and Romans could not be surpassed. With this in mind, the material, or *matière*, was unimprovable.[1] The meaning, or *sens*, was the only aspect that could be altered to enable a more accurate and subtle understanding of their thoughts. With the development of secular literature, this practice was continued, though in a modified form.[2] The presence of the concepts of *sens* and *matière* in a prologue, and an understanding of those concepts, allowed for a great deal of poetic license. As long as one used an old tale (*matière*), one was free to give the material any presentation (*sens*) that the author chose.[3] At the same time, by following monastic convention and claiming to be making use of an old theme, the poets molded the prologue into a standard humility theme. The prologue was also used to praise the largesse of one's patron in hopes of additional financial reward.[4] Chrétien's use of these two terms, then, implies only his proper education in the medieval form of writing.

What little may be directly gleaned from his poems about his contributions and the nature of his source material may leave the reader wanting more. However, his writings have produced modern criticism from many different perspectives and especially from Celtic and French scholars. These two fields have combined to give a good indication of Chrétien's material, and the true significance of *matière* and *sens*. The focus of these studies has been chiefly literary in nature. However, critical focus has included other, broader scopes and topics. The main interest in this chapter will be divided between the Celtic and French schools of thought on Chrétien's sources and his use of them. These two schools of thought will be shown to be compatible.

The Celticists, led by Rachel Bromwich, have developed the idea that the hero Arthur and a discernibly British cast of characters were transferred to the continent in conjunction with him. To quote her: "This body of names constitutes the most important and incontrovertible evidence for the Celtic contribution to Arthurian romance." (1991b, 281).

The focus of their studies has mainly been in the geographic and chronological origin of the material, and in determining what form and manner it was transmitted. To this I will add the theory that the *Northern Memoranda* or some allied material could have been the original source for these tales. The evidence gathered in Chapters V, VI, XIV, and XV will support my theory. It has also been generally agreed upon that the material was transferred both orally and by manuscript, though proper names were almost exclusively of oral origin. To quote Dr. Bromwich: "It is surely legitimate to conclude that the Nennian *Arthuriana* section came from a source closely related to the *Northern Chronicle* that underlies *Annales Cambriae*, even if this source was not the same." (Bromwich 1976, 175-6).

Deriving a point of origin for the British-based literature is nearly impossible. If the tales evolved from heroic-age poetry, then one might reasonably believe that the corpus had begun near where Arthur and other prominent chiefs lived.[5] One can imagine a petty king generously rewarding the fortunate poet who had most recently extolled him. There are, however, several complications with this simple equation.

First, around 550 the British language shifted so significantly that the vocabulary that antedated this watershed would have become archaic and, very quickly, incomprehensible to contemporary speakers. Any original bardic verse composed around 450 would be obsolete by around 600, and thus any literature written in 450 or before would not have been understood well enough to be recopied after 600.[6] These written poems would have been lost.

On the other hand, it may very well be that certain of the living poetry would not have survived beyond this point, either. The poetry would have been limited to the Old North. Several prominent chieftains are known, from their inclusion in several triads of *Trioedd Ynys Prydein* and the references of later poets, to have been associated with extensive sagas. Yet these sagas have not survived. For Professor Jackson, this can easily be explained by the extinction of the Cumbric language, and with it much of the oral history of the northern British regions.[7] What remained of the sagas apparently became the basis for oral tradition that has endured the centuries, as one may assume any literature pertaining to most of the British heroes similarly would have survived.[8] Therefore, any territory in British hands up to around 550 could have been the point of origin for the tales that eventually became tied to Arthur.

The argument that Wales is the earliest location for this material is the easiest to defend on literary grounds, so the review will begin there. The linguistic evidence points to the conclusion that *Preiddeu Annwn* and *Culhwch ac Olwen* had been in what is now Wales prior to Chrétien de Troyes.[9] Loomis admitted that a Welsh point of origin was suggested by the less popular names, which he believed came directly from Wales without alteration.[10] He listed well-known names such as

Gauvain and Modred which he saw as adaptations made when translating the story to French (Loomis 1941, 376).

The evidence for Cornwall and Somerset as a source of Arthurian information is most apparent in Geoffrey's account of Arthur's conception in Tintagel. However, there is also some place-name evidence in honor of some events of Arthur's life (Padel 1994, 4-12). In addition, the Tristan element of the Arthurian legend was clearly from Cornwall. This may also be seen in the place-names embedded in the Tristan romances.[11]

The Bretons could also have developed the legend of Arthur. Loomis saw the Breton names Ivanus (Yvain), Moraldus (Morhaut), and Winlogee (Guinloie) as intermediaries between their Insular and French counterparts.[12]

In addition to the Welsh, Cornish, and Bretons claim to being the founders or continuators of the Arthur legacy, certainly what had been Roman Scotland cannot be excluded from the search for source material. Parts of the area fell under the domination of the Anglo-Saxons some decades after Arthur's traditional obit (516x542), indicating military activity during his proposed floruit.[13] The Arthurian characters and place-names Rion, Yvain, Tristan, and Perceval, and the place-names Galvoie, Loenis, and Cardoel are of northern origin in the form of Urien, Owain, Drust, Peredur, Galloway, Lothian, and Carlisle. It has also been noted that all the earliest poets were predominantly northern figures,[14] indicating a substantial and influential body of knowledge on northern history.

In addition, there is here the possibility of a written, historical source from this region. Thurneysen was the first to argue the existence of the material from which such a body of lore as Arthuriana could have evolved. It was his belief that such a resource was in the form of literature. This corpus may have been a source for the *Historia Brittonum, Annales Cambriae*, the two extant lives of St. Kentigern and possibly other literary works now lost. This theory has been accepted by several prominent scholars.[15] Because of the work of Professor Dumville and Dr. Hughes about twenty years ago, one may be assured that there were written records kept in the North with some degree of antiquity. In addition, one may also manage a reasonable theory of the development of this document from the eighth century on (see drawing below).

Chrétien's Known Sources and Influences

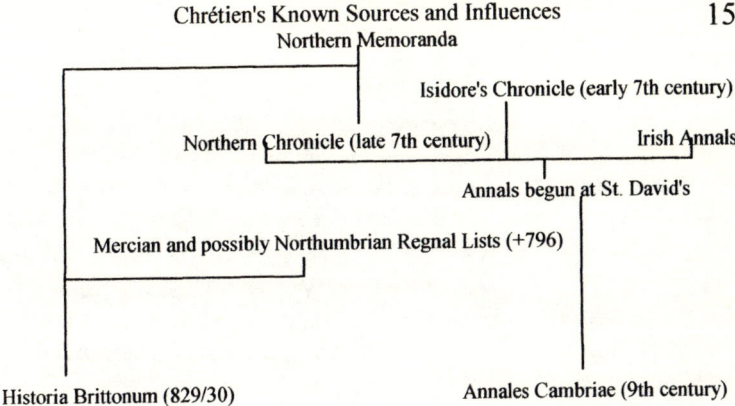

First, the general locale of the above works favors a "northern Britishness." The kingdoms of Mercia and Northumbria were located in what is now northern England. The early events of *Annales Cambriae* may be located mainly in the North. Finally, the northern British section is devoted entirely to British leaders of *Y Hen Ogled*. Professor Jackson made the following observations in favor of the antiquity, bias, and region of origin of the document *Historia Brittonum* that have come to occupy a solid academic position:[16]

1) Names of places and battles are not of Germanic origin. In some places they are ancient.
2) Sympathies are strongly British.
3) Details pertaining to the five poets the author associates with Outigern would be of no interest to Northumbrian English.
4) Even the inclusion of Gwynedd kings in this section pertains only to the North.[17]

The third of these observations also argues for the existence and use of a source of some age. No independent record of the poets the Ninnius compiler speaks of is in existence. It may be assumed that all but Aneirin and Taliesin would have been forgotten relatively quickly. Therefore, the person who recorded the names of the other three poets surely lived well before the late-eighth century, possibly within living memory of all their obits.

Nora Chadwick came to the same conclusion by different means: "there can, I think, be little doubt that many of the picturesque details of the narrative and the static epithets are of this [sixth or seventh century] origin." (1958a, 70). She continues that *Historia Brittonum* ends with Penda who died at or before 655 and its last battle is that of Nechtanesmere in 685 (1958a, 71). Therefore, according to her the source ends with the last years of the seventh century and was most likely last edited shortly after Nechtanesmere.

The location of origin for the *Northern Memoranda* is easy enough to find. A clue comes in the same sentence that tells us the date of the original *Historia Brittonum* manuscript. Ninnius, one reads, wrote in King Merfyn's fourth year of rule.[18] Merfyn and his heir Rhodri are known to have taken a considerable interest in North British history in order to build a national consciousness and gathered and published much of its records for this purpose. Since the only surviving British state in ninth-century Scotland was Strathclyde, it seems most probable the *Northern Memoranda* was kept somewhere within its borders. It must have been stored there for several decades at least. Its specific location of storage is unknown, and unnecessary to discuss for this chapter.[19]

As to the nature of the *Northern Memoranda*, it was most probably written down,[20] and may have been much larger than what one finds in *Historia Brittonum* (Jackson 1963, 57). The evidence from *Historia Brittonum* and *Annales Cambriae* indicates it contained historical, pseudo-historical, and literary material. In addition Dr. Bromwich, along with Professor Thurneysen and Professor Bruce have added the Arthuriana section to the segment of *Historia Brittonum* that derives from the *Northern Memoranda*.[21]

There is some evidence for the existence of additional literary material within the *Northern Memoranda*, as Dr. Thurneysen and others have hypothesized (above); this is to be found in the Scottish *vitae*. Professor Jackson would date the *Life* of Kentigern back to the eleventh or possibly the tenth centuries based on the language of the vitae (1958, 273-357). MacQueen (1956, 107-131; 1959, 175-83), Carney (1955, 79), and more recently Koch (*The Gododdin of Aneirin*, ed. Koch 1997, lxxvii-iii) have used other methods and postulated a date in the seventh century for the first version of the legend.[22] Clearly a large body of historical and pseudo-historical data existed in the North by the seventh century.[23] This was in both written and oral form, and was undoubtedly to be found in independent and isolated sources.[24] It may not be too bold to suggest *Glas* and *Dysgyl* may have originated from the *Northern Memoranda* or similar sources as well.

As uncertain as the geographic origin of the legend of Arthur and its subsequent heroes are, the precise form in which this corpus made its way to France is fairly certain; it was primarily oral. The Arthurian scholar R.S. Loomis was for many years the biggest proponent of this belief. He devoted the majority of his first chapter in *Arthurian Tradition and Chrétien* to listing the widespread evidence for oral transference in during and before Chrétien's period.[25] This is the best assembly of evidence to my knowledge.

Several motifs found in Arthurian literature also bring this out. E.g. a blow is delivered to the head to finish a combat, regardless of the height of the opponent. Several lances are used in jousts with a good opponent and only one for a poor one. These suggest the use of oral formulae. Since the phenomenon is to be found in other Welsh tales as well, it implies a system of techniques that is the signature of a Celtic bard (Middleton 1991, 153-4).

Dr. Bromwich asserts the debt to oral transference by stating that the French/Welsh equations were unknown to Geoffrey and his adapters, yet can be found in Welsh and French stories. Some of these equations are Girflet fis Do/Gilfaethwy fab Don, Maheloas/Melwas, Mabonagrain/Mabon, and Caradues Briebras/Caradawc Freichfras. Dr. Bromwich then proposes that oral tradition was probably the reason the names used by Chrétien and his successors were unrecognizable. She puts this succinctly in *The Legend of Arthur in the Middle Ages*.

> Although a proportion of names in Chrétien correspond with names in existing Welsh poems and triads and native tales, the large number of names in the French romances which cannot be explained, and which have obviously been borrowed in forms which are corrupt, favours the belief that oral transmission was by far the more frequent and widespread means of transference of Celtic names and stories into French; though we must allow always for several significant instances of written borrowings. (Bromwich 1983, 44)

This is indeed what one would expect to find if the material was transported orally.[26]

Finally, the question of whom past the British information on to poets such as Chrétien has been the subject of many debates. Two major theories have been created to account for the phenomenon. They all involve different intermediaries in primarily the same role. The proponents of each have been roughly equal. In these proposals, the protagonists are the Bretons, Welsh, and the unskilled tradesmen and military personnel of the Angevin England realm. A brief review will outline the main points of each.

In 1055 a Gwynedd king named Gruffydd ap Llywelyw united the kingdoms of Gwynedd, Powys, Deheubarth, and Margannwg under him (Bullock-Davies 1966, 19). In the eleventh century, these countries constituted most of Wales. Gruffydd's political unity allowed an interstate travel to the people of the bardic class that had previously been closed. The boundaries of the various countries had for centuries contained the local traditions of the Welsh nations because they had not allowed their bards to cross those borders. The stability that Gruffydd's kingdom gave allowed both bards and legends full range throughout all of Wales (Williams 1944, xl-xli). The exchange was such a lucrative one that it created a renaissance of British culture and Wales became a receptacle of northern British, Cornish, and Irish historical, pseudo-historical, and literary materials (Loomis 1936; 1965).

The mid-eleventh century produced a large corpus of material about Arthur in Wales. By the end of the century, the vehicle for easy transference to the continent was in place. In 1066, William the Conqueror of Normandy assumed the English throne. By the time he died in 1087, William had control of a large part of Britain and his hereditary estates in Normandy. By 1100, this Angevin empire stretched over much of France and the South of Wales, not to mention Scotland and England. At this point all the necessary ingredients were in place. The literature needed only an anima in the form of Geoffrey of Monmouth to send it pouring forth on the continent.

Angevin Empire, c. 1100

The Arthurian material could have found its way to the continent by several means; soldiers, monks, crusaders, or noblemen each could have brought Arthur to France, and undoubtedly many representatives of these groups did.

The Welsh were the keepers of British history and legend. It is known that there were bi-lingual communities in the South of Wales who spoke their native language and French fluently (Bullock-Davies 1966, 20). Professional storytellers from these communities, known as *Latimari*, could have translated the Arthurian material to French and Welsh as the situation required. The *latimari* were renowned for their linguistic prowess and often served as translators in Britain. These men may have served in France as well.

It is also possible the Bretons translated the material. It is known that the Bretons were among the more numerous of William the Conqueror's allies. After his assumption of the throne, the Bretons were allotted territory in Wales, England, and France. This act made them one of the more powerful groups in the Angevin realm. Their language was also intelligible to the Welsh at this point, helping them form a bond in English- and Norman-dominated Britain. What is more, southern Wales was under Norman control by the twelfth century, allowing for unimpeded transmission of material from the homeland to the continent.

The *troubadours*, professional storytellers of southern France, are also part of the Arthurian equation. Undoubtedly, they were bearers of early versions of Arthurian stories. *Troubadour* poetry is known to have predated Chrétien and all extant Arthurian romances. Tristan was known to them before 1145 and Perceval is referred to in a poem prior to 1160, anticipating Chrétien by some twenty-five years (Lejeune 1959, 396). An overwhelming number of references to Arthurian characters are to be found in the *troubadours*' literature (Lejeune 1959, 398), indicating a strong and early foundation in southern France.

It was also probably the *troubadours* who modified and softened the Welsh literature involving Arthur. It was they who created what can be considered the framework for the romance pattern that is now associated with Arthur and made him fully palatable to the French courts. It was in their tales that Tristan became the best lover, Yvain the first model of fashion, and Arthur the courtly standard for kingliness.

This is not to say, however, that the troubadours in any way created the plots. The vast majority of what is integral to the romance literature of the period found its impetus in the Celtic tales. As Alfred Nutt put it a hundred years ago: "What is claimed is that the spirit of the age, akin to the Celtic, recognized in Celtic tales the food it was hungering for" (1888, 235). Regarding the poets of northern France (the *Trouvères*), this statement has gone generally unchallenged, and in the South the work of Dr. Joseph Anglade and Dr. Rita Lejeune have greatly substantiated this claim.[27]

One can be certain that some of Chrétien's data for *Le Chevalier de la Charrette* originated in Scotland, Wales, Cornwall, or Brittany (or any combination of these places). It was transmitted by professionals through Breton and/or Welsh bards/translators, in oral and, possibly, written form. Informally, Breton soldiers, settlers, or any class of people who traveled throughout Henry II's empire transmitted the data, specifically the names of the heroes. It was softened and made more courtly by the *troubadours* and *trouvères* of Chrétien's native country. This is the extent of Celtic research on the transmission of Arthurian material.

The French perspective is based mainly on the relationship between *matière* and *sens* of which Chrétien speaks in his prologue, what little is known of his personal life and his literary influences, and his patrons.

Professor Gaston Paris admitted to Celtic influences of some sort and of some degree (both undefined).[28] Still, he saw most of Chrétien's work as being influenced by the classical writers, which is one reason Chrétien is often labeled a clerk, priest, or holy person.[29] The following pages of this chapter will demonstrate the degree to which Chrétien's learning has molded his poetry. Demonstrating how he successfully integrated his vast knowledge of Latin, Greek and contemporary scholars with the Celtic motifs and names he is known to have used will show this.

The Roman poet Ovid was most clearly one of Chrétien's guiding forces in technique and manner of presentation. In addition, Ovid was the expert on the topic of love for the twelfth-century reader (Guyer 1921, 217-18). His belief that the instutions of love and marriage were in opposition permeated much of the thinking. Chrétien himself claims to have written a version of several Ovidian poems -- *The Art of Love, The Shoulder Bite, The Metamorphosis of the Hoopoe, Swallow,* and *Nightingale* (*Cligès*, ll. 2-5). In two of his poems, part of *Cligès* and *Le Chevalier de la Charrette*, he seems to follow Ovid's principles of love. Lancelot and Guinièvre and Cligès and Fenice both have relations out of wedlock, and in spite of the fact that both women are otherwise married.

However, Ovid was clearly not a welcome influence. In *Cligès*,[30] Chrétien protects his conscience through a constant denunciation of the heroine of the *Tristan* cycle, Isolde. In *Le Chevalier de la Charrette*, he disclaims responsibility for *matière* and *sens*. Curiously, he did not finish this poem. He gave it to Godefroi de Leigni to finish. Ovid's love-philosophy was something Chrétien apparently could not personally accept.

On the other hand, four of Chrétien's Arthurian poems -- *Erec et Enide, Yvain, Le Conte du Graal*, and part of *Cligès* -- extol marriage, a non-Ovidian ideal. This betrays a moral sense Chrétien shows in his poems. The creations under scrutiny here are two of three works in which he does not show the same concerns.[31]

There are, then, strong indications that Chrétien had a consistently negative view of Ovidian love philosophy. Dr. Guyer's thesis, *The Influence of Ovid on Chréstien de Troyes*, only reinforces this proposal. He believes that the following acts of semi-insanity by Lancelot are directly due to Chrétien's influence by Ovid's love-philosophy: 1.) Lancelot's wish to jump from the top of a tower to rescue Guinièvre. She is at that moment safely and slowly riding and by. 2) Lancelot's mental absorption with Guinièvre during his first duel with Meleagant. He becomes so enraptured with seeing her that he allows his opponent to work his way around and face Guinièvre, forcing Lancelot into the error of turning his back to his foe (*Le Chevalier*, ll. 113-14). In caricaturing Lancelot, the personification of the perfect lover, Chrétien is belittling courtly love. Peter Noble's book *Love and Marriage in Chrétien de Troyes*, lists many examples of excessive behavior from Lancelot that demonstrate Chrétien's personal belief in marriage.

Noble also gives further evidence of the Roman poet's influence on the poem, however. Ovid's method in *Heroide* of capturing the emotional thoughts of the characters and then commenting on them is well matched in *Cligès* where Soredamors allows us a glimpse at her thoughts (ll. 475-523). It is also to be found in *La Charrette*, when Guinièvre ponders suicide on hearing Lancelot is dead (ll. 4177-4262). He further sees the couples Lancelot and Guinièvre, and Yvain and Laudine as Ovidian lovers. This is because the male is obedient to the whims of his idol, the female, who is most willing to test those feelings.

Following Ovid's lead, and formalizing and adapting it to the twelfth century, Andreas Capellanus systematized the ideology now known as courtly love. A few of his rules will be sufficient to clarify its main theme:

I. Causa coniugii ab amore non est excusatio recta.
XI. Non decet amare, quarum pudor est nuptias affectare.
XII. Verus amans alterius nisi sui coamantis ex affectu non cupit amplexus.
XIV. Facilis perceptio contemptibilem reddit amorem, dificilis eum carum facit haberi.
XXIV. Quilibet amantis actus in coamantis cogitatione finitur.
XXVI. Amor nil posset amore denegare. (*De Amore: Libri Tres*, ed. Trojel 1972, 310-11)

1. Marriage is no excuse for not loving.
11. One should not love another whom one should be ashamed to court.
12. A true love desires only his beloved.
14. The more difficult love is the more it is prized.
24. Every act must end in the thought of the lover.
26. Love can deny nothing to love. (*The Art of Courtly Love*, trans. Parry 1959, 184-6)

It is within this fashionable concept that Chrétien began to create the poems for which he is praised today. The evidence of this courtly code is clearly marked, especially in *Le Chevalier de la Charrette*. The entire love element in the story would not be possible without Capellanus's first rule. And though no-one can love two people, he does say that two people may love the same person.[32] This is not in Ovid's works but is central to *La Charrette* and therefore is the product of Capellanus' influence.

Chrétien did not write with only Ovid and Andreas Capellanus in mind, however, as has been demonstrated on numerous occasions. Geoffrey of Monmouth, great progenitor of the legend of Arthur to the reading world, gave Chrétien his setting. Wace was also an influence. In *Erec* (l. 83), Chrétien mentions the Round Table which he first introduced. Dr. Owen saw the treason episode of Count Angres in *Cligès* as based on the Modred affair from Wace, too (1968, 507). Margaret Pelan's *L' influence du Brut de Wace sur les romanciers français de son temps* elaborates on these comparisons throughout (1931).

La Chanson de Roland, progenitor of the *Matière de France*, also gave Chrétien inspiration. The retreat of the traitor Angres, descriptions of resplendent tents, jousting among the enemy are all reminiscent of similar themes in the French epic (ll. 2635-7). So is the segment when the hero of the story combats the enemy in the Alexander section of *Cligès*. Alexander names each of his comrades in turn, beginning with a close friend, as in *La Chanson* (l. 793). Both lists include an epic pair.[33] In both cases the enemy attempts a night raid that is defeated by a premature rising of the sun.[34] None of the above is from Wace or Geoffrey.

Other details of Chrétien's romances that relate directly to *La Chanson de Roland* include two heroes named by Chrétien. Fernagut and Forre were both killed by Roland.[35] A comparison Chrétien makes between Yvain and Roland makes it clear he was familiar with *La Chanson de Roland*'s general form (*Yvain*, ll. 3235-7). The similarity of the Roland-Oliver-Aude relationship to that of Gauvain-Alexandre-Soredamors in *Cligès* and the reference to Ganelon are also plainly derived from the French epic and later romance (*Cligès*, l. 468). Finally, Owen detected a great similarity between Arthur's statements about the betrayer Angres and Charlemagne's comments about his traitor in the respective poems, thus indicating a definite influence from *La Chanson of Roland*. It seems most obvious in *Cligès*, though possibly this has some connection to the relative independence of *Cligès* from Celtic influence.

Chrétien also drew from the Tristan legend. He claims to have written a version of it in *Erec* and inserts in the same poem a comparison of Enide with Iseut's blonde hair (*Erec*, ll. 404 and 424, respectively).

He also uses the theme of the beloved being recognized by her golden hair in this poem, a concept he borrowed from either Virgil's *Aeneid* or the *Roman d' Eneas*. Chrétien refers specifically to the Old French version of this poem (*Roman d' Eneas*, ll. 5337, 5891), and uses the name Lavinia of Laurentium — Aeneas' wife (*Roman d' Eneas*, ll. 5891). The actions of the two maidens in preparing Enide's hair are strongly reminiscent of a similar scene in *Aeneid* involving Dido and her maidens.[36] Even the monologue Soredamors develops in *Cligès* seems to be based on the *Aeneid*'s Dido monologue (IV: 19).

The great poet had a heavy debt to other classical writers as well. Dr. Laurie saw evidence of Propertius' stream of erotic poetry in *Elegiae* (33-6, 79). In Alexander's lament for Soredamors she saw a resemblance to Lucretius' *De Rerum Natura*.[37] A link to Caesar's *De Bello Civili* can be seen in the rise of Erec and his subsequent problems (*Erec* l. 23), and Enide's self-examination resembles the Cornelia character of Lucan (VIII. 156-7). Chrétien mentions Macrobius, author of *Saturnalia* (*Erec* l. 6738). Chrétien has also been seen to mimic Quintilian in his treatment of the queen in *Cligès*. Her manner of detecting the signs of love between Soredamors and Alexandre are similar to Quintilian (*Cligès*, ll. 547-51). The wedding scene of *Erec et Enide* is blatantly from Statius' *Venus* (*Erec*, ll. 2021-3). Chrétien even touches on mythology with his introduction of Medea, wife of the famed Jason.[38] Other notable connections, though of lesser strength, have been made to Plato's philosophy (Laurie 1972, 215), Cicero (Laurie 1972, 25, 60, 90, 174), and the later writer Boethius (Laurie 1972, 148, 156, 167, 215, 216, 217).

Christian writers also influenced Chrétien. Dr. Laurie detected the Augustinian concept that "the will finds rest in knowledge itself" in Chrétien's poem (1972, 63). She also discovered that St. Augustine's *Confessions* was Chrétien's source for the motif of deliverance from evil (IX l.1). The concept that a "touch of resignation is real enough" given to Lancelot about Guinièvre (*Confessions* IV xii. 18), and the belief that the soul is informed of the world through the body is also taken from St. Augustine's *Confessions*.[39] The sequence of the plot in *Cligès* is similar to a hymn attributed to St. Bernard.[40] It is stated here that natural science is not necessary to the pure of heart (Laurie 1972, 106-7). The axiom is followed by a biblical sequence.

In addition, the trees in *Yvain* covered by sweetly singing birds seem to derive from those of *Navigatio Sanctii Brendani* and its Anglo-Norman version (Owen 1968, 516). Dr. Owen found one comparison between *The Gospel of Nicodemus* and *Le Chevalier de la Charrette*; Lancelot's trip to Gorre imitates the gospel's version of Christ's crucifixion and Harrowing of Hell (*La Charrette*, ll.1841-3937).

Some of these comparisons may be highly subjective, but they do bear out a common trend. One may see that Chrétien made use of the works of Ovid and Andreas Capellanus, as well as those of Wace, the early Tristan romances, and scores of classical and ancient Christian authors. One may also see that he is able to take these ideas and manners of presentation and place them out of their intended contexts.

One must now turn to Chrétien's major and most watchful influence -- his feminist patron the countess Marie de Champagne. What little is known of her character tells us a great deal about her. Her mother, Eleanor of Aquitaine, was one of the most formidable women in all of Europe. Her most noteworthy action was when she had decided to marry King Henry II of England after being divorced by King Louis VII of France. This was not only a personal affront to Louis VII, but it effectively gave one quarter of France to England and Henry II. Her actions had great personal and political repercussions to all of western Europe. Her later divorce from Henry again altered the political scene. After her second divorce, she created her own court at Poitiers. Here she went on to fund the maturation of the romance movement. She did this by making her daughter the head of a court devoted to courtly romance which ruled on romantic issues and commissioned tales of romance. It is here where Marie, through Eleanor, created the ambiance which allowed for the movement which created Arthurian literature (Kelly 1950, 157-67).

Marie was also a figure of note throughout Europe. She was a widower of the Count of Champagne. She was a woman who commanded respect, if not love among her male peers. Letters were written not only to, but about her. One letter was written to the bishops of Sens, Reims, and Meaux as Marie lay on her deathbed, and spoke of her contributions to society and her death.[41] Two contemporary historians describe her as acting *viriliter*, that is, "in a manly fashion".[42] Marie was seen as a woman with a man's qualities. She actively and repeatedly took charge of situations, as when a small group of nobles was gathered on her property to decide how best to control the young King Philip Augustus. After peace had been made with the king, she approached the sovereign and made use of his weighty influence. She asked the sovereign to intervene when a treaty that had assigned her son and daughter a wife and husband was in danger of being ignored. The matter was conducted to her satisfaction.

It was this decisive woman for whom a succession of poets worked, and it is quite apparent she took an active role in the creation of many of their works. Her commission of a translation of *Genesis* points this out most of all. Three versions of this work have survived in manuscript ("A", "B", and "C"), but they may be used to point out her level of influence on those she patronized.

Dr. Henderson concludes that manuscripts "B" and "C" are later versions of "A".[43] This is because of the intense feminist attitudes in "B" and "C" that are not found in "A". Henderson believes this feminism was due to Marie's direct supervision (Unpublished Ph.D. thesis, 1977, 69). Considering this assumption, Dr. McCash believes the third book of *De Amore* tells us something more of Marie. Andreas Capellanus finished writing his thesis in c. 1186. From this point on, he is not to be found in any of Champagne's legal charters, implying he no longer was a part of Marie's circle. Whether he was allowed to finish the book in her court or was expelled before he wrote it, the third book of *De Amore* was not condoned on Marie de Champagne's property. It seems that the author of such writings was not allowed, either (McCash 1985, 243).

With the completion of *La Charrette*, Marie must have reached the height of her power in the cultural world. Her brothers Richard the Lionheart and John Lackland would fight their father and later, each other. She could not do this. She was condemned to marry a Count and be a wife and later a widow. She was forced into the role of a woman in a man's world, and she must have hated it. In the literature her court produced, though, and particularly in *La Charrette*, she got some measure of revenge. In it Lancelot is the perfect knight in all respects, bowing to every whim as though Guinièvre were his master. This was the *sens* which Marie wanted to integrate into the British tales, and the *sens* for which Chrétien wanted no credit. This is also the influence which helped create the Arthurian romance, and which must be accounted for if one is to gain an accurate view of the original British tale.

As I wrote at the beginning of this chapter, the Celtic and French approaches are not mutually exclusive, in fact they occasionally complement each other. No French scholar claims that the impetus for much of the early Arthurian romances derived from anywhere but Britain. The French scholars do not argue the tales could have been transferred to the continent by any oral or written means, either. Scholars see many Celtic themes and names in the early romances, but the references to classical writers make it clear that Chrétien was also aware of them and made use of his knowledge. Therefore, it is clear that Chrétien used British sources for the plot and many of the individual scenes. It is also clear that he integrated other sources, both classical and contemporary, when it suited his personal tastes or the desires of his patrons.

The accumulated facts allow the critical analyst to gain some perspective on Chrétien's creativity concerning the material that influenced him. Much of where Chrétien gained many of his themes and perspectives are known. He was unmistakably well read in the Greek, Roman, and medieval authors and especially the *chansons de geste*, *Historia Regum Britanniae*, and Wace. It appears that Chrétien re molded the Celtic stories in his poems and elaborated on his source with the techniques of literary scenes, and figures of the classical and medieval worlds. As Dr. Owen, translator of the poet, has remarked: "At times his memory of some narrative appears to condition his presentation of important sections of a romance as he takes elements from it, adapts them to his needs and insinuates them into his text." (Owen 1981, 140).

However, there are minutiae that are not from the literary masterpieces of the ancient or medieval worlds. As has been noted, the names and several motifs and themes are Celtic. There is also much more which remains unconnected to the classical or contemporary worlds. Much of this, and the energy of the romances, derive from British sources. This is because the primary source is British. The other influences on the poems are generally transitory and appear to have been superimposed on the plot.[44] A first step toward proving this thesis has been taken by demonstrating Chrétien's dependence on a large number of classical scholars. A second step was taken in establishing the existence of an early body of historical and literary material from which the Arthurian abduction and grail romances may have derived. Finally, a survey of possible transference manners to the continent has provided the means by which Chrétien may have accessed them.

In the following chapters I will show evidence, both motival and historical, why several early forms of the abduction scenario were not totally dependent on Chrétien. In addition, I will bring forth evidence to show that at times these alternative forms drew on one of the British sources directly. Thus, several different romance writers drew on British sources independently. This in turn means that each writer may be employed to define the Arthurian abduction prototype.[45] I hope to show that there was one post-Roman British tale from which the various authors of the abduction and grail romances drew.

---

[1] This is an often addressed aspect of medieval writing. Of course the religious writings were also beyond reproach, and therefore monks were often hardpressed to interpret the Greeks and Romans in such a way that they did not conflict with the Christian theology.

[2] The practice was continued undoubtedly because the most efficient way to educate oneself in this period was through the monasteries. Therefore, those who were writing fictitious poems were most probably the product of some religious instruction.

[3] (Nitze 1915-17, 30; Warren 1901, 384; Faral 1911, 185, 187).

[4] (Nitze 1915-17, 28; Hunt 1971, 327-8). However, Dr. Rychner has argued *sens* may have been used by Chrétien to mean his motivation (1967, 1-23).

[5] *Y Gododdin* and *Pa gur?* implies that the fifth to seventh centuries were heroic (Chadwick 1912, 32). The praise poetry of later figures of Y Hen Ogled-Urien of Rheged, Owain, and Gwallawg only supports this position. Thus, a society similar to that which produced the lyrics of the court bard Aneirin and the other four poets listed by the Ninnius compilation (Chapter 62) can be postulated for the turn of the fifth century and, by deduction, a similar body of poetry can be hypothesised for Arthur, the first and most praised figure of Welsh lore.

[6] (Jackson 1953, 690; 1955, 77).

[7] The last date at which Old Cumbric was practised is, of course, impossible to determine precisely. There is almost nothing known about the kingdoms of Strathclyde and Cumbria between the seventh and tenth centuries. Professor Jackson's best guess about the last use was right around 1092 (Jackson 1953, 9).

[8] Indeed, *Trioedd Ynys Prydein* (*The Welsh Triads*) and *Culhwch ac Olwen* are treasure stores of such names, but their identifications have generally eluded scholars.

[9] (Haycock 1984, 57); (Bromwich and Evans 1992, lxxxii). Professor Sims-Williams (1991, 39) will only give the dates 1100-1160 for *Pa gur?* which, though probably before Chrétien, are not necessarily before him.

[10] (Loomis 1941, 376); Gonemans, Bron, Palamedes, and Arioel.

[11] (Padel 1982, 53-82; Bromwich 1991b, 220-1.)

[12] (Loomis 1936, 207-8); First recorded in 1083, pre-1083, and from 1099-1106, respectively.

[13] *The Anglo-Saxon Chronicle* assigns the year 547 to the capture of Bamborough.

[14] (Lewis 1976, 31, 34, 35, 40, 44). Taliesin is believed to have begun his career in Powys, but the majority, and the more mature poems, are in praise of Gwr Hen Ogled. Therefore, he too may be considered a northern figure.

[15] (Thurneysen 1896, 85, 87; Bruce 1923, 9; Jackson 1959, 6; (Hughes 1973, 237-9; Bromwich 1976, 175-176; Dumville 1976, 23-50; Charles-Edwards 1978, 63).

[16] In the main, Professor Dumville has accepted the thesis, though with some modifiations. These changes have been inserted into the drawings.

[17] In this foundation legend, the royal house of Gwynedd is made the descendent of Coel, a king of *Y Hen Ogled*. Therefore, all entries pertaining to Gwynedd are also a part of the northern history.

[18] (Chadwick 1958a, 91-2). Dr. Chadwick suggested specifically Bangor Fawr on the basis of the Elfoddw of Bangor named in the preface and this site's proximity to the Gwynedd court.

[19] (Chadwick 1958a, 66-72). Dr. Chadwick believed the document would have been kept in Cumberland (most probably Hoddom (Chadwick 1958a, 64-5) because the saga hero Rhydderch Hael's death is not recorded in it, *Historia Brittonum* gives the Strathclyde king the epithet "Hen" (as opposed to MS 536 Hengwrt), and because Urbgen is here killed by treachery, as opposed to his fate as recorded in the Llywarch elegy. Here he is killed in battle. Professor Koch has attempted to date the records to the period 685x700 on the basis that this was the period when the northern British nations would have most benefitted from the lapse in Northumbrian aggression. The English genealogies and chronological tie-ins between English and British events could thus be explained by the conquest of Cumbria and the subsequent increasing influence of English religious men; support of this theory could be found in the Chartres manuscript, if it could be proved to be the oldest version of the *Historia Brittonum* compilation and in fact a precursor to it (*The Gododdin of Aneirin*, ed. Koch, 1995, cxxv). However, Professor Koch fails to explain how such information could have come into the hands of the Gwynedd dynasty. (Jackson 1963, 53) argues for Glasgow as the religious capital of Strathclyde, the last British kingdom in what is now Scotland.

[20] (Jackson 1963, 6; Hughes 1975, 237-9; Bromwich 1976, 175-6; Dumville 1976, 23-50).

[21] (Thurneysen 1896, 85, 87; Bruce 1923, 9). Jackson opposed the inclusion of this text from the *Northern History* on the basis of Beulon's request that the Anglo-Saxon (meaning also the *Northern History*, apparently) genealogies be omitted. This was done to his satisfaction, though *Arthuriana* was left intact. Therefore, *Arthuriana* is not a part of the *Northern History*. I think it more accurate to conclude that Beulon did not believe that the *Arthuriana* was a part of the *Northern*

History. His opinion carries no more weight than that of a modern historian.

[22] These dwell upon the fact that the hero's birth and childhood are spent in Lothian (German as of the early seventh century). The place-names are definitely Celtic, implying the source was in circulation before the conquest of Lothian.

[23] Undeniably, a similar body of literature could be assumed because of the existence of many of the vitae of the Cornish, Breton, and Welsh saints, but I am not aware of any. Instead, the consensus has been that these came from folk memory. (Roberts 1991, 82).

[24] Undoubtedly, similar arguments could be made for many of the *vitae* of the Cornish, Breton, and Welsh saints, but I am not aware of any. Instead, the consensus have been that "Their Latin lives, although containing traditional elements and perhaps some historical features, are compositions of the eleventh and twelfth centuries and constitute a well-defined genre of semi-biographical writing." (Roberts 1991, 82).

[25] For a convenient summary of the linguistic and historical evidence see Chapter I of *Arthurian Tradition and Chrétien*, (1949).

[26] However, names which have obviously been orally learned do not imply that the material with which they are associated was oral as well.

[27] (Anglade 1929; Lejeune 1959).

[28] This line of thinking was originated in 1883 (Paris 1883, 459-534).

[29] The discussion is hardly settled, nor is there a general agreement. As recently as 1976 Eugene Weinraub interpreted the grail ceremony as based on the Jewish religion and thus Chrétien was a Jew or a man with Jewish sympathy. (Frappier 1959, 158; Vigneras 1934-5, 341f. and sources therein cited).

[30] The main characters, *Cligès* and his lover, are Ovidian, but *Cligès*'s parents, Alexander and Soredamors, represent traditional love and are married.

[31] *Cligès* appears to be the most graphic demonstration of his two different ways of portraying love. Soredamors and Alexander get married and live happily ever after, while their child Cligès and Fenice are lovers while Fenice is otherwise married.

[32] Rules no. 184 and 186, respectively.

[33] (*Cligès*, l. 1289; *La Chanson de Roland*, l. 794).

[34] (*Cligès*, ll. 1704-12; *La Chanson de Roland*, ll. 2456). The term "epic pair" is to be found in many epics and foundation myths. It signifies brothers whose names mean roughly the same thing. Thus Hengest and Horsa both mean horse. One of an epic pair is usually invention.

[35] Known from, respectively, *Erec* (l. 5779) and *Yvain* (l. 597).

[36] (*Erec*, ll. 1655-69; *Aeneid* IV: 138-9).

[37] (*Cligès*, l. 635; *De Rerum Natura*, III; l.1056; Laurie 1972, 78).

[38] The references here are quite terse, and influences which might be suggested could only be guesswork.

[39] (*Confessions*, VII. xvii. 23; Laurie, 1972, 63, 68, 81).

[40] (*Cligès*, 4346-7; BN fonds Latin 2931).

[41] (Helinand de Froidmont, *Les vers de la Mort*, trans. Boyer and Santucci 1983, XIX, 349). However, one wonders if this is a note of sympathy, or whether "the frailty of the female sex" (2-3) he speaks of is an intentional irony with regard to Marie's feminism. (McCash 1985, 244-5).

[42] (*The Chronicler of Tours* and the contributor to the *Annales de Rouen*).

[43] Thus "A" was first, apparently Marie critiqued it, and "B" and "C" are either copies of the original or one of them is the final version.

[44] The other influences are transitory with the exception of Marie de Champagne and Andreas Capellanus, whose consistent influence stems from Marie's patronage of Chrétien and her insistence that he follow Andreas Capellanus' rules of courtly love.

[45] The consistency with which Keu, Ginover, Arthur, Gauvain, and Melwas appear in the abduction, in similar roles, argues strongly for a common original source or at least a common tradition. This will be thoroughly demonstrated in the following chapter.

Chapter III: The Characters and their Roles[1]

The previous chapter has shown evidence that a significant percentage of the material in the Arthurian stories came from Britain. In this essay, I will focus the reader's attention on the main characters of the tradition abduction story. No one denies that the names of the chief actors -- Meleagant, Guinièvre, Keu, Gauvain, Arthur, and Lancelot, and their occurrence in the literary material present incontrovertible evidence for the ultimately British origins of the story.[2] However, there are three topics that it is necessary to discuss in order to fully understand the story. These are the strange imposition of Urien/Valerin as the alternative abductor, the exact role of each of the main characters in the presumed original tale, and the birthplace of the name Lancelot. All the above topics will be discussed forthwith.

Lanzelet and *Diu Crône* employ an alternative Valerin/Urien as the antagonist.[3] As all the other characters are consistently present and retain their functions in the different versions, it seems reasonable to assume that either Melwas or Urien is a later intrusion on the story. Most likely Urien is the later addition.[4] The fact that Urien of Rheged was a member of the same heroic age as the Arthurian figures and was a memorable person for early Welsh history is the key. It is quite likely he was superimposed on an already existing theme in the Arthurian corpus as his persona was drawn to it. However, the lingering doubt to this answer is why is there no evidence of this happening in Britain, where his memory was stronger? Etymology offers a neat solution.

Professor Sims-Williams translates *Melwas* as "honey-youth" because the earliest and overwhelming majority of the sources use *Mel* for the first syllable (Sims-Williams 1991, 59). This name then fits into a pattern whereby Melwas is a King of the Isle of Glass. Honey was the main ingredient of the Welsh ale *bragawt*, which is generally suggested to be in excess on the island. Also, the aging process was known to be nearly absent on the Isle of Glass. The other theory, proposed by Dr. Bromwich, is that of Melwas< mael 'prince' + gwas 'lad, servant'.[5]

The translations "prince-lad" and "honey-youth" both sound like titles or nicknames. In the context of *Ymddiddan Gwenhwyfar ac Arthur* or *The Dialogue between Gwenhwyfar and Arthur*, such an appellation would be quite applicable as the nickname of a well-known character, or simply a poetic invention for a nameless hero. Apart from this story and the second *vita* of Gildas, he is unknown in Britain.[6]

Considering his absence in British versions, Urien was possibly given the abductor role when the original antagonist of this tale was forgotten on the continent. Urien would have been superimposed onto the existing story because of his fame, as often happens in heroic cycles, or simply because his name sounded British to a German ear.[7]

Guinièvre seems like a very obvious and necessary element of the tale. She is in all versions both Arthur's queen and the victim of a kidnapping. However, there is some negative evidence that this character was not an old one. Both Guinièvre and her progenitor Gwenhwyfar, are unknown in any tale whose orthography dates before the twelfth century. She is not to be found in the oldest group of triadic material. She is only to be found in *The Dialogue between Arthur and Gwenhwyfar*, the *Modena Archivolt*, *Culhwch ac Olwen* (ll. 161, 330, 358), and the later *Vita Gildae*.[8] There are four tales that have elements that certainly predate Chrétien and possibly Geoffrey. However, one cannot with any certainty date the introduction of Guinièvre to these works much before 1100; she could well be superimposed.[9] It should also be remembered that the names of famed kings' wives were rarely kept, and then only when they were the daughters of famous kings;[10] the father of Gwenhwyfar is unknown.[11]

On a more positive note, however, the often opposing elements in the four British versions suggest that Gwenhwyfar was considered to be Arthur's queen before the transference of the Arthurian material to the continent.[12] However, it is also possible that their agreement here is a direct result of the overwhelming influence Geoffrey of Monmouth had on the development of the Arthurian legend.

Keu's role in the abduction is much simpler to determine. With the sole exceptions of the *Vita Gildae* account and the heavily edited story in *Iwein*, he is always present. Further, the Welsh *Pa gur?*, *Ymddiddan Gwenhwyfar ac Arthur*, and *Culhwch ac Olwen* indicate that Cei was a formidable warrior in Arthur's troupe. If, as the majority of the abductions say, Gauvain and others were away when Melwas/Valerin came to court, Keu would have been an acceptable substitute for him and in no way an unworthy opponent. It is likely he was an original element in the tale, and acted as Guinièvre's protector.

Arthur is the king and husband to the victim. In Irish lore this is a common phenomenon and thus an explanation of his role requires a review of the abduction theme in Irish myth. In the typical abduction tale there is a one-year delay between the kidnapping and the abductor's death, or surrender of the wife (see below). This is so with Chrétien and the *Vita Gildae*. However, in the Irish tales the king is usually the rescuer. In *La Charrette* and most of the other variants Arthur does not have this role. From a literary standpoint this is intriguing.[13] From an historical standpoint, Arthur's role in the plot as it stands is inconsistent regarding the degree of his power and his representation as a warrior. I would suggest the Arthurian world has at one stage added Gwenhwyfar's abduction from another heroic age source.[14]

Any thesis that explores the Celtic aspect of *Le Chevalier de la Charrette* must also address the question of Lancelot. Did he exist in the British tradition prior to the Arthurian rebirth? If so, why is he not visible in Geoffrey of Monmouth's *Historia Regum Britanniae*, *The Pictish King-lists*, the oldest Welsh poems, or any other British tradition? To date, no-one has linked him to any twelfth-century personage Chrétien may have wished to extol. Is he present in one of these works, but the linguistic intricacies are so great one cannot distinguish him? Where did Chrétien get the information about Lancelot saving Guinièvre? Did he or Marie de Champagne invent the name? Lancelot does not rescue the queen in the other abductions -- except for *Lanzelet*. Even then he is only one of many. Clearly Lancelot was not the traditional rescuer.

In a recent article, Dr. Lloyd-Morgan has summarized the argument concisely; Lancelot did not have a past before Chrétien invented him in *Cligès*.[15] However, she does add a single, potentially damaging corollary to her conclusion. Tristan was not a prevalent figure, either. Dr. Lloyd-Morgan suggests the two may not have been common in Welsh lore because their themes both undermine beloved kings (1994,

178). Thus, in her argument she allows for a reason why Lancelot was not a popular character in Wales, yet his absence there is the crux of her argument. The window is still open and Lancelot may have been a part of Welsh lore at one time. If Lancelot was a traditional Arthurian character, his and his story's extreme unpopularity there are thus explicable.

Lancelot has occupied scholars and Arthurian enthusiasts alike for generations. There is no abduction tale in Welsh lore that assigns this character the same role of rescuer as in Chrétien's *La Charrette*.[16] Therefore, one cannot simply link him to Welsh tradition by a comparable personality or adventure. It would indeed appear that Chrétien probably invented Lancelot, but theories abound. Tatlock claims that Geoffrey's book contains *Anguselaus — L' Ancelot*.[17] He is Lleu Llaw Gyffes of the *Mabinogion* (Loomis 1949, 92). He is Lleog/Lleminog of *Preiddeu Annwn* (Loomis 1956, 161-2). Such theories are linguistically challenged.

There are some things one can be certain of, however. In 1842 Viscount Hersant de la Villémarque began the discussion of *Le Chevalier de la Charrette* with a theory based on a long-standing problem in French manuscripts -- the *L'*. When this rule is applied to the Chrétien poem, the *L'* in Lancelot could be *L' Ancelot*, "the Ancelot", as many manuscripts read (Villémarque 1842, 50).

It is known that Old British was in a period of extreme development between the mid- and late-sixth centuries.[18] Any writing in this period would have become obsolete within a few generations. It is also known that many local oral legends of *Y Hen Ogled* would have been lost with the extinction of Old Cumbric some time in the eleventh century.

Third, if one can accept some part of Chrétien's story was of heroic-age character (see Chapter VI), one can make further assumptions. H.M. Chadwick gives us some idea of what happens to the memory of a person or significant event in its early stages of metamorphosis. It would seem that fictional incidents can be attached to characters as soon as they die (Chadwick 1940, 201), or even within their lifetime. For example, it is known that literature about Davy Crockett circulated before his election to Congress. It was claimed that he had outwrestled a bear.

Indeed, proving a saga figure lived at all is difficult. Professor Chadwick is quite skeptical. However, he believes if a figure in a saga did exist, he is to be located in the same period and general location as the central figure of the saga (Chadwick 1912, 334). All this tells the scholar is that an invented figure may be difficult to spot, but if he did exist he lived in the same heroic period as that of the central figure.[19] His statements have been to some extent validated in Celtic studies.[20]

Finally, the main Arthurian romance characters all have an equivalent British name in the opinion of the leading scholar in British Arthuriana, Dr. Bromwich. All are to be found first in the British heroic period, and some are even attested to independently of Arthur.[21] Still the question remains, what about Lancelot?

Is Lancelot the sole non-British figure among the chief of Arthur's men to be invented? Is the critic to believe he is a "bit-part" creation of Chrétien or his translator in *Erec* (l. 1694), and that this same invented character was later used in *Le Chevalier de la Charrette* and *Lanzelet*? It hardly seems likely Chrétien invented him in the 1160s. This is because twenty years later two men wrote independent stories (see Chapter III and below) about the same minor personage, at roughly the same time and in different countries. One can safely say the Lancelot character had a predecessor before his inclusion in *Erec* and therefore before 1160. The fact that Lanzelet's education is by fairies in *Lanzelet* is evidence of the story's extended existence in an oral environment.[22] In turn this is a further reason for postulating an origin of pre Norman character.

In Dr. Bromwich's edition of *Trioedd Ynys Prydein* she states authoritatively that:

> because of the absence of any convincing resemblance in the name forms, I feel no hesitation in rejecting the derivation of "Lancelot" <Elyflath<Eliwlat proposed by T. Gwynn Jones and also that proposed by R.S. Loomis in which he associates "Lancelot" with "Lluch Llauynauc" of *BBC* 94, 13-14 and so derives the name ultimately from that of the Irish god Lug. (*The Welsh Triads*, trans. and ed. Bromwich 1978, 415)

The examination will begin where Dr. Bromwich does. In a concluding remark following several well-researched and generally accepted Arthurian matches, Thomas Jones informs us that Middle Welsh *Eliwlad* is "a kind of rendering of Lancelot".[23] He gives no literary, historical, or referential support for this theory, nor does he explain the word change by oral or written means. I am in total agreement that Jones' argument is unsupported and weak.

In *Celtic Myth and Arthurian Romance* Professor Loomis theorized that Lancelot was in reality the Irish god Lug descended through several men listed in the Welsh Arthurian poems (1927, 190-5). He continued this belief throughout the rest of his career. The Welsh intermediary, he said, could be found in *Culhwch ac Olwen, Pa gur?*, and two versions of the same triad of *Trioedd Ynys Prydein*.[24] In Loomis' words:

> The puzzle may be explained by the fact that the person and the name were borrowed from some foreign people, probably from the Irish since the Welsh are known to have borrowed a few figures famed in Irish saga and enrolled them among Arthur's warriors, e.g. Manawidan ab Llyr in *The Black Book of Carmarthen*, and Cynchwyr mab Nes, Cubert mab Daere, Fercos mab Poch, Lluber Beuthach, Corvii Bervach, and Sgiliti in *Kulhwch*. (Loomis 1941, 929-30)

Thus, his true name was Llwch, transferable to Irish as Lugh. His last name was originally Lonnbemnech that, for some reason Loomis does not explain, the linguistically related and culturally tied Welsh could not understand or even translate. For Loomis, this accounted for the varying surnames. The theory does explain the otherwise unmentioned Lleog/Llemenawc of *Preiddeu Annwn*. Further, the first syllable of the character, "llem<llam 'the bounding or prancing one'" does have some affinity with the athletic Lancelot (*The Welsh Triads*, trans. and ed. Bromwich 1978, 420). However, there remain difficulties with accepting this proposal. For one, such arguments rely heavily on linguistic evidence, an uncertain tool.[25] Besides, even on linguistic grounds, Loomis' argument that Lancelot derives from Lug is not feasible.

Even if the etymologies of Jones or Loomis are correct and there is a connection to one of the mythical characters of Irish or pan-Celtic mythology, this proves nothing. The character Lancelot does need to have been transposed from myth. There are many instances where people have been named after deities of an extinct religion. Current religions observe this practice. The name Bridget among the Welsh and Irish is still well loved, as is Thor or Freyr among the Germanic countries and as was Oswald and other compounds containing *Os* among the Anglo-Saxons.[26] From an historical perspective, any connection of the old gods to a precursor of Lancelot proves nothing. Through the textual variant Arcturus, King Arthur himself has been linked to Ursa Major (*The Welsh Triads*, trans. and ed. Bromwich 1978, 544), yet no one continues to see him as a god of directions.

This brings the critic to the most recent challenger of the theory that claims Lancelot is an invention. Professor Goodrich, as I have mentioned in passing earlier, bluntly reminds us that in Geoffrey's book the brothers Uryen of Moray and Loth of Lothian are both unmistakably Celtic. She believes the third brother, Anguselaus, was too. She suggests that the name would normally lose its middle syllable in metamorphosis from Latin to Old French if it were in a weak and unaccented position, which *gu* is. This change would leave *Anselaus*. This opinion is supported in Dr. Pope's *From Latin to Modern French with Especial Consideration of Anglo-Norman* (1934, 147). However, it should be noted that the author here speaks of alterations to words that occurred over a period of one thousand years and Goodrich speaks of an outright translation from Latin to French. Still, the adjustment of Anguselaus into Old French *Anselaus* is linguistically plausible. From here, Chrétien's talent must have controlled the fate of the name. From a literary standpoint, *Ancelot* in French means "servant", giving "the servant" (Goodrich 1986, 172). Chrétien would have enjoyed the possible duality of meanings with his poetic mind and the fact that several manuscripts have the form *L'Ancelot* supports the theory that this was his intended meaning. Chrétien, one must remember, was a man who needed to satisfy his patroness.

Anguselaus' British form would be *Unguist* (Clancy, personal interview, 1996). This name matches two figures in the *Pictish King-Lists*. The most likely candidate of the two to have been drawn into the Arthurian milieu is probably the son of Forgus. Forgus succeeded in conquering Dalriada and reigning approximately 31 years (Anderson 1980, 88). He was a very powerful and warlike king and most likely inspired heroic stories about himself that could then have been brought into Arthur's literary court. Of course this does not preclude other possibilities. *Unguist* could represent the cognomen of any British hero or subking who existed sometime between 400 and 1200 (See Appendix III).

With Unguist/Anguselaus/Lancelot one has a scribal solution. There are, though, two problems with Professor Goodrich's theory. As Professor Tatlock and others have made note, there was an Angus of Moray killed in 1130 who claimed to be a king of Scotland, just as Geoffrey's Anguselaus of Albany does (Tatlock 1950, 154). It has been argued Geoffrey could have been using the rebel's name for a humorous element in the story. However, this cannot be a joke. Albany normally represented the land North of the Firth of Forth (*The Four Ancient Books of Wales*, trans. Skene 1868, 2). If this was Geoffrey's meaning, the plenary court held by Arthur shows Albany as a geographical complement to the other kings who are there present.[27] If Anguselaus, king of Albany, was inserted to be amusing, it is very well hidden.

Second, Goodrich fails to make a connection with anything or any one who is listed in the Welsh manuscripts. And while her theory that Lancelot was a noble Pict may account for this phenomenon, it seems unreasonable to simply assume Lancelot exists because of linguistic arguments.

The fact is that Lancelot is a large mystery as a character. It is difficult to say whether he became confused later with Arthur or was initially a part of the early corpus. He probably was not originally associated with saving Guinièvre from Melwas (below). There is no concrete, or even tenable ground in the Welsh oral sources, though it is possible he may have been a Pictish or British king. He may have helped steal a cauldron under the appellation Llenlleawc, as Loomis suggested (above), but there is no tangible proof. Regardless, the literary figure Lancelot probably existed in some form prior to 1100. Dr. Bromwich follows Loomis in suggesting an eleventh-century *Lancelin* of Brittany as a prototype, and I think this name is the most important clue about Lancelot's beginnings (*Lanzelet*, ed. Loomis, trans. Webster 1951, 11).

It can be assumed that the abductor, Kei, the abducted, and the hero were in the sources of all the versions of the abductions.[28] One can also be reasonably certain they performed the same basic functions. This, as Dr. Bromwich has often pointed out, is remarkable.[29] Such a faithful preservation of a foreign culture's heroes with or without that region's stock features is, to my knowledge, unique in ancient and medieval world literature, both oral and written. Yet there it is, present in French, German, Italian, and later Dutch, Spanish, Icelandic, Irish, and Scottish romances with all the accouterments of Celtic literature. This is because *Glas* was a probably written source that each author felt a need to reinterpret to a greater or lesser extent.[30] The abduction story, however, has more to offer an inquisitive scholar, as I hope the next three chapters will demonstrate. A penetrating examination of the first full-length version of the abduction will reveal elements in the story that could be historical, followed by a chapter devoted to certainly historical material. The aim of these chapters will be to establish the dates of the earliest elements in the abduction sequence.

---

[1] I have here assumed some knowledge of other abduction romances on the part of the reader in order to maintain the fluidity of my argument. A more detailed discussion of each of the pertinent romances will be forthcoming in the next chapter.

[2] Gauvain's presence in *Le Chevalier de La Charrette* will be discussed fully in the following chapter.

[3] Melwas occurs in both British and continental versions. Therefore, his name was known on the continent and in Wales.

[4] The only instances where Guinièvre is made the victim of two kidnappings are *The Vulgate Version of the Arthurian Romances* and Mallory's *Le Morte d'Arthur*, both late and conglomerative works. It is safe to assume tradition only assigned her one abduction.

[5] (*The Welsh Triads*, trans. and ed. Bromwich, 1978, 382); this theory is based on the Maheloas of (*Erec*, l. 1947). It is interesting enough to note here that the enemy of the isles whom Arthur has confrontations with in *Historia Regum Britanniae* is Gillomarus (or a derivative thereof), whose *Gilla* or *Gil* translates also to young man or servant.

[6] Chambers (1927, 85) is the sole supporter of a theory that the Maylwys mab Baedan of *Culhwch ac Olwen* (l. 178) is Melwas.

[7] Several instances of transplanted heroes come to mind. Theodoric the Great and the Burgundian kings at Attila's court in *Nibelungenlied* and William the Conqueror at Arthur's court in *Culhwch ac Olwen* are the most notable. This is a common feature of heroic age tales.

[8] A full introduction to *Culhwch ac Olwen* is reserved for my discussion of the grail story, below. Here I refer to the story because of its integral nature in understanding the quandary. It is sufficient here to state there are at least three stages in the development of *Culhwch ac Olwen*. The first is a myth known as "Six go around the world", (*Culhwch ac Olwen*, eds. Bromwich and Evans 1992, xliii). The second is represented by the Arthurian characters, was added progressively before the fourteenth century (*Culhwch ac Olwen*, eds. Bromwich and Evans 1992, ix, xliv), and can be dated no later than the tenth century. The third stage is one of constant introduction of

characters from the historical world of the twelfth to fourteenth centuries (*Culhwch ac Olwen*, eds. Bromwich and Evans 1992, lxxxii).

[9] Dr. Bromwich, personal communication, 1997. She promises to write on this subject in her new edition of *The Welsh Triads*.

[10] This is so in the Norse sagas *Beowulf*, *Volsungasaga*, and *Nibelungenlied*.

[11] Gwenhwyfar is given three fathers in *The Welsh Triads*.

[12] Theoretically, if all versions name her as the abductee, and the versions have clearly developed very different plot twists, the base story must have included her and been old enough to allow such diversity to develop.

[13] I would suggest that, for this reason and the weakness of Gwenhwyfar's connection to early Arthurian lore, Gwenhwyfar's abduction has been added to the Arthurian corpus from a tradition external to Arthur.

[14] This would clearly place the abduction tale outside the realm of a literary source for Arthur. However, it does remain a source for the fifth or sixth centuries.

[15] Her argument is based on the fact that there is no existing Welsh version of the Lancelot rescue, or of Lancelot, accept in translations where Lancelot is prominent and his presence necessary.

[16] In fact he is absent except for Welsh recensions of continental Arthurian romances.

[17] (Tatlock 1950, 154). This would make the character's English popularity particularly ironic. Professor Tatlock believed Geoffrey created this name to make fun of an Angus of Moray, a Scottish rebel killed in 1130.

[18] He has done this particularly in *Language and History of Early Britain: A Chronological Survey of the Brittonic Languages 1st to 12th c. A.D.* (1953, 4-6, 9), with an update in his chapter in *Studies in Early British History* (1954).

[19] See Chapter IV of the author's *Arthur: Historicity and Location*, forthcoming.

[20] O' Rahilly based his history of early Ireland on the myths and legends of the Irish (1946, v).

[21] Modred-Medrawt (*Nennius*, trans. Morris 1980, 45), Geraint-Erec, Peredur-Perceval (Bromwich 1991, 281), Owain-Yvain (Bromwich 1991, 281), and Drust-Tristan (Bromwich 1991, 281).

[22] (*Lanzelet*, ed. Loomis, trans. Webster 1951, 27; Chadwick 1940, 763-4). This is a stock feature in an oral tale.

[23] (Jones 1936, 37). He compares the figures Morgan Hud-Morgan le Fay, Banw-Ban of Berwick, and Melwas-Meliagraunce.

[24] These are Lluch Llenlleawc the Irishman et al, Llyauynauc, Lludd Llurugawc, and Llyr Lluyddawc, respectively.

[25] Particularly hazardous in Arthurian research. In this corpus, it involved transference of material to the romance authors through several languages (Latin-French, Scottish-French, Scottish-Breton-French, Welsh-French). A safer connection in Arthurian studies relies minimally on exact linguistic compatibility. Instead, ties focus on the motifs and stories associated with a character.

[26] The *Os* prefix refers to the gods and is related to the Norse Aesir.

[27] The Moray of which the Angus of history was king has a delegate named King Uryen.

[28] Although, based on the traditional material, it is certainly possible that Kei may have been an early hero.

[29] (Bromwich 1961b; 1983, 41-4; 1991b, 276-81).

[30] The simplest reason for this is that Celtic bards had a habit of transposing characters and themes, so that such consistency can hardly be thought to have occurred in an oral environment.

Chapter IV: Literary Tools for Supplementary Material

In the last chapter, it was seen that the material that made up the plots of the Arthurian stories came from Britain and that the characters were remarkably consistent. This in turn argued that they were all originally from a common tradition, whatever its form and from whatever point it began to mutate. Building on this conclusion, I will be using the other abduction romances in conjunction with the Chrétien version for comparison. When there is a question regarding the original sense of a *Le Chevalier de la Charrette* episode, I will employ the other romances to clarify a scene. To do this, it is necessary here to briefly examine all the major versions of the Arthurian abduction one at a time. This will have two results. Most importantly, one can learn which works were, at the least, not solely the derivative of any now-extant earlier version. Second, I will demonstrate that several tales involving Guinièvre's abductions are not simply adaptations of one another. This will help formulate a theory of a common source and begin to determine when that source may have first taken a recognizable form. I shall, however, refrain from speculation as to its place of origin at this time.

The first of the pre-Galfridic versions of the abduction is ascribed to Caradoc (*Two Lives of Gildas*, trans. Williams 1990, 102), a monk of Llancarfon who was a professional hagiographer (Rider 1990, 6). Caradoc's rendition is fraught with improbabilities, which makes it clear the *vita* was adjusted to serve Glastonbury's purposes.[1] Foremost, it places Gildas in Glastonbury, whereas the earlier, anonymous *Vita of Gildas* does not. In fact there is no other reference to Gildas living in

Glastonbury, which would not be an abbey till the eighth century.[2] Here the reader may begin to suspect the Glastonbury monks of deception, and such a scholar would have a healthy amount of support.[3] Arthur and his wife were "discovered" there in the twelfth-century. *Perlesvaus*'s source was from Glastonbury. Together, these two are ample demonstration of the lengths the monks of this period would go to so that they might maintain their pilgrim standing. Even Caradoc's authorship is questioned. Only one of the two manuscripts list him as the author.

There is a gleam of true antiquity in the story, though. Caradoc's statement that Arthur searched for the queen about a year is most enlightening.[4] The period of time seems unnecessarily long, and does have similarities to Celtic motif. The one-year hunt for the abductor has numerous parallels in Irish myth;[5] it is an obvious sign of some aspect of Celtic oral handling. Glastonbury has here used the motif to its advantage.

The inclusion of a king as rescuer is a common device in Saints' Lives, so it should not lead one to believe there is a serious divergence from the later versions.[6] With this in mind, the *Vita Gildae* has some notable parallels to Chrétien's *La Charrette*, such as Melwas as the kidnapper, Gwenhwyfar the victim, a removal to an island, and a restoration to the king.[7] However, it predates Chrétien, which means it was independent of Chrétien's influence. The story was written in Britain. Because of this, Caradoc's version was probably independent of all French tradition.

Of the three Gwenhwyfar/Guinièvre abductions which could be prior to Geoffrey, that from the *Life of Gildas* is by far the most complete. The other two, *Ymddiddan Gwenhwyfar ac Arthur* and *The Modena Archivolt*, share a common problem for this comparison: They portray only one scene.[8] However, they both contain material independent of Geoffrey and Chrétien and are therefore worthy of study.

The first of these, *Ymddiddan Gwenhwyfar ac Arthur*, is found in two versions. Both involve mainly a conversation between Gwenhwyfar and Cei, and have enough dialogue similarities to be considered two products of a distant original. How far back the work should be placed is a different matter. The height and prowess accorded to Cei throughout the confrontation points much more toward a traditional Welsh origin than the romances.[9] The placement of Arthur in Dyfneint, or Devon could also be from native tradition. The prominence of Cei and the probable absence of Arthur from a speaking part[10] make it clear the dialogue was not based on the Caradoc version. However, this work has Glastonbury influence; the location of Melwas in the "Isle of Glass"[11] can only have been due to the church's influence (above). Still, aware of the probable motivations of the author, one can make good use of the dialogues.

The other pre-Galfridic abduction -- found in the Archivolt relief of an Italian church -- is more problematic in nature. It is a picture of one scene, and from it one may gather that a certain Caradoc has imprisoned Gwenhwyfar in a castle. Meanwhile, Arthur, Cei, Gwalgavius, and Isdernus are attacking it from both sides (below). Unfortunately the only hints as to date can be gleaned from the armor etched on the figures and the spelling of the names, and it is not solid enough evidence. Caradoc and Isdernus are never connected with the abduction, and Arthur only in the Caradoc of Llancarfan version.

Together, these three versions of the Guinièvre abduction demonstrate a consistent plot. In it the following common story may be seen. The protagonist challenges and wins the queen. He is allowed to take her to his region without further threat of violence. Arthur's men and possibly Arthur himself rescues her and returns her to Arthur's hall. In this respect *Le Chevalier de la Charrette* is clearly a fourth variant of the abduction episode. It is quite apparent that the material in the four versions goes back to a common oral and/or literary source. This source was undoubtedly to be found in the British literature prior to Caradoc's book (c. 1130). It is this collective knowledge from which I believe Chrétien drew.

However, there are more versions of the abduction of Guinièvre. Geoffrey of Monmouth can be said to lead this second collection for two reasons. First, he wrote the first internationally read Arthurian history. Second, that "history" had a tremendous impact on Arthurian literature as a source of inspiration throughout the Middle Ages. However, the abduction contained therein bears little resemblance to what I have postulated above as a prototype, and the chapters pertaining to Modred have no basis in Old Welsh literature.[12] The kidnapping of Guinièvre in this version actually contains a dearth of historical, motival, or nomenclatural knowledge regarding Dark Age Britain.

There is not much detail in his narrative. Instead of the casual story pace one generally finds in Welsh tales such as *Owain* (Thomson 1991, 166), the events seem hurried, as in *Yvain*. Arthur rushes from France to combat the pretender to his throne and fights two battles in two days, the last ending in his death. There is little detail as to protocol or the specific weapons of combat, methods of fighting, or rights of inheritance that would indicate a place of origin. The only real hint one is given that the French and Roman campaigns, and the quelling of Modred's rebellion are not simply the creation of Geoffrey's mind is in several battles. Here those who fell and the manner in which they died are recounted.[13] Geoffrey simply generalizes and passes from one event to the next too quickly! He probably knew of an abduction of Guinièvre and used it as a plot device to help cause the end of the Arthurian realm he had presented in such extravagant terms. However, as to his sense of politics or chronology, his opinion is hardly dependable.[14] His tendency to displace and rearrange segments of British history even as he claimed to be representing it is too well established. On top of this, Geoffrey is known to have been writing to further his political career and was promoted to bishop soon after *Historia Regum Britanniae*'s publication. One will be on safer ground avoiding Geoffrey, and Modred's abduction of Guinièvre.[15]

In sharp contrast, Ulrich von Zatzikhoven's *Lanzelet*[16] is a document that offers a wealth of Celtic material. This in support of Ulrich von Zatzikhoven's statement that his source was a *Welsche* book, and in contrast to the general opinion that condemns him as a German redactor of Chrétien.[17] In addition, something more is known of Ulrich Zatzhikoven's source than Chrétien's. Its owner was a Hugh de Morville who was brought to Germany in 1194 as a surety for the rest of King Richard's ransom (*Lanzelet*, ed. Loomis, trans. Webster 1951, 151). This Hugh was a man of Cumberland or south-western Scotland (*Lanzelet*, ed. Loomis, trans. Webster 1951, 5). If Ulrich Zatzikhoven's book is to be thought of as a direct translation and interpretation of Chrétien, it was at no less than one remove from the French poet.

Its direct correlation to *La Charrette*, however, must be viewed with skepticism. Zatzikhoven makes fifty-three appeals to authority and without exception each is in a section with traditional material (Webster 1934, 22 fl.). Often these invocations are for elements of which *Le Chevalier de la Charrette* offers no parallel. In *Lanzelet*, Guinièvre's love interest. Further, in the *Lanzelet* redaction Cei helps in the rescue instead of being the cause of the abduction. Bademagus' counterpart, Malduz, guides the heroes to Guinièvre, as opposed to holding her captive. These and other variations (below) from Chrétien of strongly

Literary Tools for Supplementary Material

Celtic provenance make it difficult to believe *Lanzelet* was based in any significant way on Chrétien's poem.

Lanzelet also offers hints of the societal structure of the culture from which it originated. The fact that the niece of one of the rulers Lanzelet kills inherits her father's lands would have been highly unusual to Ulrich von Zatzikhoven and all of Europe's medieval culture. Succession by the eldest son, primogeniture, had been the rule for several centuries in Germany during Ulrich's lifetime. A woman ruling major property would have been a last resort to keep land in a family. Ulrich Zatzikhoven could not have understood that Celtic law gave the husband of the last ruler's daughter the authority (see Chapter V). Instead, he has the lovesick girl give Lanzelet her property. Lanzelet collects three kingdoms by seducing two more women in this manner (*Lanzelet*, ed. Loomis, trans. Webster 1951, 55, 42, 100).

Chrétien de Troyes' *La Charrette* (c. 1185)
|
Hughe de Morville's text (c. 1194)
|
Ulrich Zatzikhoven's *Lanzelet* (c. 1200)

Lanzelet, one may conclude, seems to have too many Celtic peculiarities that do not come from *Vita Gildae* or Chrétien de Troyes to be considered derived from Chrétien.[18] The often contradictory actions of the characters Keu/Keii and Bademagus/Malduz and the absence of the romantic element in the main plot of *Lanzelet* argue for a great deal of separation between the two. Further, *Lanzelet* reveals a large amount of preserved heroic-age ideals in this supposed romance. Therefore, I shall rely on it for confirming Old British elements in *La Charrette*. In the words of Hendricus Spaarnay:

> Though it is true that Lanzelet possesses the virtue of courage, axiomatic in a medieval hero, and is capable of loyalty, sacrifice, and liberality, he takes life much as it comes. He has no conscience in love; religion is as foreign to him as it was presumably to the author of Morville's book. His biography is an Arthurian romance in its most elementary stage. (Spaarnay 1959, 439)

Despite *Diu Crône*'s relatively late publication (1200x1250), this document, too, is highly useful. In it Keii is shown the same respect accorded him in the Middle Welsh tales. He is the one who most greatly laments the supposed death of Gawein (ll. 16862-17092). It is he who leads Arthur's army to meet with Gawein "as was proper" (l. 22221). It must be admitted that Heinrich Türlin indicates strong influence from Chrétien, but Türlin is quite certain of Keii's prominence in Arthur's court.

> Although Keii might be unpleasant and quite mannerless, he still had not lost the pride of nobility. Indeed, he was so brave that he wouldn't avoid any monster: He dared fight it no matter how large it seemed to him and whatever his chances of success. You should also know that Arthur was zealous in virtue and in his faultless youth had chosen such attendants as were free of deceit. How could Keii have remained one of them for a short time if he had been as evil as many have said? The truth is that he liked to scoff and spared no one. That was his chief failing (ll. 1521-45).

This scoffing and wit were an acclaimed part of a Celtic warrior's abilities, not a liability.[19]

Diu Crône also has an interesting scene reminiscent of that in *Pa gur?* In it, a gatekeeper makes Arthur prove the worth of all of his comrades in order to gain entrance. *Diu Crône* likewise makes Gawein prove his worth. Also noteworthy is the repeated use of decapitation (ll. 12957-8, 13386, 16713, 17762-72), and Gawein's promiscuity (ll. 8423, 8659, 13181), though these can be thought of as common Arthurian motifs at this stage. In his *ALMA* contribution, Dr. Sparnaay concluded: "On the whole, one gets the impression that Heinrich created very little out of whole cloth, that much of his material came from lost sources, but that he made his own combinations and exercised considerable freedom in the invention of detail" (1959, 442). This precarious source will be employed only for comparison, and with due caution.

In c. 1205 Hartmann von Aue wrote a German adaptation of Chrétien's *Yvain*. It largely follows the storyline and specifics of Chrétien or alters them to the taste of a German court, but he does at times show signs of an independent Celtic source. Gawein alone is mentioned as Guinièvre's rescuer (*Iwein* ll. 15-17, 267). Also, the cloak, which is so prominent in Celtic law and myth (below), is added to the story in two places where it does not appear in Chrétien.[20] When dealing with Chrétien, one can easily see why this piece of clothing is mentioned less regularly. It must have been an essential garment for the British people and the coastal French with the constant precipitation in these regions. However, the Germans, who have no access to the Gulf Stream, are therefore in less damp climate and are hardly in more need of protection from rain. Admittedly, this is fragile evidence, but the more complete details regarding the abduction scene also lend themselves to this conclusion. It must be admitted, however, that the evidence for it as an independent variation of the abduction is nearly, if not fully, untenable.

From this group of abductions that are known to have derived from at least one common source (see Chapter III), three relatively safe assumptions may be made. First, the abductions of *Ymddiddan*, *Vita Gildae*, *Modena Archivolt*, *Diu Crône*, and *Lanzelet* all contain many unique details of British provenance that are unknown in the previous extant manuscripts. This evidences at least partial independence from Chrétien and each other. Second, the consistency with which the independent elements of each version may be linked back to a much older British culture argues for a common source.[21]

Third, the diversity of detail in the abduction theme and the earliest dates for some of the abduction redactions are telling. They allow for the conjecture that the tradition of the abduction of Arthur's queen was an old one by 1100.[22] Finally, the consistency with which Gwenhwyfar/Guinièvre is made Arthur's queen implies that either she was a part of the oldest Arthurian tradition or that she had been attached to it before the development of the abduction theme. Again, this would have happened well before 1100. The date at which this prototype first emerged is an important one and the question will be explored as fully as possible. In the next two chapters evidence will be brought forward to help prove it was in existence before 900. This evidence will be of an historical nature. It is hoped that the establishment of historical elements in the poem may reasonably allow one to link the abduction prototype to some of the material from the *Northern Memoranda* or another, related source of early British history.

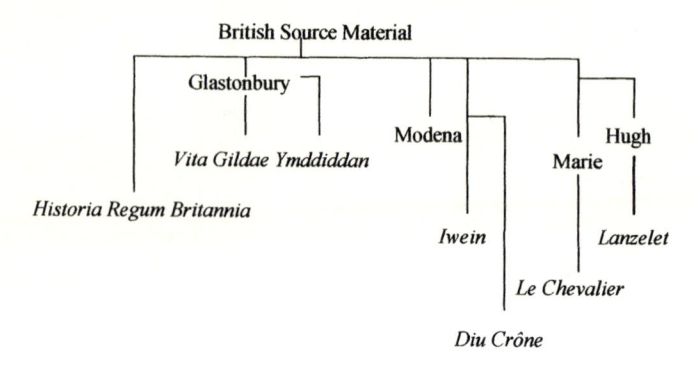

```
British Source Material
├── Glastonbury
│   ├── Vita Gildae Ymddiddan
│   └── Historia Regum Britannia
├── Modena
│   └── Iwein
│       └── Le Chevalier
│           └── Diu Crône
└── Hugh
    └── Marie
        └── Lanzelet
```

[1] It is, in fact, the episode involving Arthur that is the main purpose of the Life. His gratitude at recovering his wife and the act of giving territory to Glastonbury was regarded as contractual, while the antiquity of the act gave the monastery sanctity. However, as there are so many abduction stories, each with their own blend of Celtic customs, and motifs, one must assume the tale was in existence in tradition before Caradoc wrote (Roberts 1991, 82).

[2] (Foot 1991, 167, 169; Finberg 1967, 346).

[3] I list here only the major authors; for a more exhaustive list see Abrams and Carley, (eds.) *The Archaeology and History of Glastonbury Abbey. Essays in Honour of the Ninetieth birthday of C.A. Ralegh Radford*, (1991). (Crick 1991; Davies 1981; Loomis 1953; *Didot Perceval*, ed. Nitze 1934).

[4] Similar tales in Irish myth and legend have many variations (e.g. the king's men search for a year, then the king finds the prison of his wife immediately; the king is told to be at a specified place in one year, etc.), but all somehow contain the motival one year. (Cross 1970, 51).

[5] Examples of this form of literature are to be found under titles including *aitheda* (elopement), *tochmarc* (wooing), *longes* (exile), *echtra* (adventures in fairyland), *Táin* (cattle-raid), and *Tóruigheacht* (pursuing).

[6] The saints of the vitae rarely deal with anyone but kings. This is so that when the antagonist admits he is less powerful, the saint gains a maximum amount of prestige from the confrontation. On the other

hand, it seems the earliest abductions (more specifically those found in *aitheda*) always have the king and an army in pursuit of the wife (Cross 1970, 52).

[7] The alternate *vita* has no abduction.

[8] For a full discussion of the Modena relief, see Loomis in *Medieval Studies in Memory of Gertrude Schoepperle Loomis*, (1927b).

[9] Version A, line 10. Hereafter the two conversations will be referred to as simply "A" and "B".

[10] This is a point of dispute. (Williams 1938).

[11] l. A2; this is intended to mean Glastonbury.

[12] Exception being made for the atypical account in Historia Regum Britanniae that Modred is Arthur's nephew and he is Arthur's heir. Tatlock suggested that this scenario might be a reflection of events contemporary to Geoffrey. In 1135, Stephen had refused to accept his uncle's daughter Matilda as sovereign. Similarly, Modred refuses to accept the sovereignty of his aunt over him and claims the kingship (Tatlock 1950, 426-7).

[13] This is a well-recorded feature of heroic age battles. Note *Mahabharata*, *Nibelungenlied*, the Ulster, Gilgamesh, and bogatyri cycles, and the elegy of Owain mab Urien.

[14] Tatlock (1950), has been the strongest critic of Geoffrey in this century.

[15] Bromwich authoritatively states there is no linguistic relationship between Medrawt and Melwas in her edition of *The Welsh Triads* (1978, 384).

[16] Only available translation is by Webster, edited by Professor Loomis (1951).

[17] Which both Webster and Loomis translate as French, though in light of its Celticity this conclusion should be rethought. I do not deny some elements derive from Chrétien, but the vast differences in ethos and plot between the two argue for a more ancient source for Zatzikhoven's book.

[18] Though the fact that *Lanzelet* includes the fostering of the hero by a fay, and Lancelot in *La Charrette* (ll. 2347-62) has a ring from a fay would lend itself to believing they both may have had a common source.

[19] (Chapter IV; Gowan 1988, 16-17).

[20] (*Iwein*, ll. 15-17, 267).

[21] The names of both the abducted and the abductor are linguistically compatible in all versions. In addition, many of the elements culturally belong to a period before 1100 and probably before 900. It is most economical to believe that there was only one such source.

[22] Caradoc of Llancarffan and Geoffrey of Monmouth both wrote in the 1130s. The abductor and rescuer are both different, as is the setting in both versions. It is safe to assume that such diversity in a story which is essentially the same would have taken something more than thirty years.

Chapter V: Motifs and Details: Clues of Celtic Origins

Onomastic study provides a useful tool in the search for Celtic origins in Chrétien. Here it has established a common tradition for the abduction legend. A survey of those elements in the other early abduction romances that are Celtic and probably non-motival has confirmed their independent use of *Glas*, the probably written British common source. Certain motifs and themes, some of which may be pseudo-historical, are also visible in the lines of Chrétien's verse. I will survey both the Celtic motifs and themes to understand better the extent and nature of Chrétien's debt to the ancestors of the Britons. This has, unfortunately, never been done before, but in doing so I feel a great deal may be learned.

The Arthurian hall, as Chrétien paints it, could very well be ancient as well as modern in Chrétien's day. The poet describes the structure in two passages -- at the Cart Castle and the Castle of the four Axemen. I shall first argue that the description of the castle in each episode was not altered to improve Chrétien's plot and then explain my reasons for claiming that it had Dark Age British origins.[1]

The dining hall of the Cart castle has three beds on which the two visitors Gauvain and Lancelot retire, then the hostess leaves for a room in another chamber. One can assume that the two guests are not being insulted, because Gauvain is otherwise treated with the utmost courtesy. Why does the damsel make these warriors sleep in the dining hall and not a guest room? Certainly there were more rooms in the royal contemporary castle that Chrétien could be expected to portray.[2]

The other instance is the Castle of the four Axemen, where a lady offers to shelter Lancelot in return for sexual favors. Lancelot is again left to sleep in the hall of the castle (l. 1292). What is more telling is his surprise at not finding the woman there waiting when he goes there to sleep.

It is a moot point that older castles of the lower nobility were in existence in the twelfth century. It is also quite probable that some of their dining halls had the dual use of eating and sleeping which is implied in this poem. It should not be forgotten, though there is also evidence that royal halls in the centuries following the withdrawal of Roman troops had this dual use, in German as well as British sources.

In *Beowulf* the sleeping arrangement of the hero and his men is clearly described: the king moves to separate quarters while the guests and his retainers remain in the hall. This is more precisely articulated in *Hrolf Kraki's Saga*, where it is stated that the lord of the dwelling and his wife were to sleep in a separate chamber in the hall.[3] All other men, even such distinguished guests as Beowulf, then slept in the same room in which they had dined (*Beowulf*, trans. Crossley-Holland 1982, 35).

Early Welsh tales rarely speak of the architectural arrangements. However, post-Roman archaeology in Britain supports the theory of dining/sleeping halls, though the agreement has been anything but uniform.[4] Beginning with Professor Alcock in Dinas Powys and Cadbury Castle, Somerset (1963, 62; 1995), many archaeologists have come to the conclusion that halls were in existence and used as both consumption and sleeping facilities.[5] Professor Charles Thomas is willing to term site D of Radcliffe's dig a potential hall (1993, 90-1). Dr. Brian Hope-Taylor's Yeavering writing is another notable agreement with this proposal. Dr. Selkirk's finds at Birdoswald also concur with these verdicts (1990, 288-91). In Dr. Kenneth Dark's *Civitas to Kingdom*, the author reasons back why such structures were a necessary part of the late Roman world (1994, 178-81). Dr. Laing has not only accepted the proposal but has produced an article "Timber Halls: Some Problems", which survey the various obstacles in detecting a hall on a site (1969, 110-127). Though currently not accepted by all experts, the idea is accepted by most. The theory of halls is an established part of Dark Age Britain. *La Charrette* contains them as well.

On the other hand, there is reason to doubt Chrétien's halls were contemporary. The setting he portrays bears little similarity to the contemporary, royal Norman castle as is it is understood today. These structures featured living quarters adjacent to the dining hall, not generally within them.[6] The dining hall Chrétien would have known was simply not designed as a sleeping quarters.[7] For the upper echelon of nobility to retire to the drafty dining room the servants slept in would have been uncomfortable and degrading. The addition of several extra rooms above or beside where the residents ate had become the norm in defensive structures of Chrétien's time. The conveniences of private quarters were simply expected by visitors. If one cannot state with impunity that the castles which Chrétien describes are British and date to well before 1100, one may be secure in believing that they may well have been.

A second aspect of Chrétien's poem that is surprising is Lancelot's military behavior; in particular the way in which all duels seem destined to end, decapitation. Lancelot beheads a man at the request of Jandrée just after crossing the stony passage. He does so again to Meleagant himself (l. 5034).

The prescience that this is Celtic, even common in ancient and Medieval societies, is easy to verify.[8] Herodotus tells us that a Celtic warrior could not receive his share of the booty without a head (*The Histories*, IV. 64). Livy records that one important general Postumius was taken to a temple by the Celtic tribe Boii where they decapitated him. They made a gold-mounted cup of his skull (*Ab Urbe condita*, XXIII. 24: 11-12). Again, speaking of the Early Republic, Livy writes that the Romans received no word about a particular battle until: "in conspectu fuere Gallorum equites, pectoribus equorum suspensa gestantes capita et lanceis infixa ovantesque moris sui carmine." "...some Gallic horsemen came in sight, with heads hanging at their horses's breasts or fixed on their lances, and singing their customary song of triumph." (X:26: 11).

Irish myth contains the same theme of decapitation. All of Cú Chulainn's battles seem to end with a head dangling from its own hair. Such is the case with the renowned warriors Nadcranntail, Loch, and many others (*Taín Bó Cuailgne*, trans. Kinsella 1969, 124, 126, ad infinitum). *The Legend of Brân*, two instances in *Peredur* (*Mabinogion*, trans. Jones and Jones 1974, 192, 226), and the elegy to Urbgen's head provides confirmation. The Welsh had a cultural fascination with the human head. It seems reasonable to believe that heads had some sort of mystical or religious meaning to the Celts even after Christianity.[9]

It may be argued, and with some cogency, that such things as decapitations were familiar to the twelfth-century mind and therefore beheadings are not a uniquely Celtic practice. War has always been ghastly in its treatment of mankind -- before and after death -- and decapitation is a motif of both heroic-age societies and medieval Europe. On the other hand, neither the Greek nor Germanic/Norse heroic ages have recorded such a fascination with the head.[10] Achilles drags Hector's entire body around Troy and Sigurd's head becomes no man's trophy. It is possible that this facet of the romance has purely Celtic origins.

Another point that must be made concerns the sexual habits of the Celtic peoples. Herodotus was the first man to record their marital customs. Of the Massagetae he wrote that each man married a wife, but these wives were common to all (*The Histories*, 1.216). Caesar was quite appalled at the sexual promiscuity of the women, saying that a female might share between ten and twelve men, mainly brothers, fathers, and sons (*De Bello Gallica*, XIV. 1). Strabo went so far as to say the Celtic women were carnally active with their own sons and brothers, though he admits it is only hearsay (*The Geography*, 4.5.4). Dio Cassius claims a Celtic woman proudly stated that her race only mated with the strong men (*Dio's Roman History*, lxvii: 16). Later Dio Cassius writes that the Maeatae and Caledonians shared their women (lxxvii; 12).

Similarly in Insular lore: In *Culhwch ac Olwen*, a woman is offered to the hero at the gate right after food, wine, and song (*Mabinogion*, trans. Jones and Jones 1974, 98). There is a legend that Hercules was the progenitor of the Galatian family during one of his travels. He is said to have slept with the founding mothers of the various tribes. The compert stories,[11] illustrated in Mongan, MacBeth, and Sts. Kentigern, Ambrosius, and Dubricius all demonstrate the widespread practice of this feature in the Irish and British regions after Christianity had become established.[12] Several instances in the Irish tale *Tochmarc Emere* contain relevant examples in Irish myth that indicate its social acceptability.[13] These are only a few examples. To quote Dr. Kelly: "The large numbers of sons begotten by kings indicate widespread polygyny among royalty". (*Críth Gablach*, ed. Binchy 1970, 70).

This obsolete coupling tradition is somewhat confirmed in Old Irish Law as well. Here there was only one "form of matrimony that is fully legitimate and honorable", that of *cét muinteras* -- a lifetime marriage with a woman who thereby acquired full status in her husband's family. Along with this, there were many semi-legitimate contracts. In the laws of *Crith Gablach* (c. 600) one is told that *lanamnas* was a legal term for " ... neither permanent nor monogamous" marriage, and a *dormuine* was a "temporary concubine". Kelly tells us this differentiation was common to most tracts, as was the concept of seven forms of marriage (*Crith Gablach*, ed. Binchy 1970, 70-1). The temporary concubine was an established part of the Irish way of life. The coming of Patrick and Christianity had pressured the Irish customs. Because of them, a series of modifications were made to marriage laws from the fifth century onwards. However, the practice clearly persevered.

The Welsh Laws also contain evidence that the taking of a wife could be both of a temporary or permanent nature:

> Whoever sleeps three nights with a woman from when the fire is covered until it is uncovered on the morrow, and from then on wants to leave her, let him pay her a steer worth twenty pence and another worth thirty pence and another worth forty pence. And if he takes her to house and home and she is with him seven years, he is bound to share with her from then on as with a wife with bestowers.[14]

Even when she was fully married as a *gwraig briod*, a woman might legally go outside the common bounds of monogamy.[15] One of the three cases in Welsh Law in which a husband could not receive compensation for his wife was "if a man from afar from a strange country should fondle her before knowing the law of the country".[16]

All this points to a strong Medieval Celtic tradition of princes arriving in foreign lands and mating with the royal women there for a night. It is a pattern to be found throughout Celtic lore, and one to be condemned by the new ideals of love formulated by Andreas Capellanus and adored throughout Europe.

With this in mind, one may recall that the heroes Gauvain, Lancelot, and Perceval seem to be romantically associated with a substantial number of women.[17] Considering the Celtic customs, perhaps we may also better understand what has happened in the poem at hand, and increasingly in the Arthurian tales that followed. A Celtic theme is being carefully hidden. Chrétien's first leaves us a hint in *Le Charrette*. In the moments when Lancelot watches Guinièvre and attempts to jump to her, the author makes a coy remark about Gauvain being occupied with the Lady of the Cart Castle.

> A l'autre fenestre delez
> estoit la pucele venue,
> si l'i ot a consoil tenue
> mes sire Gauvains an requoi
> une piece, ne sai de quoi (ll. 544-8).

The maiden had come to the next window, where my lord Gauvain had chatted with her for awhile in private, though I do not know what was said or the subject of their conversation. (trans. Owen 1989, 192).

Lancelot is not totally free of this behavior, either.

> Il lor done, puis si s'an va
> tant que de bas vespre trova
> une dameisele venant,
> molt tres bele et molt avenant,
> bien acesmee et bien vestue.
> La dameisele le salue.
> Come sage et bien afeitiee
> et cil respont: "Sainne et Heitiee,
> dameisele , vos face Dex."
> puis li dit: "sire, mes ostex
> vos est ci prés apareilliez
> se del prandre estes conseilliez;
> mes paritel herbergeroiz
> que avoec moi vos coucheroiz
> einsi le vos ofre et presant."
> "Plusor sont qui de presant
> li randissent cinc cenz merciz,
> et il an fu trestoz nerciz
> et li a respondu totel:
> "Dameisele, de vostre ostel
> vos merci ge, si l'ai moltchier
> me soferroie je molt bien."
> "-Je n'an feroie autremant rien,"
> fet la pucele, "par mes ialz."
> Et cil, des que il ne puet mialz,
> l'otroie li cuers le dialt
> quant itant seulement le blesce,
> molt avra au couchier tristesce (*La Charrette*, ll. 931-960).

Then he goes on his way until, late in the evening, he met a damsel coming his way who was exceedingly beautiful and attractive, elegantly dressed and adorned. This damsel greets him discreetly and politely, and he replies: "May God keep you healthy and happy, young lady!" Then she said to him: "My home, sir, is all ready for your lodging, if you're prepared to accept it. But you'll be given hospitality on condition that you sleep with me: Those are the terms of my offer." Many people would have thanked her five hundred times for this favour; yet it leaves him quite miserable, and he gives her a very different reply: "I thank you, damsel, for your offer of hospitality and am most grateful for it. But, if you were agreeable, I could well do without the sleeping arrangement." - "By my eyes," says the maiden, "My offer depends on that!" then, as there is nothing else for it, he agrees to her condition. (*La Charrette*, trans. Owen 1989, 197).

Can one believe that the territory Lancelot is passing through demands he stay in the Castle of the four Axemen? It is not practical; he is in friendly territory and will be for several days according to Chrétien. Besides, a Medieval knight, especially the best knight, was not so pampered as to need an inn every evening. It is not necessary in Chrétien's romances, either. Later Arthurian knights often sleep in forests quite often. Perceval will do so in *Le Conte du Graal* and Gawen in *Syre Gawen and the Grene Knight*. Yet this is the sole reason Chrétien gives us for Lancelot consenting to the lady's conditions (*La Charrette*, l. 959).

Later in the poem, one finds the wife of Meleagant's Seneschal bargaining for sex with Lancelot (*La Charrette*, ll. 5500-15), and then quietly accepting that she will not receive her end of the bargain. Why? Even Jandrée, who saves Lancelot from the tower where Meleagant imprisons him, gives us little doubt that she would consent to more intimate relations as well. Her attraction is useless, however. Jandrée is described as repulsive, so it does not raise Lancelot's esteem in the reader's eyes if she is attracted to him.

All the above examples point in one direction, towards a different view on male sexuality. Chrétien undoubtedly develops a theme about Lancelot's devotion to Guinièvre in this poem. However, it is also clear he has attempted to smother another Celtic tradition. The poet most probably had before him a source where the protagonist of the tale was a typical carnally active Celtic hero. This theme was neither acceptable to his own moral conscience, nor to Marie's wishes. To rectify the situation, he altered those portions of the story that conflicted with his thematic purpose and made use of the romantic ideals of Capellanus' book to conform with Marie de Champagne's wishes. However, the stitches in the patchwork remain. In the independent and more British *Lanzelet*, the hero is unrestrained by Marie's fetters and often finds new lovers.

Another action of Chrétien's characters is helpful in understanding his material; the phenomena of the taunting knight who provokes a fight with the protagonist could have its precursor in heroic tales.[18] It need hardly be said, however, that making every knight opposed to the protagonist rude only heightens the hero's appeal, but the later French Roland romances do not treat the antagonists like this. The villains often seem more polite than the heroes.

In the prelude to a near-confrontation between Lancelot and a king's son in which the Lady of the Castle of four Axemen is present, the monologue of the over-confident prince is as follows:

qu' adés vos en maing gié.
Un mui de sel avroit maingié
cist chevaliers, si con je croi,
einçois qu'il vos desraist vers moi.
Ne cuit c'onques home veïsse
vers cui je ne vos conqueïsse.
Et quant je vos truis ci an eise,
mesque bien li poist et despleise,
vos an manrai veant ses ialz,
et s'an face trestot son mialz. (*La Charrette*, ll. 1583-92).

And a poor escort indeed it is, for I'm about to take you off! I fancy this knight would have eaten a bushel of salt before he could protect you from me: I don't believe I've ever seen one from whom I couldn't win you. And since I conveniently find you here, though it may very well vex and displease him, I'll take you away under his very nose, despite all his efforts. (*La Charrette*, trans. Owen 1989, 206).

One is a bit mystified when one finds the same man later admitting he was fortunate to have been saved fighting such a knight as Lancelot. Such modesty is hardly a stock quality of the rash challenger, yet it is highly chivalric. In addition, it is also an heroic age quality.

Honesty and respect toward one's adversaries was a cultivated aspect of the ideal warrior's personality in heroic age culture. In *Taín Bó Cuailgne*, at that point in the story where Cú Chulainn is holding off Queen Medb's army with duels (*Taín Bó Cuailgne*, trans. Kinsella 1969, 114-205, every warrior who is asked to fight for her freely admits Cú Chulainn is more skilled than him.[19] Such modesty of speech can also be seen, to some degree, in *Mahabharata*[20] and the *Iliad*.[21] The heroic ages of the Norse, Japanese, Greek and other, similar cultures demonstrate a like attitude. It is most definitely an heroic age, and in this instance probably a Celtic, notion.

In conjunction with honor and respect, gentility was a praised feature in Chrétien's time. Chaucer's description of his Knight being "meek as a maid" is as unforgettable as it is ironic. How odd it is that a man who had fought in so many campaigns and lived in the brutal climate of warriors should be described "meek as a maid". The picture, however, has a long thread in the literary tradition of twelfth-century Europe. The knight of great prowess who is cowed by the woman he admires is a common theme with Chrétien as well -- in the personalities of Yvain, Alexander, Cligès, and Perceval. Marie must have rejoiced in the thought of a great warrior being absolutely obedient to the woman he loved. Such was the attitude of Eleanor and her daughters.

The British heroic age also contains a parallel in the near-contemporary evidence of *Y Gododdin* (see Chapter II). In it the warrior Ywain mab Marro is praised as "Diffun ymlaen bun, medd a dalai;" "... Breathless in the presence of a girl, ..."[22] Later in the same stanza: "Rhag pebyll Madog pan atgoriai, Namyn un gûr o gant ni ddelai;" "... when he used to come back to Madog's tent there used not to return but one in a hundred".[23] In a praise of Ceredig it is said: "cyn dyfod ei ddydd, gowychydd ei wybod;" "... his refined manners were perfection".[24]

These two distinct qualities are treated as equal in importance. There are further examples in Irish legend. The *Taín Bó Cuailgne* portrays Cú Chulainn as the unquestioned champion of Ulster, but he is clearly not of the romantic mold. He sleeps with Aífe after making an oath with his bride-to-be Emer to remain faithful. Still, he shows a clear bashfulness around women of his native court. Conchobar's only solution to Cú Chulainn's battle-fury is to send naked women out to greet him (trans. Kinsella 1969, 91-2). He is also slowed in his approach of the Munstermen by the satirist Riches, who strips for Cú Chulainn to hinder him ("Mesca Ulad; The Intoxication of the Munstermen" trans. Watson 1994, 117). The Janus-like qualities of the perfect warrior are expressed in praise of the northern hero Urien Rheged.

Gnawt gweled ymdanaw   am teyrn gocnaw
Amdanaw gwyled   a lliaws maranhed

eurteyrn gogled ar benhic teyrnwd.
(*Canu Taliesin: gyda Rhagymadrodd a Nodiadau*, ed. Williams 1960, 23-6).

Courtesy is usual around him,
around the provocative chief.
Courtesy surrounds him
and plentiful wealth,
golden chieftain of the North,
foremost of kings.
("Uryen Erechwyð; Urien of Erechwyð", trans. Koch 1994, 340)

Such a dual personality of terror in battle and courtesy in noble company is not a characteristic of the typical Germanic hero of saga. It is not common in any other cultures to my knowledge -- except the Celtic and the literature of Europe that had been influenced by the Celtic bards directly by the Bretons and Welsh.[25]

The British hero was supposed to have a mildly "schizophrenic" nature. He was not to be a drunken oaf whose sole benefit to the king was his ability to go berserk against the enemy, as Adhil's warriors do in *Hrolf Kraki's Saga*. He was to be equally adjusted to the king's court and the terrors of the battlefield. This duality of personality was equally a Celtic and later medieval quality that was admired in their respective cultures.

Another commonplace in Chrétien's poetry with Celtic affinities is that a knight is given free lodging wherever he may find a house. Erec, Cligès, Yvain, and later Perceval are all beneficiaries of this custom. In addition, there is no mention of Gauvain and Lancelot paying their hostess on that first night at the Cart Castle. These characters do not give money when staying with King Bademagus, either. For one intent on writing a fairy tale, these things only add to the dreamy background that makes the Arthurian world so memorable. The mere inclusion of money would bring the reader back to the world from which she is trying to escape. For the more historically oriented, it does not seem unlikely that a stranger knight might be offered hospitality by a regional ruler. However, Gauvain is posing as a merchant when he is offered a room in *Le Conte*.

There is also a connection to Celtic law and custom. Binchy defines *Biathad* (a freeman title) as one who has the "general obligation of supplying hospitality to all persons, together with their appropriate company" (*Crith Gablach*, ed. Binchy 1970, 76). Further on in the same entry Binchy informs the reader that refusal to do so by anyone above the rank of minor householder or *ócaire* (young landowner) would be considered an illegal offence. The fine was the honor-price of the person refused (*Críth Gablach*, ed. Binchy 1970, 77). This concept was integral to the society. There was a class of people with the sole responsibility of giving hospitality. A *Briugu* was "a rich landowner whose property is reckoned in the hundreds" (*Críth Gablach*, ed. Binchy 1970, 79). He was an hospitaller, and was to make his home situated near an easily accessible position and give unlimited hospitality to all. In return, he was given the "honor price" of a *Rí Tuaithe* (king of a country). The free room and board concept is reiterated in Irish myth, most conspicuously in *Togail Bruidne Dá Derga*.

The Irish were obviously very intent that a stranger should not be left hungry or wet if he had no wish to be. One cannot doubt that those areas of Britain with little Roman intervention would have the same ancient Celtic custom; Welsh law evidences its retention in Wales during the later Middle Ages. It may be that this Arthurian theme is due to influence from France or any other continental culture. However, it is equally possible that its inclusion in the Arthurian romances is a direct response to native British influences.

Bademagus's speech to his son when he nears Lancelot after the "Sword Bridge" episode is also noteworthy.

> Et si vos praing, cui qu'il enuit,
> Vers trestoz homes an conduit,
> Ja mar doteroiz de nelui
> Fors que seulement de celui
> Qui la reïne amena ça
> Onques hom si ne menaca
> Autre con ge l'ai menacié
> Et par po je ne l'ai chacié
> De ma terre par mautalant
> Por ce que il ne la vos rant
> S'est il mes filz, mes ne vos chaille
> Se il ne vos vaint an bataille
> Se il ne vos porra sor mon pois
> D'enui faire vaillant un pois. (*La Charrette*, ll. 3375-87).

However indignant anyone may be, I place you under my safekeeping against all men. You need fear no man except the one who brought the queen here. No man ever threatened another as I threatened him. Because he did not hand her over to you, my fury almost caused me to drive him from my land. Yes, he is my son. But do not worry. Unless he defeats you in combat, he can never, against my will, cause you the least harm. (*La Charrette*, trans. Owen 1989, 230).

Why does Bademagus grant such generosity? Is this a mere politeness? Is Chrétien just using Bademagus's words as a contrast to his headstrong son Meleagant, and as a balance against the highly emotional, though more controlled Lancelot?[26] It is very possible. Contrasts are an excellent tool in all forms of literature. On the other hand, why should Chrétien allow Bademagus, father of the enemy, to be looked on kindly? Why make the father support the man who has come to kill his son? Again, heroic-age ideals and Welsh and Irish laws give us another clue.

Whatever the "sword bridge" incident was (below), the successful conquest of the bridge obviously drew the attention and admiration of the spectators by its audacity, sheer bravery, and/or physical difficulty. This feat commanded some measure of respect and delicacy of diplomacy. It would not be to Bademagus' advantage to overwhelm Lancelot with numbers when he had made the crossing, as no bard would praise any but Lancelot for the act. So Bademagus safeguarded himself from reproach by formally putting Lancelot under his protection. This reading fits the facts well. When it is heard in Bademagus's presence that Lancelot has died retrieving Gauvain, the protector promises death by hanging, burning, or drowning to the perpetrators of the crime. Curiously, when Lancelot is found to be a prisoner and Meleagant the probable cause, Bademagus makes no such threats. There was no way of knowing if he was injured or not. Chrétien only tells us that Bademagus will hand over Lancelot if he finds him. Because Lancelot is not under the cloak of protection (he is not known to be injured or dead or even to have remained in Gorre) Bademagus's honor is not at stake.

This also helps explain why Meleagant did not attempt to have his adversary killed or maimed in prison as well. He wanted to win Guinièvre, but to injure Lancelot physically while he was formally under Bademagus' protection would mean dishonoring his father.[27] By imprisoning him, he hoped to win Guinièvre and avoid any complications.

There are, however, other aspects of the romance that bear evidence of strong British influence. The Celtic cloak was an item of longstanding use and great pride among the Celtic people. Diodorus Siculus noted that the Celts wore striped cloaks with a checkered pattern fastened with a clasp (*The Bibliotheca Historia of Diodorus Siculus*, trans. Skelton, ed. Salter and Edward 1968-71, 5.30). The writers of *Culhwch ac Olwen* as well as the *Taín Bó Cuailgne* and other surviving Celtic tales repetitiously (and monotonously) describe this item in much the same manner. It plays a key role in *The Boyhood Deeds of Finn*, where the hero grabs the brooch of a girl. Her cloak falls off and she is forced to return to Fionn, presumably to grant him a wish of some sort ("The Boyhood Deeds of Finn" trans. Carey 1994, 190). Dá Derga's men are described as each wearing "a short cloak to their buttock" ("Togail Bruidne Dá Derga; The Destruction of Dá Derga's Hostel", trans. Stokes 1994, 167).

The Law of Hywel Dda confirms that the famed cloak of the British Isles was not just a pre-Roman feature. The statutes are clear that both parties in a divorce retain their own cloaks, though all else is to be divided equally (trans. Jenkins 1986, 46). The cloak was and remains a climactic necessity for the Celtic peoples in the British Isles. The damp nature of the regions that they inhabited called for the use of it. The practice of wearing a cloak continues today. It is only rarely that Scots leave their homes with but one layer of clothing and no umbrella.

It must be admitted that any coastal region, such as France, could be expected to have some form of equivalent. However, such clothing is rarely if ever mentioned in the Germanic tales, and it is entirely absent from the Roland romances, except as part of ceremonial clothing. The source where the cloak comes from is probably of Celtic origin. The cloak can be found in the Arthurian romances throughout Europe. Lancelot is more than once given the cloak (Fr. *mantel*) by a woman (*La Charrette*, ll. 1020 et al), as is Perceval (*Le Conte*, ll. 1549 et al).

Of the remaining scenes and passages in *Le Chevalier de la Charrette*, two strike one as particularly romantic and synthetic in comparison to the rest of the narrative because of several details. These are the bridges and the bed scene. They are most probably the result of the Chrétien's diplomatic compromise between *sens* of Marie and the original British tale. They were inserted for artistic purposes or simply plot devices. They are, therefore, likely to contain relevant evidence in the present discussion. Chrétien, the *latimari*, the *trouvères*, and the *troubadours* rarely invented any particular detail or episode unless it made the action of the scene more contemporary. Neither the bridges nor the bed scene perform this function.[28]

What is to be made of the plot devices the *Pont Éspée* and *Pont Evage*? Truthfully, they are too much the expression of romance to be seen easily as part of any pre ninth-century historical or literary source. On the other hand, the two bridges do not have any known literary predecessors on the continent. They are too original (and unique) to be a product of a romance movement that is based on the Celtic myths and legends. However, they seem to be too romantic to belong in a Celtic hero's tale. Despite this, several details argue for a Celtic and heroic origin.

The reader is told that Gorre is the land of no return and it is clearly difficult for a mortal to cross into it.[29] These two facts have led a number of scholars to believe the Sword Bridge is a passage to the land of the dead. In this respect it would be similar to the Orpheus or Heracles adventures of Greek mythology. Others have suggested it is the Celtic equivalent of the Bridge of Souls of Christian theology. This gives us two alternatives, but there are some problems with both these hypotheses.[30]

As Laura Hibbard pointed out in her "The Sword Bridge of Chrétien de Troyes", the Bridge of Leaps is not a test for acceptance into the Underworld for several reasons.

1.) Cú Chulainn does come to be taught by Scáthach, but he fights nothing and no guardian to get to her kingdom, as traditional underworld heroes must.[31] He simply proves his worthiness as a student by crossing a feat bridge.

2.) One of Scáthach's daughters and she herself actively pursues Cú Chulainn. If sexual interest in a hero is a motive in myth, it is always the action of the underworld ruler that brings that hero to the realm of the dead.[32] This is not the case here.

3.) One can observe that Scáthach needs the aid of Cú Chulainn to help defeat another leader in Alba. The ruler of the underworld never has contenders.[33]

4.) There is even a hint of non-underworld connotations when Cú Chulainn decides to leave Alba. He is not asked or pressured to remain, neither is he impeded from leaving. In fact, all seem pleased to be rid of him (1913, 185).

The location of the place Cú Chulainn enters is also much too well defined to be magical. He visits Scáthach in Alba, or northern Britain. The location of a traditional underworld is partially or totally undefined in myth,[34] but this should not be the case here. The concept of the Irish Sea province is generally accepted, and with it the idea that there was a constant exchange of ideas between Ireland and Britain in this period.[35]

Alba would hardly be a totally unlocatable place to an Ulster native. It is highly debatable whether there even was a Bridge of Souls in Celtic mythology (Ellis 1992, 177-8).

Gorre does not even have the same basic taboos as an Indo-European underworld should have. To use Celtic myths as a guide, Cú Chulainn, like Lancelot, is not abducted by any infatuated underworld woman and can freely leave the castle at any point. More important, Lancelot has no obstacle or any being obstructing his path when leaving the castle. The crowd who follows Lancelot has none either, but all have presumably eaten of the castle's food and with it the mythical pomegranates since their arrival some time ago.[36] If this were a realm of the dead, the crowd could never leave and Lancelot would need to fight his way free.[37]

As a Celtic parallel to a Christian Bridge of Souls the *Pont Èspée* has little more substance. The first instance of an underworld bridge in the British Isles is found in *Fís Adamnan* (L. Loomis 1913, 170). This work does date to the eleventh century. It is five hundred years later than the Bridge of Souls in Gregory the Great and Gregory of Tours and therefore could be of Christian origin through influence or direct knowledge of their writings. This does make it "highly improbable that the Irish visionaries were borrowing or dating the idea of the soul bridge from any surviving pagan lore" (L. Loomis 1913, 170).

However, the Sword Bridge is hardly a Christian adaptation as the values are different here from the test of moral worthiness one finds in the Bridge of Souls. The desirable qualities of one who crosses a marvelous bridge such as Cú Chulainn's in *Tochmarc Emere* or Lancelot of this poem are honor and courage, not the moral strength and virtue of a Christian. If Chrétien found a wonderful bridge in his source, it does not have the qualifications for a Christian soul bridge. Lancelot's moral virtues are hardly mentioned here.

The Sword Bridge of *La Charrette* is two lance-lengths. Chrétien tells us that Lancelot crawled over a sword bridge of sixteen to twenty feet. This is a flaw in the plot; a twenty-foot jump is not an excessive one. This scene is something Chrétien has modified for his purposes, which implies his source here was probably of British, and one must therefore look to Celtic literature to better understand the scene.

Cú Chulainn defeats Curoi in *Bricriu's Feast* by hovering around him in a swooping feat (trans. Henderson 1899, 109). The sword bridge episode is not also a sword feat as it stands. The heroes who do this marvel walk across the blade and are famed because they are so light of foot they do not cut themselves. This would have impressed an audience, and a British Guinièvre, far more than crawling.

This Sword Bridge, then, is not some Bridge of Souls or the passage to the Celtic underworld. There are, however, other possibilities, and here one must take leave of Dr. L. Loomis, who could only conclude:

> As a Perilous Passage, the sword bridge, however amazingly elongated and strangely used, has little real analogy with the much more incredible marvels of Celtic story. Moreover the form, the realistic quality of an actual sword used as a bridge, and its connection with the romantic episode of Guinièvre's rescue, remain unexplained. (L. Loomis 1913, 185-6).

It is conceivable that the original designers of the sword bridge incident made this a feat for Lancelot to cross on a par with one of Cú Chulainn's many abilities. Alternatively, it could have been the traditional sword feat, where a hero crosses a blade as a test of skill. Chrétien conceivably could have added the details of the river and Lancelot on his knees for romantic effect.[38]

Gauvain's place in the poem, however, is a question. Here, the pride of *Erec et Enide* and *Yvain* is made a blundering failure. This is very different from the description of him in *Culhwch ac Olwen* as a man who never came home without accomplishing his quest (*Mabinogion*, trans. Jones and Jones 1974, 108). Dr. Weston found a more acceptable answer to this quandary long ago. He, she believed, was the original hero of the tale. She points out that Gauvain is a key figure in every Guinièvre rescue, Lancelot is not.[39] That, and Hartmann von Aue's peculiar modification to Chrétien's *Yvain*, are indicators that one is on solid ground.[40] There must be some reason for this and one must accept the possibility that he was the original hero.[41] A look at the "water bridge" is in order.

Chrétien uses the word *pont evage* to describe Gauvain's means of landing in Gorre.[42] This difficult term is never further described by Chrétien, so one can make only perilous guesses as to its nature. However, Chrétien's evasive attitude toward the word leaves two options. Either there is a textual problem with the word or he has again modified something that he did not fully understand or care to understand.[43] Invention seems more likely here. A textual problem has probably not occurred for reasons of consistency. In all the extant MSS *pont evage* is always the word employed.

The episode -- Gauvain's embarrassing situation, the ease with which Lancelot aids him, and Chrétien's mysterious reluctance to explain Gauvain's *pont evage* -- is strange if one takes *pont evage* at face value. However, it is very possible Gauvain's original position has been usurped by Lancelot (see Chapter IV). In this case, Gauvain would inevitably become the foil to Lancelot, and Gauvain's bridge the invention of Chrétien or a chronologically near predecessor. "Water bridge" would then be an irony and would simply mean that the "bridge" Gauvain took was through water, whether the sea or a lake, between Galloway and Gorre. In other words, he either tried to take a boat (which must have capsized) or swam. Chrétien has not explained the bridge further because the joke is clear enough; Gauvain fails to cross it. Thematically speaking, this is his punishment for refusing to jump into the cart with Lancelot earlier.

To Chrétien and his twelfth-century French audience, a fabulous entrance was needed to justify Lancelot's instant respect in Gorre, so he made one. He could not have known getting past the *porthawr* would have been just as impressive a British audience. He put the original hero in his usual role as foil, and used the crossing to further belittle Gauvain and emphasize Lancelot's peerlessness and devotion to Guinièvre; this was done to artistic perfection.

The most prominent theme of all, more basic to the plot than any one episode, even the Sword Bridge, is the theft of the queen. Is the kidnapping of the queen of an important kingdom a myth, motif, or historical possibility? A mythological source must be entertained, if only because of the preponderance of similar tales in Celtic lore.[44] However, Celtic myth has relatively few rescues by a lover; it is usually the husband.[45] These exceptions are unusual, and Dr. Cross felt comfortable in claiming there was no rescue by a lover (Cross 1930, 52). If one is to call *La Charrette* a myth, one must first deduce a reason why such an unusual role transformation occurred. Then, one must prove the abduction could not have happened. This is something that I think a redoubtable task.[46]

The possibility that Guinièvre has been imposed on an established theme is also reasonable. Any recurrent mythic element may find its way into a bard's repertoire. However, problems abound with this proposal. Chief among them is the inconsistency of the motif. Certainly Meleagant could be Valerin, but his nature does not fit the motival pattern. The abductor in the archetypal kidnapping is always a benevolent wizard or god,[47] and Melwas in the most ancient versions --

Vita Gildae and *Ymddiddan Gwenhwyfar ac Arthur*-- is certainly not.[48] Further, the combination of Guinièvre and the abduction is one of the few instances where a character and basic motif were passed to the continent in tandem (Bromwich 1961, 441). It is the rare case where the main elements remain intact, implying that this may not have derived from an oral source.[49]

Finally, the option of history must be attended to in this discussion. The only reasons for the inclusion of this contingency is the fact that the first two possibilities are tenuous and abductions were common and an accepted part of Celtic society. This may be demonstrated in the myths of Ireland and Britain.[50] They are to be found in the Welsh tales as well as those of the Ulster cycle. It is conceivable that an historic king of the fifth or sixth century could have had his wife abducted, though it is in no way probable or provable.

There is, then, more that could be Celtic in Chrétien's narrative than the names. The above list, one of motifs and themes that fit equally (and better) in the context of heroic-age Britain rather than twelfth-century France, is unexpectedly large. Without the Celtic-derived material and any of his continental resources, Chrétien's poem is very much reduced.

Admittedly, Chrétien could have either invented these elements based on his culture, or taken the motifs and themes from sub-Roman British life. At first glance it would appear that basing these items on his period is the simpler answer. If he was so creative there are more questions. Why has he chosen so many distinctive characteristics that were a part of the British culture. How has he created an entire world that looks similar to post-Roman Britain as seen through the eyes of a twelfth-century poet. Considering his heavy influence from the classical and contemporary writers, should it be granted that he had that ability along with his tremendous literary skills? Should one not assume he did the same thing with the Celtic source he had access to as with what he already knew. Is it not likely that he followed it very closely and reinterpreted only when he needed to deepen the emotional content of a passage?

One should not be alarmed at the proposal that the greatest poet of the French Middle Ages was heavily dependent on previous literature. It is well known that medieval writers thought of themselves as merely presenting older data for the better understanding of their audience. In this sense, Chrétien was no different from any other medieval artist. If a story had been original, the poet would have been forced to invent a source. To quote Geoffrey of Vinsauf:

> And in the degree that it is more difficult so also it is more praiseworthy to treat such material well, namely, common and familiar material, than to treat other material, namely, new and unusual" (*Documentum de modo et arte dictandi et versificandi*, trans. Parr 1968, 132).

This chapter has demonstrated that the Celtic influences on Chrétien were much greater than has hitherto been acknowledged.[51] Beyond the names and a basic plot, several episodes have elements that are very possibly Celtic and seem logical in an historical or pseudo-historical context. This suggests at least one source for the poem that was, in turn, historical or pseudo-historical in nature. To date, *Glas* has only been chronologically placed well before 1100. However, a study of the historical elements of the poem will reveal a date much earlier. It will also demonstrate the British point of origin for this tale and its oldest characters. In conjunction, these two proofs will allow for the possibility that the source of *Le Chevalier de la Charrette* and the other abduction tales could originally have been a part of the *Northern Memoranda*, or a related text. In other words, it will give evidence that the abduction story is derived from a literary source that dates back to 900, and possibly earlier.

---

[1] It should also be noted that French *la salle* is a general term which includes any public building. The associations Chrétien makes with the structure allows for a free-standing Dark Age hall, or the banquet room of a later medieval hall. The reader is told Arthur's residence is near a garden in one passage in *Le Conte du Graal* (l. 1051).

[2] Chrétien tends to go extremes in his descriptions, e.g. Those of the maidens and the dwarf who drives the cart that Lancelot comes into town in. He is also very positive in his description about any noble-oriented ceremony or structure. Apparently this added to the perfect ambience he creates for the Arthurian reality.

[3] (*Hrolf Kraki's Saga*, trans. Anderson 1988, 31). In both cases, a hypothetical prototype would date to the fifth or sixth centuries through two of the characters, Hugleik (*Beowulf* and *Hrolf Kraki's Saga*) and Hengest (*Beowulf*).

[4] Alexander Curle was quite adamant in his paper on the Mote of Mark that there was no ale-hall of any sort there or elsewhere (1914,

125-69). And though his paper was written over eighty years ago, the party in favour of an absence of post-Roman halls in Celtic Britain is no less strong now.

[5] Though he does have reservations about Alt Clut (1991, 95-149), and admits that there are no other structures like those he proposes at site 1B of Dinas Powys (1963, 68).

[6] (Kenyon 1990, 126-30). This is with the exception of servants.

[7] As understood by the present awareness of archaeology. He may have known of "lower class" castles, but certainly would not intentionally affix one to a noble character in one of his poems.

[8] Though it should be noted that Professor Hector and Dr. Nora Chadwick's summary of all heroic age societies concluded that this custom was not consistent, except in respect to the Celtic peoples (1932, 94).

[9] The Picts would not be Christian till after Arthur's death. It should come as no surprise that their rivals the Britons did not choose to accept all the Christian values and Roman customs till long after their first introduction. Dr. Anne Ross devoted an entire chapter to the subject of the Celtic head cult in *The Pagan Celts* (1967, 61-126).

[10] Later sagas seem to employ the concept of beheading a dead enemy for a trophy on occasion,
but *Beowulf*, the *Prose Edda*, and the *Poetic Edda* contain no such instance.

[11] A traditional compert story is one in which the subject is given divine conception.

[12] The birth of MacBeth is described in the doubtful testimony of *Andrew of Wyntoun's Chronicle* (Book VI, Chapter xviii, verses 1953-84 (Cotton) and 1913-44 (Wemyss)).

[13] The warrior-queen Scathach has three children, but there is no mention of a father-living or dead. Cú Chúlainn demands Scáthach's enemy Aífe for one night without giving wedding gifts. This is after he has made a mutual pledge of devotion with Étain before leaving Alba.

[14] (*The Law of Hywel Dda*, trans. Jenkins 1986, 50. This last statement means that the woman in question will be treated as though her family had given her to him with a bride-price.

[15] A woman who has lived with one man seven years.

[16] (*The Law of Hywel Dda*, trans. Jenkins 1986, 48). The term "Fondle" is MW *gofysio*; alternatively *dodi bysedd ynddi* "putting fingers into her", (1986, 241).

[17] I have not made use of Dr. Busby's exemplary work on Gauvain (1980). While it does do a good job in charting Gauvain's literary progress from the *troubadours* through the Middle Ages, it is not relevant to this book, which attempts to see how the romances may have develeoped before the *troubadours*

[18] I use here the term as defined in H.M. Chadwick's *The Heroic Age* (1912), in which he carefully shows that the period of heroic culture in Indian, Greek, Irish, Norse, and British legend all contained the same basic values and motivations. This system is a combination of chivalry to compatriots and opposing warriors and brutality to defeated foes.

[19] This is the only means by which the mighty, solitary Cú Chúlainn can be kept from killing thirty of her army at night. The salvation of the army is provided by Medb and Ailill, who summon the best of their warriors, get them drunk, and promise the men their daughter as reward. Refused, they accuse each of the men of cowardice. The proud warriors submit quickly thereafter. But cowardice is not the reason for their desire to avoid Cú Chúlainn. Every one of these hapless men accepts the death blow in silence.

[20] Especially Book VI, which contains the *Bhagavad Gita*.

[21] See in particular the duels in Books III, VII, and XXI.

[22] (*Y Gododdin*, A2 l. 22; *The Gododdin: The Oldest Scottish Poem*, ed. Jackson 1969, 116).

[23] *Y Gododdin*, ll. 28-9; *The Gododdin: The Oldest Scottish Poem*, ed. Jackson 1969, 116).

[24] *Y Gododdin*, A28 ll. 33-4; *The Gododdin: The Oldest Scottish Poem*, ed. Jsckson 1969, 128). These two examples are considered ancient by Jackson (1969) and Charles-Edwards (1978, 78). On the basis of his reconstruction of the poem, Professor Koch dates the first to between 655 and 700 and the second before 638. However his opinions, and his reconstruction of the poem, are highly debatable with the scholars of the Celtic field.

[25] This dual quality of ferocity and bounty is not spoken of by the classical authors, one would have to live within a culture to understand

why such a personality as this was so highly praised. Besides, one may see why the Romans and Greeks would have found no space to praise the courtesy and bounty of people they considered barbaric, even if they had understood.

[26] With characteristic ingenuity, Loomis saw Bademagus as yet another representation of Brân in Arthurian literature (1949, 240-50).

[27] I assume Lancelot was still on Gorre because it is nowhere stated he has been moved, or even that Bademagus owns land outside of Gorre.

[28] I refrain from the problem of the "Bed Scene" here. For a review of various possiblities and an extremely tentative conclusion. See Appendix II.

[29] In this instance Gorre is only the land immediately surrounding Bademagus' castle.

[30] Dr. Brusegan has made the argument against Gorre being an other world by alternative means in "L' autre monde et Le Chevalier de La Charrette" (1995, 77-85).

[31] In Greek myth, one must go past Charon and Cerberus. This is typical of polytheistic religions.

[32] I use as comparison the Indo-European myths of the Norse, Greeks, and Romans.

[33] This is, to be truthful, exactly what happens in the Welsh underworld story of Pwyll Pendeuic. (*Mabinogion*, trans. Jones and Jones 1974, 5). However, this seems to me like a ritual which is paralleled in Greek myth. Here, for instance, the mortal Heracles defeats the Titans for the gods. This assumption is supported by Goetinck (1975, 214-15), who believes Arawn and Hafgan are the same person.

[34] Annwfn is a mystical island West of this Isle of Britain. Anubis' realm is totally undefined, as is Hades's (as opposed to that of Pluto).

[35] See Moore, *The Irish Sea Province in Archaeology and History*, (1970), specifically the articles by Professor Alcock and Dr. Chadwick.

[36] In Greek myth it was the fruit of the pomegranate that condemned the dead to remain in Hades and caused them to forget their previous life.

[37] Heracles and Orpheus were the only Greek heroes to go uninvited and return to this world through their own prowess. It is unheard of in

Norse tradition and only a Japanese god attempted it in that country's mythology.

[38] It would be romantic from the point of view of his patroness, Marie, who saw man's role as one of being absolutely submissive to his lady. Thus, showing one's physical agility would be acceptable, but crawling on one's knees would be better.

[39] Apart from the scene of *Ymddiddan Gwenhwyfar ac Arthur*, the corrupted *Vitae Gildae*, and the much later *Le Morte d' Arthur*, where Lavaine is the second hero.

[40] Here one of Hartmann von Aue's characters briefly describes the abduction and recovery of the queen from *La Charrette*, using only Gauvain's name as a rescuer.

[41] *Diu Crône* allows him passage to the island without mishap. The other versions of this "adventure" do as well.

[42] *Pont evage* translates as "water bridge".

[43] The absolute dearth of suggestions from Celtic experts is most telling. Loomis could only suggest it represented a crannog.

[44] (Cross 1952, 91). See Cross (1930, 52), for a more exhaustive list.

[45] (Cross 1930, 61; 1952, 466-9, R151-151.1, R161-161.1, F322.2).

[46] It is possible that Lancelot was drawn from *Cligés* to replace Gauvain in this role, and the continental writers followed him to a man. This proposed theory of blind imitation can be seen in the grail legend (below). However, it would be a formidable job to prove an abduction was not conceivable in British culture of the post-Roman era.

[47] Such is the case in the most famed abduction myth, "Echtra Chorbmaic uí Chuinn" or "The Adventure of Cormac [son of Art and] grandson of Conn".

[48] With this problem, however, one must acknowledge the very real prestige of Arthur and his ability to reduce other characters-even magicians-into minor role-players. However, a similar prominence did not keep the great kings of Irish myth from suffering the misfortune of being openly manipulated by otherworldly beings.

[49] For the purpose of further elucidating the argument contained in this paper I intentionally refrain from further supposition on this question at this point and will take it back up when there is a greater weight of evidence laid out in the next chapter.

[50] The fact that myths represent a culture's accepted morés is an established one, and I have no desire to again prove their usefulness and acceptability in historical study. The myths, and particularly those of the Irish, are the product of several cultures, and are therefore not a pure representation of the Celtic peoples who ruled in Ireland during the Iron Age and after. However, the theme of abduction is such a commone one in Irish myth that it seems prudent to believe that abductions were a part of everyday royal society during this period.

[51] The standard works on the topic of Celtic influences on continental romances are Dr. Bromwich's "Celtic Dynastic Themes and the Breton Lays" (1961, 439-74) and "First Transmission from England and France" (Cardiff, 1991, 273-98).

Chapter VI: The Sixth Century in Chrétien

Up to this point in my study, I have discussed the influence of continental authors on Chrétien and the significance of the names and some motifs that Chrétien employs. This has helped explain the origins and nuances of much of the romance, but many remain that have been untouched by Celtic and French scholars alike. To resolve this dilemma I will now inspect the poem by utilizing the knowledge derived from archaeological finds, law tracts, and documents as well as legend and the vitae of the Irish and Welsh saints. This will uncover the most important historical elements and will aid in the formulation of a more precise date for *Glas*.

The most likely places to look for Celtic material is in scenes that betray Ovid's and Andreas Capellanus's unmistakable influence. It has been shown (Chapter II) that these two influences were inserted last, under Chrétien. It is likely that he displaced the original matter that the sophisticates of Marie's court would have found displeasing in favor of a more contemporary source. Here one can assume Chrétien was superimposing Ovid's and Andreas Capellanus's material upon what was originally more complimentary to the hero, from a Celtic perspective.[1] The cart episode itself comes to mind in this respect. In it Lancelot, as a slave to the Roman poet's views on love, steps into a cart and knowingly degrades himself to hear word of Guinièvre.

As far back as Sir John Rhys' contributions, scholars have taken a skeptical view of the charrette episode. "How far the cart incident is to be regarded as the poet's invention, it is difficult to say" (1891, 142). It is too much a fairy tale for many, while others point out the absence of mythic and romantic precursors. However, Chrétien gives the reader two vague hints of something more tangible when he writes that it was a *pilori* -- "pillory" (*La Charrette*, l. 322), and that "en oren a plus de trois mile, n'en avoit a cel tans que une;" (*La Charrette*, l. 325-6) "In every fair-sized town where now one finds over three thousand of them, there was at that time only one" (*La Charrette*, trans. Owen 1989, 189).

Chrétien continues that this unusual four-wheeled cart making its way slowly into town was a vehicle of dishonor, the transport of the condemned. However, Lancelot is not killed, neither is he put in prison. He is given the same accommodation as his companion Gauvain.[2] He outshines Gauvain in the bed scene, as will be seen.[3] Lancelot is undoubtedly a man of some importance in the territory through which he passes. This is because of the way he is later treated at the Castle of four Axemen, and on Gorre itself. His transportation into town should, logically, reflect his status. The cart as described does not. As there is no literary or Celtic precursor to Chrétien's scene, perhaps one of two historical prototypes can help explain the cryptic cart; it could be a war-chariot or a high-status vehicle.

The possibility of a four-wheeled war-chariot like those described for Cú Chulainn and his comrades of Irish heroic epic is in accordance with Chrétien's description.[4] *Le Chevalier de la Charrette* uses the word *la charrette* to describe the vehicle, and the other permissible version that contains this scene supports this interpretation. *The Vulgate Version of the Arthurian Romances* uses *la carete* (trans. Sommer 1909-16, 162). *La Carete* and Chrétien's *la charrette* are identical words, meaning a four-wheeled vehicle (Murray et al 1961, 35).

The idea of a chariot blends in smoothly with our knowledge of Britain, too. Julius Caesar made an uneventful trip to England in the first century B.C.E. and seems to have had some trouble with their chariots.[5] Tacitus records the same vehicles in the possession of the peoples of the North later (trans. Mattingly, rev. Handford 1970, 12.1). Even though his biographical subject, Agricola, did not seem to have the same difficulty in dealing with the chariots, they were enough of a tactical obstacle to be mentioned even then (trans. Mattingly, rev. Handford, 1970, 35.3, 36.3. The chariot was traditionally a strong weapon in breaking infantry formations. It seems reasonable to assume the Picts retained it as a part of their military arsenal, especially when one remembers how oriented the Roman legions' strategy was around infantry.[6]

This assumption may be verified. There is evidence that there were chariots in Early Christian Britain. A single example of a British king owning a chariot exists. The Welsh recorded Morgan Mwynfa(w)r's *Kar*-"chariot" in the list of the *Thirteen Treasures of the Welsh* (no. 4). This implies a continued familiarity by the British with the chariot through the early medieval period, if not later. Chrétien could not have known this, and even if he had it would not have furthered his plot to say "chariot" in place of "cart". The fact that in his time it was used as a transport for the condemned was a happy coincidence for him; it was in perfect accordance with the *sens* of Marie de Champagne. This misunderstanding or intentional change allowed him to help change the nature of his chief character from an heroic to a romantic figure. In Dr. Ker's words: "It would not have mattered to Odysseus if he had been seen traveling in a cart, like Lancelot, though for Lancelot it was a great misfortune and anxiety." This was because of Chrétien's changes at Marie's command.

The cart could also have performed a more peaceful function, but here the scholar is on less certain footing. Only two sources exist which may confirm this possibility, the Meigle Stone (no. 10) and an episode from the life of Columba. In addition, Chrétien's poem does say that Lancelot rides in a four-wheeled vehicle, not the two-wheeled transport of this alternative British form of locomotion.[7]

The Meigle stone is of some use as an independent source. The writing on it is similar to other Pictish stones that have been dated to sometime in the post-Roman period.[8] There is no comparison to be made between the chariot this stone describes and those of the Romans or Irish (see Appendix I). This makes it reasonable to assume that this style of locomotion was native only to the British peoples. Therefore, a chariot similar to that on the Meigle Stone was known to the British peoples between 400 and the late-ninth century.

The theory of a high-status, wheeled form of locomotion can also be supported by evidence from a source of near-contemporary date. Several vitae refer to a transportation device in one form or another. The *Life of Saint Columba* in particular is excellent proof of their existence in the years after Arthur's floruit. In it, the saint is said to have ridden in a carriage, *currus*, with which he performed a miracle. The fable gives some providential details as to its structure that indicates it was a four-wheeled chariot.[9]

This passage has been compared to the stock incidents of Irish vitae and thus the force of this piece of evidence has been reduced to that of a hagiographic motif. However, one must remember that Adomnan was writing within a century of Columba and had as much access to Columban traditions as he had other vitae. Adomnan uses oral and written materials that are contemporary with Columba's life. Such assumptions, therefore, cannot be proven or disproven.

There is, then, an alternative to the twelfth-century cart. The vehicle could be a heroic-age means of transportation. It makes practical sense and explains both its unique quality and the attention it generates. The stone carving seems to indicate it was a noble method of traveling in luxury, though the literature and Chrétien himself favors a more warlike interpretation of the vehicle.

Following his first duel and his stay with the Lady of the Castle of four Axemen, Lancelot visits the tomb of one of his ancestors.[10] The consensus opinion has been that this is a poem designed to please Marie (a "fairy tale", if you will) and that its sole purpose is to extol women and titillate one in particular. However, this solution begs the question, why is the "prince charming" of this poem procrastinating before going to the rescue of the "fair maiden"? This episode causes him to depart for Gorre days after Gauvain, so it is not something that serves Guinièvre in any way.[11] The action temporarily relegates the heroine to secondary importance.

On the other hand, the respect of one's ancestors is of ancient tradition. Any custom that demonstrated respect was a noble and honorable way to conduct oneself, and a man of any century would be duty-bound to follow it. The Code of Bushido, chivalry, and the cultures of Egypt, China, Babylonia, Greece, the Norse, and Celtic cultures all insisted that a warrior had a sense of respect to his ancestors.

It has been said that the cemetery scene is a variation on the motif of the doughty warrior who shows the heads of his previous victims to demonstrate his bravery and intimidate foes. This is done in *Erec* (ll. 5547-6007) and *Lanzelet* (ed. Loomis, trans. Webster 1951, 234). However, Lancelot fights no-one until he leaves the cemetery and attempts the Stony Passage the next day. Not even Loomis could find a single undeniable element in the passage that might hint that there was originally a combat here. He could not give a single parallel that may make any claims to original source material, either. The argument is flawed; the reader is probably looking at something Chrétien was not using to facilitate Guinièvre and Lancelot's passion or increase Guinièvre's prestige, only to improve Lancelot's stature. He retained the scene anyway and converted it to his needs.

There is another scene in which Chrétien creates a caricature of Lancelot, and this too holds some evidence of tampering on Chrétien's part. After spending a platonic night with a damsel who has provided lodging for the hero, Lancelot accepts his hostess's request to accompany him. As he rides toward Gorre on the journey, the lady looks down another path and:

Qant la damoisel parçoit
La fontaine et le perron voit.
Se ne volt pas que cil la voie
Einz se mist en une autre voie. (*La Charrette*, ll. 1357-60).

When the damsel notices the spring and sees the slab, not wanting the knight to see them, she turned to another road.
(*La Charrette*, trans. Owen 1989, 203).

Lancelot, however, notices the boulder and fountain and makes his way to them. This is the sole reason given why he leaves the path. Conversely, when Lancelot and his companion arrive in the clearing the entire scene refocuses on a comb that is found on the grass near the boulder. The comb is evidently the central feature of the scene as it remains the locus of Chrétien's attention from the moment it is introduced, to the exclusion of the stone and fountain. This means Chrétien has transposed the comb for the boulder.[12] It is not the other way around as the stone is symbolically clearly the more ancient of the two objects; the genius of Chrétien certainly could have found something more creative than a boulder. Also, a stone in the wilderness of twelfth-century France had no symbolic value, and a comb was the basis of the moral lesson on love in the passage. Yet the stone is the vehicle of the scene, as without it Lancelot would never find Guinièvre's comb. Its consistent attributes and use in the Arthurian stories prove that Chrétien's mysterious stone is not an anomaly. These attributes of a large stone could have had two purposes in Dark-Age Britain, kingship or symbol stone.

The large stone given prominence is a recurring component of the Arthurian romances. It is a *perrun de marbre* to Marie de France.[13] Zatzikhoven terms it a "Stone of Honor" (*Lanzelet*, ed. Loomis, trans. Webster 1951, l. 5177, 96). In *Wigalois* its only quality is its selectiveness as to who touches it (trans. Thomas 1977, 120). The French generically called them *perrons*. *Diu Crône* names one a "plot of land" (trans. Thomas 1989, ll. 17331-51), and it is specifically associated with a kingship. In British Arthurian lore, it is a *glas* -- "Blue or Green or Grey Stone" and has no particular value (*Mabinogion*, trans. Jones and Jones 1974, 140).

In these romances, a coward could not touch such an article and only the most perfect could sit upon it. In the romances, it is either lain on (*Wigalois*, trans. Thomas 1977, 120), or a sword is drawn from it prior to the hero's ascension to a throne.[14] Such a monument with similar attributes is found in myth as well. Conchobar is brought forth on a prominent stone by a river ("Co(i)mpert Conchobuir [Maic Nessa]; The Conception of Conchobar son of Nes", trans. Carey 1994, 49). He is considered a man born to be the king.

Its attributes in the romances suggest its function as a kingship stone. It is a screaming stone, a *lecc*, such as those at Scone, Tara, Cruachu, Emain Macha, Mad Adair, Cráeb Tulcha, and Cothrigi. It was "an essential item of the inaugural furniture" along with an oak grove and mound -- usually of an ancient nature (Byrne 1973, 27). It had the property that none but the rightful king could stand upon it. The *perron* in the comb scene of *Le Chevalier de la Charrette* is an allusion to an item of the inaugural ceremony. The theme of a *perron* has been transferred to the continent and changed for one reason or another by Chrétien, but the indications are clear. Whatever the original context of the scene, this element of it is old. Chrétien's statement that the maiden tried to lead Lancelot away from the path that contained the stone betrays much more than a maiden's whim. It shows that behind this object of a stone, dismissed by Chrétien, was a wealth of ceremonial lore now lost.

There is, however, also the comb and fountain. The prominent boulder that drew the attention of both Lancelot and the damsel is replaced in Chrétien by the comb of Guinièvre and the fountain, which Lancelot uses as a mirror. Why these two objects and why does Chrétien so clearly switch the focus of a kingship or symbol stone to a more romantic comb and a natural object that is functionally a mirror? The answer is quite plain, namely to heighten the romantic aspect. The fact that both the stone and comb are in the scene allows the reader to consider the possibility that both were in a previous source.[15] One may see that *Glas* could have indicated a symbolic Pictish stone and Chrétien, being unfamiliar with it, failed to make the connection.[16] If the hero had seen a Pictish/kingship stone in *Glas*, one might well understand why the hero would be so deep in thought as both stones symbolized power.

The historical elements are all to be found in those places that are the most predictable; they are in the scenes where Chrétien has gone to an extreme in describing Lancelot's Ovidian response to Guinièvre. Although one can see the connections between the comb and the mirror, Chrétien's misunderstandings are understandable. One should have been surprised, on the other hand, if Chrétien had been cognizant of the customs and seen the meaning behind the symbolism in ancient Britain. It comes as no shock, then, that he made errors in judgment. It should also not surprise the reader that his guesses, influenced as they were by Andreas Capellanus and Marie de Champagne, strayed from what is known to be true of the fifth and sixth centuries in Britain. Yet they have not strayed so far as to be unrecoverable; elements of *Le Chevalier de la Charrette* can feasibly be traced back to the ninth century. This is the latest possible date of origin for *Glas*.

---

[1] As the reader has seen (Chapter II), this was to be avoided except when it directly had bearing upon Guinièvre.

[2] Though of course he is not treated with the same courtesy and respect which Gauvain receives.

[3] Because of the traditional properties of the bed of the Cart Castle in *La Charrette*, I shall delay writing about this theme until I am able to introduce the *Le Conte* material in Chapter XV.

[4] (*Tain Bo Cuailgne* II 2915; Greene, 1972, 59-73, with picture).

[5] (*De Bello Gallica*, trans. Handford 1951), XV-XVII, XIX). Caesar landed in Britain and left a short time later without having gained any extensive territory or trade rights.

[6] It must be kept in mind, however, that it is possible that the Picts simply quit using the chariot sometime in the centuries during which they controlled only the craggy Highlands.

[7] The drawing below is based on that of David Longley in Dr. Laing's article (1984, 279).

[8] A majority of scholars have argued for a date nearer the ninth century, though Dr. Laing has shown evidence for a fifth or sixth century creation for this nature of stone in "Archaeological Notes on Some Early Christian Stones" (1984).

[9] (Book II; Chapter XLIV). The *vita* states that both axles had no linchpins, yet the carriage performed its normal task. A two axle vehicle must, by its very nature, have four wheels.

[10] From the "Prose Lancelot" section of *The Vulgate Version of the Arthurian Romances* one learn's that he also removes the sarcophagus from the cemetery (trans. Sommer 1909-1916, 175).

[11] It could be argued that this is a typical romantic strategem of postponing pleasure in order to intensify it. However, Guinièvre is unaware of the postponement, thereby effectively halving the effect. Further, there is no mention of the delay in the dialogues between Guinièvre and Lancelot, nor any heightened passion on the part of Lancelot or Guinièvre as a result of it, so one must question Chrétien's intentions with regard to the tomb episode.

[12] The fountain fades in importance as the scene continues, but it is mentioned for its reflective qualities.

[13] *Lanval*, trans. Burgess and Busby 1986, l. 634). Lanval leaps upon it before becoming consort to the queen of Avalon.

[14] (*La Morte d'Arthur*, 15-16; *The Vulgate Version of the Arthurian Romances*, trans. Sommer 1909-1916, vol. vi: 11.2).

[15] If one would allow for a little literary symbolism, a mirror is also present. The comb and the mirror is the most common pair of symbols found together on the Pictish stones.

[16] The most common type of Class I Pictish stone includes the comb and mirror, though there is no way of knowing what it stood for. A. Jackson (1989, 19-25) has noted the wide use of this symbol, as well as

its consistent location at the bottom of a stone and in conjunction with two other symbols. He has also written on the consistency with which these other symbols on the Pictish stones occur within defined geographical boundaries. The symbols can be shown to appear in conjunction only with certain others, and these symbols can most normally be found within the boundaries of one of the four oldest Pictish kingdoms. The comb and mirror symbol appears regularly in conjunction with only one of each group of symbols. From this gathering of facts he has determined that the stones are marriage markers, and each of the symbols but the comb and mirror denote noble families. The symbols that are always accompanied by the mirror and comb are thereby determined to be royal in Dr. Jackson's view. This would in large measure agree with the hypothesis made here.

Chapter VII: Conclusion

In the first chapter of this volume, the academic opinion of Chrétien's poems was stated. It is believed that he had evoked an entire world for Marie de Champagne based on classical and contemporary literature and his patroness's feminism. He took only the names and a rough storyline from the British. This position is no longer tenable. How could anyone create such a visionary place that had such an uncanny similarity to the post-Roman Britain that is reconstructable from Irish and Welsh myth, legend, law tracts, historical documents, and archaeological remains? Instead, it is apparent he did what he was obviously best at, namely forming the stories, themes, and patterns of others into a coherent whole.

What do the parallels between the Celtic culture anterior to 900 and the details in *Le Chevalier de la Charrette* tell us? First, it is known that abductions were common in Celtic society, but the theft of a queen would have been an entirely foreign thought in the medieval literature. Second, these correlations are so consistent it becomes clear that the infrastructure was a British and ancient one, which I have termed *Glas*, and the other sources, e.g., classical and romantic, are additions. Chrétien may use an alternative work for many lines, but he always returns, and stays, with something Celtic. As has been seen, every scene of *La Charrette* apart from that before the Sword Bridge (an evening with a vavasour) is bristling with distinctly Celtic items. This implies a very strong and, likely, very old tradition.[1] D.D.R. Owen, the best recent translator of Chrétien, states:

> Having said that Chrétien's imagination was free-ranging, I must qualify my words by adding that there were limits to its activity. As I have suggested,

he was not happy when faced by the need to improvise important sections of his story, or extend its intrigue beyond what was in his source. This did sometimes happen, and with unfortunate results, as will be seen. He was certainly not less inventive than most medieval poets, but inventiveness was not encouraged by the literary tradition. Authority laid a heavy hand on composition; and it was more the fashion to claim a source for one's work than to assert originality, except in the manner of presentation. Chrétien was no exception to this rule. (1968, 106)

Chrétien simply was not the type of author who could invent an entire world out of his imagination. Such authors were not encouraged to develop in twelfth-century Europe.

Chrétien is not creating the world he portrays, instead he is altering the Celtic story and inserting themes and thoughts that evidently came from his background and Marie de Champagne's wishes. Could one expect more from a man whose livelihood depended on pleasing a pre chosen audience, one that wanted an aesthetic theme? Can one expect more, even if that man was the greatest French poet of the Middle Ages? His reputation should not rest on his creation of the Matter of Britain. To quote Roger Loomis:

> Is Gottfried von Strassbourg generally regarded as a mediocre rhymester because he took over with little change the *matière* supplied by Thomas? Is Chaucer considered a slavish redactor because all the Canterbury Tales except two adhere fairly closely to antecedent plots, and his Troilus is patched together from various versions of the Troy story? On the contrary, he is still regarded as one of the most individual and versatile geniuses which the Middle Ages produced. If, as I have maintained, Chrétien did not invent the *matière* which he used in Erec, Lancelot, Yvain, and Perceval, his reputation need not suffer, for no one denies that he improved considerably on his sources in style, polish, and charm. (1936, 242)

So what non-classical, non-contemporary sources did he use? There were records and heroic poems in Britain before 800, as Jackson, Bromwich, Hughes, Dumville, and others have postulated.[2] There was also interaction between the Celts and French -- directly through the Bretons, and indirectly through various aspects of Henry II's kingdoms. Further, evidence for an historical element in the poem has been found to date earlier than 900, and possibly to the fifth century. What is to bar the idea that the heroic poetry pertaining to Arthuriana became removed and copied, or orally transferred to a location in France? Its source would have been the *Northern Memoranda*, or a similar body of historical and pseudo-historical lore (below). Chrétien could then be seen as using historical (in a twelfth-century sense of the word) texts, or those on par with *Y Gododdin* or the Urien cycle. As has been seen, this agrees with the evidence at hand. Supplementary confirmation will be forthcoming in a critical study of the poem *Le Conte du Graal*.

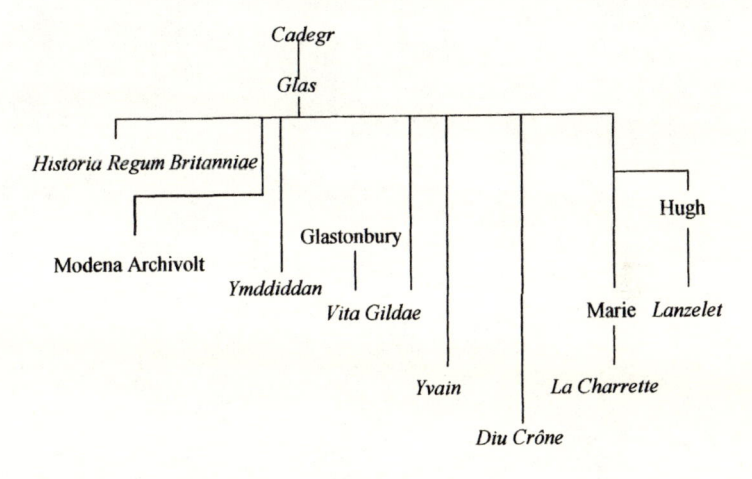

```
                        Cadegr
                         Glas
     ┌───────────────┬────┬────────┬──────┬───────┐
Historia Regum Britanniae                        │
     │                                         Hugh
     │              Glastonbury                  │
Modena Archivolt      │                          │
              Ymddiddan                          │
                   Vita Gildae         Marie   Lanzelet
                                         │
                            Yvain   La Charrette
                                 Diu Crône
```

---

[1] Even if the late addition of Lancelot and the duality of Urien and Melwas cause problems for a skeptic, the court of Arthur, Cei/Keii/Cai, Ginièvre, and Gwalchmai/Gauvain are always present.

[2] These scholars have argued for a written *Northern Memoranda* composed possibly of strictly historical data, but quite probably also of saga material and poetry like that which remains of Urien, Eledd, and Llywarch Hen. It is also known that *Y Gododdin* and some of the Taliesen poems were probably first composed by two of the filid whom the Ninnius compiler lists.

Chapter VIII: Introduction to *Le Conte du Graal*

The previous seven chapters have been devoted to the study of *Le Chevalier de la Charrette* as a potential literary source. It has been determined that this poem's progenitor, *Glas*, was probably first formed between the final departure of Roman troops from Britain and the disappearance of the Pictish culture in the years following 843. The prototype was very likely created in the post-Roman period. It would have been a bardic poem of heroism dedicated to a British figure. This literature would then have been reworked by literary and oral means for many years, and finally brought to its present state by Chrétien in the twelfth century.

It has also been deduced that the less realistic portions of Chrétien's poem can be explained in one of three manners. The two traditional notions are that the less believable scenes are due either to a cultural misunderstanding or Chrétien's interpretation of the romantic ideals of Marie de Champagne. A third possibility was elaborated upon in the introduction; many seemingly trivial elements in the poem were from or anterior to the ninth century. In the last three chapters this hypothesis was largely substantiated. The same objective is set for my study of Chrétien's last known romance, *Le Conte du Graal*. I will attempt to establish the presence of historical elements in this tale as well.

A Frenchman named Chrétien, renowned for his skills, wrote *Le Conte du Graal* in the 1190s. As in all of his Arthurian romances, here he injected his usual personal style and knowledge of the classics. In the opening lines, he again stated that he was given the *matìere* by his patron, now Philip of Flanders.[1] Because of the consistent brilliance that the poet displayed in this poem, it became a blueprint by which later writers measured their own Arthurian romances and from which they drew many of their motifs.

However, two elements in this romance are unique to *Le Conte du Graal*. First, the new patron's attitudes are quite distinct from Marie de Champagne. He has no fascinations with courtly love. Philip is a man of religious appetite and strong moral conviction, and is from a family renowned throughout Christendom for moral fiber.

Second, the theme of the poem is unique for Chrétien, namely religious piety. It will be beneficial to this study to begin by exploring these two new underlying principles. Then, I will survey the four major theories regarding the origins of the grail ceremony. The explanation of Chrétien's *graal* that each theory is able to give will favor the conclusion that all are partially correct, and that the Celtic elements make up the earliest strata of the story.[2] It will be found that each was introduced to the story individually through a process of progressive superimposition on an originally Celtic tale. This survey will also serve to support the hypothesis that the original grail and the mystique surrounding it are a conglomerate of Celtic motifs. Following the hint that this provides, I will attempt a comparison of other Celtic tales and antiquarian material that pertains indirectly to Chrétien's *graal* and the ceremony surrounding it. This will be in the hope of gaining a better understanding of the object and the ceremony that encompasses it. In conjunction with this analogous exploration, I will discuss later medieval versions of the grail story. This will prove as valuable in showing certain general patterns for all early versions of the grail story as it did in *Le Chevalier de la Charrette*. It will lead to a theory of why the different writers describe the grail and the ceremony surrounding it differently, and will in turn help further explain the grail's original nature and purpose.

A chapter devoted to identifying the original roles of each of the major characters will follow this. The most significant of these will be the indications that the Celtic god *Beli* may have originally occupied the role that became the grail-king. This, in conjunction with the traditional view that Arthur and the people of the fifth century were Christian in nature, should be cause for thought. The connection will lead to a some research pertaining to the nature and interaction of the Christian and native Celtic religions in sub-Roman Britain. In turn, this will preface a search for potentially historical Celtic material. I hope to demonstrate here that there is the same link between *Le Conte du Graal* and ancient Britain as there is with *Le Chevalier de la Charrette*. Further, I believe that this process will serve to provide an overall picture of the grail story's genesis stemming from a prototype, *Dysgyl*. It is hoped that these two objectives will help begin to define the historicity of the poem.

Unlike *Le Chevalier de la Charrette*, *Le Conte du Graal* introduces its chief character, Perceval, almost immediately. He is of royal blood and has been raised in an isolated village by his mother. The reader finds him first watching a group of Arthur's knights riding through his forest as he hunts animals for his household. The warriors stop to ask him for any knowledge of a kidnapped lady who was taken through his forest recently. In a scene of levity, the knights instead find themselves answering all of his naïve questions and telling him of Arthur's court. They do eventually receive all the help Perceval can give and finally leave. For his part, Perceval returns home and informs his mother that he has decided to become a knight of King Arthur. He rides off despite his mother's tears. With one short delay, he proceeds to Arthur's court and there insists on knighthood from the king.[3] Arthur is not immediately aware of him, however, because a hitherto unknown character called the Red Knight has just stolen the king's gold cup and dashed the wine contained therein on Guinièvre. Cei instead responds to the boy. He announces Perceval will be granted the boon of knighthood if he can prove his worth by killing the knight who is sitting on a charger just beyond the court (the Red Knight). Perceval accomplishes the task, takes the man's armor, and rides away.

Riding along, he eventually comes to one of his uncles, Gornemanz de Gohorts, who teaches him how to ride, fight, and behave in a courtly fashion. Continuing on, he arrives at the castle of a cousin in distress. He rescues her, then refuses her offer of marriage. From there he happens upon the grail castle where he witnesses the grail supper, but fails to ask the question that would end his kinsmens' suffering. Soon thereafter he stumbles across Arthur's court again. It is at this point that *Le Conte du Graal* begins to become complicated in a way none of Chrétien's previous romances are. A lady known as the Ugly Damsel brings Perceval to shame by informing Arthur's men of what Perceval has failed to do at the grail castle. His attempts to right this failure make up one major part of the plot. The Ugly Damsel pleas with Arthur's knights to lift a siege at Montesclare, and Gauvain and several colleagues take up the challenge. However, Gauvain is accused of murder by a visitor almost immediately thereafter and instead rides out to defend himself. Perceval leaves the court and goes in search of the grail castle for five years and visits no church in this period. Meanwhile, the story focuses on Gauvain. He safely arrives at the home of his prosecutor and becomes romantically entangled with a woman he soon learns is his accuser's sister; there is inevitably a conflict. To solve the social predicament, all sides agree the only proper thing for Gauvain to do is hunt for one year for the sacred lance that pierced Christ. Failure to capture and return with it will bring him back to the castle again for imprisonment. It is in this year when the tale ends, but in the meantime Gauvain manages to become lord of a castle, find a spouse for himself and one of his sisters, and anger a chieftain. Perceval arrives in time to fight Gauvain's intended opponent. The work stops abruptly in the midst of the acclaim that Arthur's court gives Gauvain.

As a piece of literature, Chrétien de Troyes' *Le Conte du Graal* has attained international status. His characters are memorable and his plot was a prototype of the grail romance of the Middle Ages. His detailed descriptions of scenery and persons make the reader wonder if he had not seen the places and the fights in his poem. The poem is a masterpiece and a cornerstone of Arthuriana. It is, however, as a literary source that I intend to examine it. I believe it, in the context of a redaction of a historical document, also functions as a source for information about the late-fifth and early-sixth centuries. In this context it will aid our attempt to elucidate the mystery of the grail.

---

[1] This is significant because the poems *Le Chevalier de La Charrette* and *Le Conte du Graal* are the only two in which he claims his patron has given him his source.

[2] The four major theories focus on the Celtic, Christian, Jewish, and archetypal universal elements of the ceremony, respectively.

[3] In the delay, he enters the tent of an unescorted maiden, takes a good share of the food and drink which is laid out, kisses the maiden, and takes one of her rings.

Chapter IX: Philip of Flanders: Life and Influences[1]

The "Phelipe de Flandres" whom Chrétien mentions in his prologue (*Le Conte*, l. 13), was from a family of some standing in twelfth-century Europe. This clan had a traditional connection with the Christian government in the Holy Land. Philip's father Robert II had gone on crusade there. Robert's predecessor Theodoric of Alsatia had once received a phial containing a portion of the holy blood for his repeated aid to Jerusalem (Adolf 1943, 601). Philip's mother, Sibyl, who also had a reputation for holiness, accompanied her husband Robert II on the Crusades and remained at the Convent of St. Lazarus of Bethany (Adolf 1943, 602). The House of Flanders was considered a bastion of Christianity in the twelfth century, and its men were greatly admired in this respect. In fact, a branch of Philip's family at one point produced several rulers of Jerusalem.

Of Philip of Flanders' life a great deal is known, because of his family and his importance in Jerusalem politics for a short time. The future count, a second son, was born in 1142 and by 1156 he was the heir. It was then that he married Elizabeth of Vermandois and gained possession of her family's holdings in a typical medieval amalgamation of property.

His character was quite powerful. His strength of faith as well as his skills in combat were acclaimed throughout Europe. He was also a good businessman, both public and private and is known to have protected the towns in his territory from economic oppression; they thrived as a result. Domestically he was just as prudent. When his wife Elizabeth was caught in adultery he neither dissolved their marriage nor did anything that might make him forfeit Vermandois. He wisely sent her instead to a convent (Diverres 1990, 28). He was not lacking in passion, either. He personally killed Elizabeth's lover.

Nevertheless, Philip made some embarrassing decisions. As was pointed out earlier, one branch of the House of Flanders family ruled Jerusalem in this period. During the early part of Philip's career the king was a sickly invalid. Knowing the conditions in Jerusalem and aware of his family's status there, Philip made the journey to the Holy Land under the pretense of seeing his mother and coyly visited the royal establishment at Jerusalem. To protect the services of the House of Flanders, keep Philip's goodwill, and add to the prestige of the state of Jerusalem, Philip was offered regency over the incapacitated monarch who was his cousin. In reality he was being handed the throne in a temporary capacity, until his cousin was deceased and the legitimate heirs, the two children of his cousin's sisters, had grown to adulthood.[2] He refused, and instead attempted to marry his cousins to two of his men. Presumably this would have ensured that Philip would remain the dominant authority in Jerusalem when his cousin died. His actions were, however, circumvented and he departed Jerusalem with no official authority in the city.

In other ways his journey was also unsuccessful. During his stay in the Holy City, Philip was persistently asked to lead a force against the Muslims in order to strike fear into the enemy, but never acquiesced. This brought negative repercussions from his family and others throughout Europe. The Jerusalem voyage, intended by Philip and his family to vault him into the position of being one of the most prominent Christians in western Europe, ended only in his embarrassment (Krey 1941, 155). Unrepentant, Philip returned to Flanders and revolted when the young Philip Augustus ascended the throne in 1180. His refusal to accept the king went on for five years until Philip of Flanders made peace with the king. After this, he was a supportive vassal. In 1192 he went on crusade and died in the Holy Land.

Chrétien is known, by references in his poem, to have written between the years of Philip's revolt and his last trip to Jerusalem.[3] A more precise date than this is not feasible, nor is it necessary to make this discussion complete. It does, however, somewhat corroborate a theory that has been developed by Helen Adolph (1943, 597-620). The evidence to be found in the pages of Chrétien has led many to a theory that has remained unchallenged for fifty years. It is generally held that *Le Conte du Graal* is a biography of the patron of the poem. Philip's direct influence on the poem is clear, but its basic plot is to be best understood in a study of Philip's life. French experts have noted the parallel development of Perceval and Philip's lives. It is also been pointed out that Philip left for Jerusalem at about the period Chrétien stopped writing, and with his hero about to return to the grail castle. The poem's consistent and often blatant parallels to Philip's actions and interactions have led to a nearly unanimous idea about the main narrative among French experts. *Le Conte* is a mirror of Philip's life. Helen Adolph went through the main points of Philip's *vita*:

1. Goes to Jerusalem, always noted for riches but given religious importance.
2. Kingdom ruled by a sick man surrounded by enemies.
3. A cousin of the king is expected and finally arrives.
4. The king's sister mourns the premature death of her husband.
5. The cousin is offered a regency; rule of country.
6. Fails to live up to his relatives' expectations and is blamed for it.
(Adolf 1943, 598).

On pages 603-7 of Adolph's article, Philip's family tree is reconstructed in genealogical terms and by events and qualities. Further, it is compared exhaustively and cogently with Perceval's family as found in *Le Conte du Graal* to underline the point.

Armel Diverres accepted this argument in principle, but also saw some political subtleties in the poem's lines. First, the genealogical similarities between Perceval and Philip's families allowed some validation of his maternal inheritance; this may be found in the manner of inheritance in Perceval's family.[4] Second, he shows some concern for the dynastic struggles of 1180s Flanders with Perceval/Philip's perceived emotional distance from Arthur/Philip Augustus (Diverres 1990, 32-42).

The influence Philip had on *Le Conte du Graal* should be readily apparent. The general reputation the counts of Flanders had, and the one Philip himself wished to engender, was one of an intensely religious spirit. This, as the reader will see, is an influence on the poem that cannot be overstated. However, Philip made mistakes of faith and morality -- a rejection of the job of Protector of the Holy Land, the blunt use of power to try marrying off his cousins for the increase of his prestige, and a revolt against the rightful king. Chrétien brings all these items to written form in the subtleties of his plot, with the full knowledge of the regretful and repentant Philip.[5] It is Chrétien's use of Philip's life as a foundation that gives the poem so many aspects that have no parallel in Irish or Welsh myth, law, or motifs.[6] As Chapter XII will show, it was this action, mimicked by following romance writers, which changed the basic format of the grail legend into something barely comparable to its Celtic precursors.

The life and influences of Philip were important factors in the creation of *Le Conte*. However, Philip's international relations, with Scotland in particular, gave Chrétien further potential information. Henry II's marriage to Edith Maud, and several lesser marriages between the Scottish and Norman royal families, had helped create an intracultural atmosphere. In this context data from Britain was often common knowledge in France (Ritchie 1954, xi-xiv). Philip's alliance to Scotland in 1173-4 made the tie there even stronger, and was tapped by Chrétien in his poem, as can be seen. The most conspicuous evidence for a Scottish contribution to the Perceval poem is the place-names. Those he uses were newsworthy in the period between Henry's marriage to Maud and the Scottish-Flanders alliance. There is also an association of ancient origin between Gauvain, Galloway, and consistent theme to be found in *Le Conte*. A brief summary of the least problematic associations and the Gauvain-Galloway connection will best point out the correlation.

First, in 1109 the Norman Count Alan Rufus took a well-known military tour to the Forth. This probably caused the English term for the Firth of Forth, Scots' Water, to come into the common aristocratic vocabulary.[7] The name appears in Wace as *Escoce Watre* and in Chrétien as *Cotouatre*.[8]

From 1124, King David of Scotland located his capital at Carlisle. It remained so until his death in 1157. David was raised by the Normans and was highly regarded by them for his prowess and manners. They considered him one of their own. His actions and location were known by the royalty of England, to whom he owed much of his power and with whom he maintained a friendly contact. Carlisle appears in Chrétien as *Carduel*, Arthur's capital (*Le Conte*, ll. 336, 839). The connection is undoubtedly valid; *Carduel* is the spelling for Carlisle in the *Anglo-Saxon Chronicle* (E-1092), and in local charters (Ritchie 1952, 9-10).

From 1110 until 1159 Galloway was in the hands of the Norseman Fergus, who was independent of and consistently hostile to the Scottish kings (Ritchie 1954, 352). The boundary of this kingdom was the Nith River. It was notorious for its inhospitality to the Scots, and this comes across in *Le Conte du Graal* as Gauvain prepares to cross the Nith.

Einz chevaliers n'an pot venir
Qui ça alast ne chanp no voie,
Que c'est la bone de Galvoie:
Einz chevaliers n'i; puet passer
qui ja an puisse retorner, (*Le Conte*, ll. 8341-45).

No knight who has ever gone that way by road or field has ever been able to come back, for this is the frontier of Galloway, which a knight can't cross and then return again. (*Le Conte*, trans. Owen 1989, 461).

The association of Gauvain with Galloway is quite ancient, as indicated in the name similarity (Newell 1902, 277-8). Gauvain's grandmother, mother, and sister are to be found in Galloway's borders in *Le Conte*, at the Castle of the Maidens. Such a state of affairs implies a connection between Galloway and its eponym Gauvain that is supported by an early draft of *De Rebus Gestis Regum Anglorum* (c. 1125). Here Gawain is specifically termed the king of Galloway (*De Rebus Gestis Regum Anglorum* III, ed. Stubbs 1889, 287, 342). This tie is demonstrably old, the incongruous presence of his family in a region famed for its anti-English sentiment in the twelfth century can be explained in no other way.

Finally, the concept of the virgin knight, which is so foreign to the *Peredur* author and the generic Celtic legends, may have its beginnings in the person of Alexander, king of Scotland from 1149-1165. Despite the incessant urgings of his advisors, legend says he remained a virgin until his early death (Ritchie 1954, 16-17).

In contrast to Marie de Champagne's influence, which was often flagrantly sexist, the inspiration of Philip was multi-faceted. His house's prestige commanded a religious aspect, and his past and regrets implied another. The friendly relations with Scotland allowed for much more diversity and in many cases offered Chrétien a number of intriguing names and places with which neither he nor his audience were familiar. He managed successfully to combine them all into a generally coherent and impressively entertaining whole, despite this obstacle. As will be seen below, the effort was so completely successful that no grail writer who followed would use any other format but the one the great poet had created.

---

[1] The main criticisms of this important figure in the past sixty years have been Helen Adolf (1943, 597-620), and Armel Diverres (1990,

13-109). There seems to have been exceptionally few disagreements between the two on the above general information.

[2] (Diverres 1990, 29). One of them was pregnant, her husband only recently dead.

[3] This is a disputed date. Conceivably, he could have become bored with the subject matter or simply found that he had painted himself into a corner. In this case there could be no definite date. Alternately, he may have ceased writing when his patron died in 1192 and there was no cash flow. There is also the possibility Chrétien's death cut the poem short; his obit is unknown.

[4] As I will argue, the intimation of matrilinear inheritance which Philip's line showed made it that much easier for Chrétien to parallel Philip's family with that of Perceval's.

[5] It should not be believed that Philip and his court could not see the similarities of relations, time, and religious outlook between Philip and Perceval.

[6] i.e. the weeping cousin who berates Perceval and the hideous damsel who humiliates him at Arthur's court have parallels in the cousins whom he had dealings with in Jerusalem.

[7] Alan Rufus was a Breton ally of William the Conqueror and member of a junior Branch of the Breton ducal family. He was made Count of Richmond by The Conqueror (Stenton 1932, 24-5; Mason, 1963, 703-4).

[8] (*Le Conte*, l. 3675; Ritchie 1952, 8; Bromwich, 1991, 277). *Escoce Watre* and *Cotouatre* are not direct translation of Scot's Water. However, the two terms are visually similar, and Scot's Water is the best translation in context with the episode it comes from. In Arthurian onomastics this is all that may reasonably be hoped for.

Chapter X: Theories for the Grail's Origins

Que qu'il parloient d'un et d'el,
Uns vaslez d'une chanbre vint
Qui une blanche lance tint
Anpoigniee par le milieu,
Si passa par entre le feu
Et ces qui el lit se seoient,
Et tuit cil de leanz veoient
La lance blanche et le fer blanc,
S'issoit une gote de sanc
Del fer de la lance an somet
Et jus qu'a la main au vaslet
Coloit cele gote vermoille.
Li vaslez vit cele mervoille
Qui leanz ert la nuit venuz,
Si s'est de demander tenuz
Comant cele chose avenoit,
Que del chasti li sovenoit
Celui qui chevalier le fist
Qui li anseigna et aprist
Que de trop parler se gardast;
Si crient, se il le demandast,
Qu'an li tenist a vilenie:
Por ce si nel demanda mie.
   Atant dui autre vaslet vindrent
Qui chandeliers an lor mains tindrent
De fin or, ovrez a neel.
Li vaslet estoient mout bel
Qui les chandeliers aportoient.
An chascun chandeliers ardoient
Dis chandoiles a tot le mains

Un graal antre ses deux mains
Une dameisele tenoit
Qui avoec les vaslez venoit,
Bele et gente et bien acesmee:
Quant ele fu leanz antree
A tot le graal qu'ele tint,
Une si granz clartez i vint
Qu'ausi perdirent les chandoiles
Lor clarté come les estoiles
Quant li solauz lieve ou la lune.
Aprés celi an revint une
Qui tint un tailleor d'argent. (*Le Conte*, ll. 3156-97).

>While they were talking of this and that, out of a room came a youth with a white lance grasped by the middle; he passed by between the fire and those seated upon the couch. And everyone present could see the white lance with its shining head, and from the tip of the lance-head oozed a drop of blood, a crimson drop that ran down right to the lad's hand. The young man who had arrived there that night saw this marvel, but refrained from asking how this thing happened, since he remembered that warning given him by the man who knighted him and taught and instructed him to beware of talking too much. He feared that, had he asked, it would have been thought impolite, and so he did not enquire. Thereupon two other youths came, holding in their hands pure gold candle-sticks inlaid with black enamel. The lads carrying the candelabras were extremely handsome. At least ten candles were burning in each candelabra.
>
>A damsel, who came with the youths and was fair and attractive and beautifully adorned, held in both hands a grail. Once she had entered with this grail that she held, so great a radiance appeared that the candles lost their brilliance just as the stars do at the rising of the sun or moon. After her came another maiden, holding a silver carving carving-dish. (*Le Conte*, trans. Owen 1989, 416-17).

Chrétien's version of the grail scene thus has a lance, candelabra, grail, and silver carving platter. The common object of all the grail ceremonies is the center of a procession that passes in front of the hero.[1] Though most versions assign the grail a cornucopic property, the procession itself causes anguish to the residents of the grail castle.

This entire spectacle that revolves around the grail has puzzled scholars for centuries. The various redactions produced in the sixty years following seem to combine the strange beauty of the Christian Mass with the seemingly ageless, incoherent conglomeration of the fairy-like world of Celtic mythology. The grail romances have moral purity and religious fervor coupled with ancient kingship rituals. They show a fixation on an object held in a maid's hands, a barbaric concept of human life, and the dead warriors' symbolic importance. The combination is striking and at times overwhelming. Theories as to the explanation of this wonderful object of the grail, the event of the ceremony, and location of the grail castle have only reflected this. It has been described as a Christian, Celtic, Greek, or Jewish rite. It is a beautiful example of the extinct "Celtic Christianity", or the invention of Chrétien's mind. The ideas are limitless and the solutions which Chrétien's ambiguous *graal* have provoked have been incalculable as well. However, there is an answer, and it is ascertainable with the knowledge available, as I hope to show in the following pages. This solution will best be facilitated by first reviewing the chief arguments of the major camps. Therefore, in the following pages I shall summarize, analyze the chief and most compelling points of the Christian, Nature Ritual, Jewish, and Celtic theories. This done, I shall reject that any one of these is the pure solution to the puzzle of the grail.[2] I will then develop what is in essence a theory that complements them all to some extent.

The Christian theory has primarily evolved from later grail romances, which are overtly Christian,[3] and the judgment that anything written for one of the most famed Christian families in Europe must be of Christian origin. It now has few supporters.[4] The theory is often based on Christian phrases that superficially dot the poem.[5]

There is pseudo-historical evidence that such a story as one finds in Chrétien could have been originally Christian, and quite old, however. Since the late Middle Ages, Britain has considered itself one of the earliest Christian countries. The seeds that would later develop into Joseph of Arimathea's legendary immigration to Britain had appeared as early as the 700s. The *Chronicle of Freculf* states that St. Philip and St. James sent twelve disciples to convert the island in the middle of the first century. Glastonbury later claimed that the leader of this mission was the same Joseph who buried Christ on his property (*De Antiquitate Glastonie Ecclesie*, ed. and trans. Scott 1981, Books I and II). Such a claim was only strengthened by extending it to somehow encompass the most famed king of British lore.[6]

It is argued that Perceval seems a very Christian character because of the general ambiance of the poem. The place he is raised is portrayed as a community in many ways comparable to a monastery. It is isolated from society and contains only the servants of the household, and farmhands. There is none of the leisure activities of a royal center. The central figure, Arthur, is unanimously a Christian king in all the early romances. However, the same or more spartan childhoods may be attributed to Fionn, Enlil of Babylonian myth, and the Tarzan of fiction, none of whom are Christian or demonstrate strong Christian values. In addition, when Perceval implies that he has kissed his mother's chambermaids (*Le Conte*, ll. 706-10), he is not explicitly admitting to anti-Christian behavior. However, this not-so-innocent act does not seem like the action of a boy raised in an idyllic Christian community, nor was the act of kissing a peasant one of an innately noble person.

The manner in which Perceval is instructed also highlights the sense of Christianity in the poem, so the argument goes.[7] Early in his career, Perceval is taught by Gornemant how to fight well, but warned not to kill in accordance with Christian ideals (*Le Conte*, l. 1627). As his experiences mature him, he comes to find a deeper form of belief in God. He begins to have an understanding of right and wrong, and a realization of his place of importance as a holy knight of God. On Good Friday pilgrims recall him to the faith from his wanderings. He spends the next few days cleansing his spirit along with his uncle the Hermit King. The reader is made to understand that when he has reached the proper level of understanding and demonstrated his devotion to God, he will be the next grail king. The religious views of Arthur's knights toward the grail and the reverence they hold it in indicate the object must be Christian.

Again, this is hardly strong evidence; heroes of any nation or faith know right and wrong and learn to understand their importance. They do kill, contrary to Gornemant's advice, as did the holy men who went on crusade in the Middle Ages. The judgment that faith is the necessary element in becoming a grail-king is a notion that can be attributed more to the life of Philip and its influences on the poem than to the values of Christianity (see Chapter IX).

The Christian ambiance of the poem is stressed to the point of nausea. Perceval refers to God and figures surrounding the Christian afterlife constantly in puzzling over the knights he sees in the forest.

> Par m'ame,
> voir me dist ma mere ma dame,
> Qui me dist que deable sont

Plus esfreé que rien del mont, (*Le Conte*, ll. 113-16).

By my soul, my lady mother spoke the truth when she told me that devils are the most hideous things in the world. (*Le Conte*, trans. Owen 1989, 375).

Unable otherwise to describe their beauty when he has seen their armor, he later concludes they are angels. Such a scene is intended only for humor and has no place in a discussion of the religious outlook of the grail.

There was a large volume of trade that took place between the East and the West of Europe in the twelfth century due to the crusades. Because of this, critics who support the Christian theory have felt justified in using Orthodox as well as Roman elements of the mass to explain the grail ritual as they find it in the pages of twelfth- and early thirteenth-century writers (Bruce 1923, 258-9). It is believed that Chrétien would have been exposed to Byzantine merchants or a returning crusader as a member of Philip's court. It is further theorized that the unusual quality of the eastern ritual would have made it an exciting element of the grail ceremony. The use of evidence here by those who follow the Christian Theory is an extremely liberal and at times almost whimsical interpretation. Because of this, the theories thereby formed have been necessarily highly optimistic and often have disregarded simpler solutions. As will be seen, however, there are stronger points to the theory.

These scholars believe that the objects involved in the grail ceremony are to be found in the Byzantine rite. There the blood of Christ is carried on a platter, the lance of Longinus follows, and a bowl, which catches the blood from its tip, ends the procession of religious objects.[8] This neatly explains away many of the pagan elements of the poem. With this done, all the other anomalies of the poem seemingly fit into place behind the theory of Christian origin. The strange titles of Perceval's uncles can be explained away using this theory. The Hermit King is clearly one who has found Christianity in the wilderness. He represents the easiest way of finding God, through penance and by avoiding the temptations of civilization. He is the one to lead Perceval from the ways of the world and to the path of religious observance. The Grail keeper, known as the "Fisher King", is a name originally rendered from a literal interpretation of *Matthew* "Follow me and I will make you fishers among men" (IV: 19).

However, this aspect of the theory is flawed as well. The grail ceremony does not strike one as particularly Christian. The grail and lance are kept in a castle, not a temple where they should be.[9] There is, too, the fact that the place is associated with Judas. Yet no grail writer who followed him disputed this; these properties which Chrétien gave to the grail appear from this point on as common grail attributes.[10] In addition, no aspect of Christianity satisfies the asking ceremony at which Perceval fails. There is none in the Roman Catholic, nor to my knowledge in the Orthodox Church.

There are other nuances of the grail ceremony that remain unanswered by this theory. A woman carries the grail of Chrétien. Dr. Peebles believed this seemingly pagan detail could be shown to be one of a number of exception instances in which the general ban on women holding religious objects was overlooked. However, the small number of examples and their limited geography only weakened her argument (Peebles 1911, 209-13). A long line of conciliar decrees and episcopal edicts support the contention that women were not allowed to touch holy objects in ceremonies. The grail scene of later versions replaced the maiden with a youth or priest, apparently because the romancers realized the discrepancy as well.

The lance, too, is most definitely not of Christian derivation. Chrétien says nothing of its part in Jesus' crucifixion. It simply precedes the grail and drips blood amidst mourning. Its literary connection to the Spear of Longinus was a result of many stages in the grail legend.[11] The first continuator gives it a Christian quality.[12]

The castle where Perceval comes upon this object also seems pan Celtic and unChristian in disposition. Chrétien's hero can only find it by chance even after he had been there. This implies the young man was either very bad with directions or, more probably, that the grail site had no set geographical setting. This castle is not a Christian one as mystic locations are the property of Hy Breasail, Annwfn and many more otherworld locales of pagan religions.

One can be much less certain about the other, less tangible aspects of the world Chrétien shows us. However, certainly the stone chair which splits as Perceval sits on it in *Didot Perceval* (ed. Nitze 1932-7, 150-1), and strange symbols such as the recurring combination of the colors white, red, and black, are not specifically Christian. The Waste Land and the dead knight motifs of later versions are also certainly incongruent with Christianity (Weston 1913, 64). Even the episode with the Hermit-king indicates exactly how little the tale originally was

Christian. That scene in *Le Conte du Graal* is directly borrowed from an episode in the Irish hero Fionn's life (Loomis 1963, 62), and thus is yet another Celtic element.

The reader may look to the history and literature of Insular Christianity as well, but it offers no support for a Christian Theory. The fifth and sixth centuries were the Age of Saints in Britain, when every significant Celtic country in Britain that existed between the years 400 and 600 boasted a holy individual who could claim sainthood.[13] Numerous vitae were later written in which these saints were given credit for every conceivable miracle. Folktales, legends, and other *vitae* were all used to make each saint appear more holy than others. No hagiographer should have allowed a tradition of such beauty and significance as the one surrounding the grail to be unconnected with a saint, if it was indeed Christian. Strangely, no grail, chalice, or cauldron ceremony or procession is included in any *vita*. This can only be because there was no such Christian object in Britain. Support for this observation comes from the Catholic church, which has never accepted the grail rite as a Christian ceremony (Remy 1907, vi: 7211). However, it is clear that both Arthur and Perceval are Christian characters. This is perhaps the strongest evidence for the Christian Theory, though the Christian resonances contained in the poem are unmistakable.

These problems have led to the introduction of other theories. The possibility that Chrétien was Jewish has led Dr. Weinraub to the theory that the famed grail ceremony was a ritual celebrating the evacuation, by the Jewish people, of Egypt. He believes it is a celebration of the Hebrew event known as Passover.[14] The comparisons he makes are numerous and intricate and have led to a theory that, while never attaining the prominence of the Celtic or Christian hypotheses, has attained some degree of strength.

Circumstantial historical evidence is not wanting for Chrétien's Jewish affinity. Troyes, an important economic center, was famed for its renowned Jewish citizen, the Pentateuch master Rashi (1040-1105). The school he left behind was his legacy. In addition, there is evidence that fairs were held in Troyes concurrently with synods (Weinraub 1976, 81). It is quite possible that the religious schools of learning begun in the tenth century, as well as traveling scholars contributed to an awareness of the Jewish religion in France, and especially Troyes. Chrétien would have lived in a city renowned for its Jewish learning and would have had easy and open access to the Jewish culture and customs.

There is no dearth of textual evidence; Weinraub sees parallels to the Jewish religion in *Le Conte du Graal*'s general storyline. Moses' exile from Egypt is duplicated in Perceval's departure from his mother. The crossing of the Red Sea can be seen in miniature when Perceval crosses the grail castle drawbridge (l. 623). The Jews' inability to cross the Jordan because they have not been purified is duplicated by the *Le Conte* hero, who cannot ford a stream because of his sin at the grail castle (l. 2985-3023). Moses' wanderings across the desert land in which he comes to find himself are re experienced in Perceval's meanderings through a large forest or desert for some years (l. 6239). Moses' arrival into the promised land and fulfillment of his destiny is matched by Perceval's entrance to the Grail castle (*Le Conte*, l. 3050-67).

It has also been argued that the grail ceremony itself has numerous items that could be derived from the Passover meal. Upon Perceval's entrance to the castle, the grail king is found leaning on one elbow as was the custom of the twelfth-century Jew during the ceremony. The stance was a symbol of freedom and therefore significant (Weinraub 1976, 52). The dates, figs, and other foods served during the appetizer dishes of the grail supper are those which traditional Jewish meals included. The main course that followed consisted of a *gastel* (a flat round cake), pepper, and meat. In the second plate of the Passover meal, one was expected to make a sandwich of the bread and bitter herbs (Weinraub 1976, 70). In addition, the grail platter is shown three times, as is the serving plate during the Passover supper (Weinraub 1976, 76). Alternatively and more economically, all the food mentioned above would make for a typical aristocratic meal in Jerusalem.[15] The custom of leaning on one's elbow, however, is one that is a common trait for most people in any society and does not necessarily have any deeper meaning.

The two candles that precede the grail in some of the grail ceremonies are also easy to explain in the context of a Jewish custom. If Passover falls on a Saturday, the Lord's day, a boy is to lead the servants with two wicks (Weinraub 1976, 66-7). Similar contingencies allow for the various species of grail rites in the different grail tellings.

The grail maiden falls neatly into the Jewish pattern as well. Dr. Weinraub explains to his readers that the bearer of the *graal*, or main dish during Passover, could have been a Jewish woman in a twelfth-century French rite, as in Chrétien's scene. The modern-day Aleppo community follows the custom that the eldest daughter of the head of the household bears the chief vessel (Weinraub 1976, 56). This is precisely what happens in *Le Conte*, where the grail maiden is the eldest virgin daughter of the grail king. In the twelfth-century ceremony, the Jewish girl was to take the plate away before the meal began to provoke the child to ask the key question, "Why?", just as Perceval is baited by the grail maiden.[16] This manufactured question would then lead to the story of how the Jews fled from Pharoah. The reader is told this ceremony is a common feature of Jewish societies. Apparently, it was often done in the Grail society, too. However, if the Jewish boy failed to make the query, the patriarch was to tell the story of the flight from Egypt as though it had been asked. If one were to make the comparison to *Le Conte*, then the grail King is in anguish because of his error in protocol. He does not explain what is happening when the boy does not ask, so he is made to suffer when Perceval leaves. However, this is not what we are told.

After the grail procession, the king and Perceval both wash their hands, as the participants in the Jewish festival are supposed to (Weinraub 1976, 68). Also to be found in the grail castle are four noteworthy items that pass Perceval, and the number four is a key figure in Jewish ceremony. Four questions are to be asked by the youngest child and four cups of wine are to be drunk by each person during the feast (Weinraub 1976, 55).

Such is the Jewish solution. Dr. Weinraub may have a valid point, the great French poet may have been a Jew by birth, and his writings could contain Jewish elements. However, he has only two substantial arguments; first, the strange foods served do resemble those of the Jewish feast and second, the asking ceremony connection is not an incidental scene in the grail story. On the other hand, the problems Dr. Weinraub's conclusions create are unsatisfactory. According to Dr. Weinraub's theory the important question is to come from a young member of the household, not a guest such as Perceval. Weinraub also overstretches the limits of his evidence by saying there are to be four questions asked. Perceval need only make one query. There is no expected guest in the Jewish ceremony, yet Perceval is anticipated. Dr. Weinraub also fails to explain the grail maiden's dual personality, the Wasteland motif, or Perceval's expected promotion to the kingship of the grail castle. The grail scene cannot be entirely a Jewish ceremony.

There has been some postulation and a widespread common belief that the grail scene is a glimpse into Celtic Christianity. This is incompatible with the evidence. The phrase "Celtic Christianity" itself is a misnomer. It is true that the Insular Celts were isolated from the continent for centuries, and did develop their own style of the Christian religion in the period. However, there were only two major questions that were in dispute when the British were reunited with Roman Catholicism toward the end of the seventh century -- the dating of Easter and tonsure. No record of questionable rites exists. The main force of the Celtic movement, the involvement of their art in their writing, was welcomed in the monastic tradition of Europe. The theory of Celtic Christianity has no place in a study of the origins of the grail.

The two previous theories inevitably cannot account for certain aspects of the grail story as found in the various romances. This has been a consistent problem in solving the mystery of the grail for centuries. In an effort to build an hypothesis that could account for the variability of the grail ceremony itself, Dr. Jessie Weston produced yet another idea. She believed that the grail ceremony began with a celebration of Spring, the new year in agricultural terms. The year, symbolized by a person, would then progressively age and die several days before Spring the following year. The death of the person who had personified the Old Year would often be accomplished by throwing him in a nearby waterway and drowning him (Weston 1913, 82). This would be the cause of great mourning, followed shortly by the welcome of a New Year and the reunification of the male and female aspects of nature and the onset of Spring.

The festival outlined above was widespread among ancient peoples, and it is one which nearly all pre Industrial, agricultural societies observed. The reason for this is simple, because of its focus on the regeneration of floral life and with it food. Dr. Weston used this agrarian festival as a guide to account for the grail ceremony. The grail writers who followed Chrétien probably had different details about the ceremony, she believes, simply because they were adapting the tales to local variations of the nature festival (Weston 1913, 98-139).

The Nature rite is indeed quite ancient and widespread. Its first civilized record is in Babylonia, where it was associated with Tammuz. It was imitated in Phoenicia and Greece as the Adonis rites, and Greece in the Eleusian mysteries. There is also evidence of continuity into the Christian period. Dr. Weston cites modern examples from all over Europe to establish the fact of its preservation to the present day in various, often more humane forms (Weston 1913, 79). It has even found a niche in Christianity. Easter fits into the general pattern.[17]

Weston makes several associations between this popular cult and the Arthurian romances. First, that the grail symbolizes the feminine aspect of nature as a font of nourishment and a renewer of life. Second, that the spear is a phallic symbol and the other necessary component for the Spring regeneration of life. The fact that it is dipped in blood when not used indicates this connection. Blood, such as that found in the bowl that precedes the Lance, represented life itself to the medieval man of Europe.[18]

These are the chief components of the hypothesis. However, there are several secondary connections to be made. The grail king is clearly a part of the symbolism. He is the New Year whose well-being translates into the health of his kingdom. Originally his premature aging would have been the catalyst behind the Perceval quest for the grail castle; Perceval would have been seeking the castle to be the next New Year. However, at some subsequent stage the grail king was split into two characters,[19] a castrated middle age king[20] and his ancient father. The castrated character serves as the reason for Perceval's need to assume his office; the king's state causes the entire kingdom to be barren. The symbolism with both conventions is the same, however. The absence of the male element from nature is catastrophic. Dr. Weston notes that the grail king's castle is near a great lake in Chrétien. This supports her assumption of the grail king's true nature; the lake would originally represent the body of water in which he and his replacement were to be drowned (1913, 82; 1920, 47).

Another aspect of the fertility rite involved is to be seen in the grail maiden, the personification of flora. She is comely during the initial ceremony, but loses her hair and beauty in anticipation of Perceval, the symbolic new year. She will regain her luster on his arrival, much as life seems to return to its full vigor in the Spring.[21]

However, Dr. Weston seems more preoccupied with the grail ceremony itself. What one sees first has clear parallels to the nature ritual. The mourning, the terribly old man, the feminine and masculine elements of nature, and the need to ask the symbolic question in order to release Spring are all features of the Nature Ritual she describes. Much of what is not so obvious also indicates the presence of her theoretical construct. The grail seems to have three main manifestations, or levels of initiation. The first is the sexual, the forms of the cornucopia grail and lance. The second is the life-principle represented by the blood from the lance, and the third is the "holy grail".[22] The three grail guardians -- the King of Castle Mortal, the Maimed King, and the Fisher King -- stand for one aspect of the grail (1913, 94). They could also symbolize three levels of initiation, or three aspects of spirituality in the believer. The mysteries of the ancient world were not recorded and have been lost, but it does seem conceivable that they, too, had three levels of initiation -- physical, symbolic, and ethereal forms.

Many details of the grail episode can also be better understood in light of this theory, Dr. Weston believed. It is commonly known that initiates were never allowed to reveal the nature of the mysteries of which they were a part. Much of the grail scene is explicable if the witnesses were, as Dr. Weston put it, "simple-minded participants". That is they would have seen the ritual feasts and were made to believe they had seen supernatural elements (1913, 83). Dr. Weston argued that the viewer would be made to believe the symbolism of the ritual. Thus floating candles, the memory of old men looking like forty year-olds, and a cornucopia dish were implanted in a person's memory.

The Nature Ritual has some convincing points, but the hypothesis has serious flaws as well.[23] The very idea of the ceremony being a universal rite is both useless and problematic.

First, her theory is flawed because no one would claim that all religious systems originated from a common source. In addition, no one would claim that the Greek and Phoenician versions had any direct correlation to either the Christian or the Celtic rites. Yet Weston's theory seems to do so, neglecting that all the regions of the world were agricultural until the advent of the industrial revolution. The seasons were vital to the maintenance of life and therefore a prime candidate for ritualization. The nature ritual has been independently developed in many different areas throughout the world, including China and Polynesia.

Second, the theory is useless because if the nature ritual was a world-wide ceremony with one common root there would be nothing to draw from it. There are too many potential variations in the ritual to learn anything about how it would fit into the grail legend. One may deduce nothing from any grail romance because separating its authors' contributions and those of local custom would be impossible. Dr. Weston's theory would make agricultural rites of the Babylonians,

Phoenicians, Greeks, Christians, Celts, and Muslims part of a common, prehistoric nature rite (1913, 105-8; 1906, 332).

The greatest flaw in the armor of Weston's theory is its lack of tangible evidence.[24] Nowhere in *Le Conte du Graal* is there a sign that the grail king has aged according to a standard calendar, or even a great year.[25] Nowhere in Chrétien's poem is there a link between Perceval's uncles and the three aspects of the grail she conjectures. Neither is there a correlation between the two in the Welsh stories and romances, which refrain from the concepts "grail" or "grail-king" altogether. It is also true that the various redactions consistently portray Perceval's lack of action at the grail castle as the reason the kingdom is in waste. However, if he was to represent the new year or were the Spring personified there would be no need or practical desire for a first failed attempt. Indeed, this would prove unworthiness of the candidate New Year. Yet this is a fundamental element of the story. No ancient festival celebrated Spring during the first warm day of Winter. To summarize, Weston's arguments are not able to explain fully the grail ceremony, and this leaves only one major contender, the Celtic theory.

Because of the similarity of motifs and the Celtic quality of the names in the poem, Villemarqué believed that the entire episode was originally a pagan tradition given Christian window dressings by Chrétien.[26] Variations of his theory have gained many adherents. The most prominent specialists on grail studies have advocated oral beginnings in pagan Ireland and/or Wales.[27]

The argument that the grail itself and all the unreality surrounding it are based upon the Celtic myths is an old one, and it is to some extent undeniable from an historical standpoint. Irish culture was being brought to the continent in the sixth, seventh, eighth, and early ninth centuries by the Irish churchmen who were invigorating Christian Europe with their enthusiasm, knowledge, and inventiveness. Inevitably a part of their culture made its way into continental Europe's culture.

In the eleventh and twelfth centuries, the unique position of the Bretons in the Norman world enabled them to become the new conveyers of the Celtic heritage.[28] They were allowed to settle or travel to England and Wales while retaining connections with their native country. There is evidence these people spread the name of Arthur, at least, across Europe (see Chapter II).

The most prominent indications that the grail story is Celtic are the names, which are evident in *Le Conte du Graal* and the works that followed and imitated Chrétien's last poem. Gornemanz de Goorz or Goort is listed in *Culhwch ac Olwen* as Gonemans.[29] Loholt is the French version of Arthur's son Llacheu.[30] Pelles is related to the pan Celtic god *Beli/Bíle*, as is Bron, who looks and acts suspiciously like Brân (see Chapter XI). In addition, there is the usual cast of Arthurian characters: Cei, Gauvain, Yvain, and Perceval. As a proper name Perceval has no history on the continent before 1160, when it is associated with the grail.[31] However, the name is to be found on this island in the form *Peredur* as early as the British heroic age. His *enfance* has been compared fruitfully to Cú Chulainn, Fionn Mac Cumhail,[32] and even to Pryderi through indirect evidence.[33] Perceval was long ago claimed as one of the Celtic examples of the Great Fool formula in *More West Highland Tales* (Campbell 1860).

The grail itself is an indicator that there is more Celtic material in the poem than names, however. Chrétien himself leaves the size of the object vague. Hélinand de Froidmont, a French poet who wrote in the last decade of the twelfth century and the early thirteenth century, described *graal* as "scutella lata et aliquantulum profunda", which is a "fairly deep platter" of sixty or seventy centimeters.[34] As Loomis pointed out, a sacramental wafer of fifteen centimeters in length seems odd on such a wide receptacle (Loomis 1959b, 277). He suggested that something significantly larger was originally meant to be on the object. Alternatively, the *graal* vessel itself may be inaccurately named. Something about the *graal* that Chrétien speaks of was evidently misunderstood when it was placed in a Christian context.

The term Chrétien uses to describe this vessel is ambiguous as it stands. Loomis postulated a reason for the several interpretations of the term *graal* by romancers who followed Chrétien. The key to understanding the confusion was in translating Middle Welsh *corn*. Loomis's words sum up the reasoning best:

> What about the Welsh word *corn* when translated in the nominative as *cors*? *Cors* could have at least five meanings: horn, corner, court, course, body; few words in Old French were more ambiguous, and the meaning had to be guessed from the context. Though we have the Anglo-Norman *Lai du Cor* and *Livre de Caradoc* magic drinking horns, Schultz says that in connexion with medieval table service that "only seldom do I find any mention of the drinking horn." Since this rarity would tend to eliminate the first meaning

and since corner, court, and course did not fit the context, one meaning alone remained, body. This in the sense of the Corpus Christi, the sacramental wafer, though it offered difficulties, was plausible enough since there were legends about the miraculous nutritive powers of the Host. Caesarius of Heisterbach, for example, tells (Book IX: Chapter 47) how a woman lived on the Body of Christ alone. Here, then, is a possible explanation of the graal and the oiste, which sustained the life of the Fisher King's father in Chrétien's poem. The two Welsh vessels of plenty, the platter and the drinking horn, have been converted as a result of the ambiguity into the Grail and the Body of Christ (Loomis 1959b, 288).

A source had intended *dysgyl*, horn, giving the grail castle Corbenic — Castle of the Horn, but a translation that Chrétien used changed the meaning to platter because he either misunderstood or was manipulating the word.[35] Those who followed Chrétien translated the word the same way in the same context, but translated it correctly in scenes where Chrétien's poem had not influenced them. This explains the recurrence of the horn in Arthurian lore. Erec employs a horn and Perceval conquers the pagan Castle of Four Horns in *Perlesvaus* (Book XI; l. 9547).

Unfortunately, the rest of Chrétien's poem offers nothing further in the line of direct evidence to allow one to ascertain more about this *graal*. Chrétien never wrote of the second visit he surely envisioned. Luckily, many of those romance authors who followed Chrétien have also left indications of direct Celtic influence, and these authors gave the grail a plethora of new abilities and functions. Along with the grail's centrality to the Unspelling motif (see Appendix VII), the various authors assigned it the power of self-movement, of being non or partially physical, of healing the wounded and sick, and of being a source of perpetual life. All the grail romancers who followed Chrétien gave it one more trait -- cornucopia or Horn of Plenty.[36] The abilities of self-movement and being only partially physical seem to belong to a body of characteristics that are universal for mystical objects. However, the ability to heal and feed is one that is quite probably Celtic.

As the horn of plenty seems to be a universal function of the vessel, I shall examine this feature of the grail first. The property of being a limitless food giver is a telling and indicative one. Though the object may be found in a Greek/Roman context, it was not to be found in the lore of the early Medieval world. Nowhere is Alexander the Great or Charlemagne, Solomon or Julius Caesar linked to such a vessel. It was, however, a part of the living traditions of the Celts. The existence of such objects in Welsh legend is confirmed in *Tri Thlws ar Ddeg Ynys Brydain* or *The Thirteen Treasures of Britain*; items 3, 10, and 11. These are The Horn of Brân the Niggard and the Crook and Dish of Rhygenydd the Cleric *The Welsh Triads*, trans. and ed. Bromwich 1978, 240-2). In Ireland the Cauldron of Dagda had essentially the same qualities.[37]

The above evidence indicates that the chief endowment of the central object in the "Grail scene" had a cornucopic and Greek/Roman or Celtic attribute. Its peripheral functions as a life-giver and healer were probably Celtic. As will be seen shortly, the cauldron owned by the Brân of the *Mabinogion* had the former trait. *Perlesvaus* would seem to indicate that the rejuvenation feature had the same drawback in Celtic myth as it did in continental romances -- those who were revived through the power of this article lost the ability to speak.[38]

Each individual function of the grail may seem to have a reasonable enough connection back to pan Celtic roots. However, the entire range of extant Celtic mythologies contains no single item that combines all the utilities the grail seems to have. This has always been perceived as a flaw in the Celtic argument. However, from Chapter II one can safely assume oral antecedents for a sizable proportion of Arthurian lore. The nature of oral transmission can easily account for the multiple facets of the grail in various romances.[39] The multiplication of attributes to essentially the same object in the Celtic oral tradition was a not uncommon phenomenon. The phenomenon was possibly due to the nature of the bard's education, which involved memorizing motifs and learning to apply them to different heroes and stories.[40] The grail's various attributes are a product of a similar oral handling, hence its various properties and the many different combinations of those properties.

This oral transmission could also account for the many different versions of the grail ceremony, the castle, and all the Celtic figures associated with it. The constant flexibility of themes and characters in the *latimari*, *troubadours*, and *trouvères* did not encourage unity, but did support the haphazard process of sewing together various themes, objects, and characters (Bromwich 1961, 439-41). It also explains the remarkable disunity of the grail stories. The grail legend is the most widespread and disharmonic of the Arthurian tales that came to the continent because the theme of the grail was immensely popular. Each retelling would have produced new qualities for the grail, the grail ceremony, and the grail company. This, say the proponents of the Celtic Theory, is the reason the grail is a combination of a cup of kingship, a horn of plenty, and a healer of the sick and injured.[41]

The woman who transports the *graal* to and fro, traditionally the grail bearer, also has some claim of Celticity. Chrétien himself tells us very little about her, but all those who followed were more informative. She is the bride-to-be of the next grail-king and is therefore associated with that kingship. She can be either very beautiful or tremendously repulsive, depending on the state of affairs of the kingdom she is symbolizes. These traits are shared by a woman known as the Sovranty of Érin and numerous regional deities of Ireland (O' Rahilly 1946b, 11-13). The generic name of goddesses in this aspect was Medb.[42]

The Grail Castle itself has some qualities that have been linked to an Insular Celtic underworld in which unliving beings exist in a castle or on an island. The comparison is readily visible; the titles *Chastel Mortel* and *Castle of Souls* in *Perlesvaus* (ll. 38, 1081, 1646, etc.) and *Schatel le Mort* in *Lanzelet* as alternative names to the grail castle are indications of Celtic influence.[43] The grail king of *Diu Crône* declares himself and his compatriots dead men (ll. 29532-4), which is hardly something one would expect to hear in a Christian tale.

For the careful observer there is also the fact that the grail castle has some clear similarities to the typical Indo-European underworld, best exemplified by Hy Breasail and Hades. In the main, these common traits are:
1. That living visitors must neither fall asleep nor drink its wine or mead
2. That the castle often vanishes from this world
3. That the castle is unlocatable except by chance.
4. That the inhabitants of the castle are supernatural or have extended lives (Nutt 1888, 191). These are not attributes of a Christian legend,[44] and can most easily be imagined originating from an Indo-European, probably Celtic source.[45]

Finally, there is the White stag hunt to be found in *Le Conte du Graal*, *Didot Perceval*, and *Peredur*.[46] Dr. Bromwich has argued the oldest form is not contained in Chrétien but in the non-grail, Breton tale of *Graelant*. This is because here the White Stag fulfills a direct function. Instead of the meaningless episode in *Le Conte* wherein the hero is made to chop off a stag's head to atone for a crime, the animal is a catalyst in *Graelant*. It leads the hero to a bathing pool where a fairy maiden has come to seduce him. The summary given by Dr. Bromwich will best illustrate the antiquity of this form of the motif.

> A knight called Graelant is a vassal of the king of Brittany. The Queen falls in love with him, but Graelant rejects her advances and thus antagonises her. Henceforth he is impoverished, because the jealous Queen instigated the king to withhold the pay which was his due. Graelant goes off into a nearby forest, where he sees a white hart which he pursues, and is thus led into a clearing where a beautiful girl is bathing in a pool. He seizes her clothes, and so has her at his mercy; nevertheless, she quickly consents to his love, for she had come on purpose to meet him. Before leaving her, she makes Graelant promise not to reveal her name or identity. She gives him a horse, and a servant who henceforth supplies him with all the wealth he can want. At the Feast of Pentecost the king holds a great assembly, at which he calls on all the court to join in asserting the queen's pre-eminence in beauty. Only Graelant refuses to do so, and thus he is provoked by the Queen's wrath into saying that he knows a fairer woman than she. The king decrees he must prove this seditious claim on pain of death. But now that he has named his fairy-mistress he can no longer find her, nor will she visit him, and so he has to submit himself to the king's judgement. As this is being passed, his mistress comes riding into the court and confounds all by her beauty; thus Graelant is exonerated from his rash boast. The fairy leaves the court, but Graelant rides after her, until they come to a deep river. In attempting to cross it he is nearly drowned, but his lady has pity on him, and carries him across the water to her own land. Here the Bretons say he still lives with his mistress. (1961, 460-1).

The hero of the above tale has been identified as the sixth-century Breton Cornouaille king Grallon or Gradlon Mor (1961, 462-3). It should be noted that the Breton founder of Vannes (Gueroc) and one of the many eleventh- and twelfth-century León kings named Guihomarc'h are both the heroes of sovereignty tales similar to the one above. These legends do have a distant origin; Dr. Bromwich believes the Vannes and Cornouaille redactions of this story may go back as far as the sixth century (1961, 467). However, the fact that these are the earliest locations for the motif argues that the White Stag was a later incorporation into the legend of the grail.

The theme of loss and recovery of sovereignty is also Celtic and particularly British. It is in *Erec et Enide*, *Yvain*, and *Perceval*, and more apparent in their Welsh equivalents (Goetinck 1975, 129-55). Before Chrétien's period, the theme was in nearly every British tale. Gildas, *Historia Brittonum*, and *Armes Prydein* all mourn the loss of

Britain and imply the return of sovereignty to the British people. Tales of the twelfth century still speak of London as the main seat of Celtic Britain. Even *Historia Regum Britanniae*, a document of pseudo-history and invention, contains this theme (Roberts 1976, 29-40). This is also something that has probably been added to the story of Perceval as a result of oral handling.

In addition, there have been peripheral episodes revolving around the grail story that relate directly to the Celtic underworld. Rhys saw something interesting and familiar in the monster which Pellinore is often found pursuing (Appendix IX). It has the chimaera-like characteristics of being composed of the head of a snake, the body of a leopard, the hindquarters of a lion, and the feet of a hart. It has barking pups contained inside its belly. Rhys understood the beast as an Arthurian version of the creature Gwyn ap Nuð pursued with his dogs (1896, 155). This creature barks like thirty dogs, or has three heads like the Gallic altar at Oberseebach (1896, 154-5). It is an inhabitant of Celtic mythology. It is unequivocally of pre Roman origins and to my knowledge has nothing to do with any Christian document. It was also originally separate from the grail story.

The above Insular sources and their limited corroboration with the themes and motifs in the grail legend do provide evidence that Perceval's adventure was influenced by contact with a Celtic environment. However, I would not pursue the argument so far as to voice the opinion that Perceval's journey to the grail castle is a journey to the under- or otherworld, as Loomis and others have done. Such is the loose nature of oral literature that such a close-minded verdict would be inappropriate. The evidence does, however, corroborate an argument for a Celtic infrastructure of the tale.[47]

Strong as the case for a Celtic basis of the tale may be, it has had its detractors and contains its problems. If one is to accept the theory, then one must also believe either British bards or French storytellers were exchanging motifs and heroes. This is not an improbable event and does have precedent in British legend. However, the theory leaves the proponent of the Celtic theory with no direct manner to prove the existence of an intermediate form between history, pseudo-history, or Celtic literature and Arthurian romance.[48] Such a flaw hardly lends itself to widespread support. Some scholars claim no relationship between Chrétien and the Celts is beyond criticism. Dr. Brown, for instance, believed that every scene but the palace of silver and copper pillars in *Perlesvaus* was merely coincidence, or a universal motif

(1966, 25). This may be an exaggeration, but it puts the problem in perspective. Some of the evidence scholars would now consider uniquely Celtic may well have been widely known or entirely universal themes in the twelfth century.[49]

Bewildering as the diversity of these four theories of the grail's origins may seem, they all hold some truth, though the degree of each is debatable. One cannot be sure whether Chrétien was or was not a Christian. However, the Biblical explanation of the Fisher King seems the most likely.[50] The resemblances in food content of the grail castle meal seem of Jewish derivation in Chrétien, and certain motifs can be seen as Jewish. However, one may not be confident in believing that Rashi or his school's influence did or did not effect the great poet.[51] The Celtic influence on the story is undeniable, but its extent is, at best, still an unknown. The Celtic names and several themes are a certainty, and the objects of the ceremony may be Celtic, but one can go no further here. Weston's rebirth ritual best explains the Wasteland motif and allows for the most likely of the other theories in all cases.

All the grail scholars, from Professor Nutt to Professor Loomis, have been quite open about the plausibility of the other theories. In addition, all have indisputable evidence that one piece of the grail story is derived from whichever source they postulate. Bearing this in mind, it seems impossible to resist the following conclusions: First, the forms in the romances which are most likely to keep close to the traditional model are those secondary ones with which the innovating spirit, whether due to the genius of the individual artist, or to intruding Christian and possibly Jewish symbolism, has least concerned itself.

Second, the many forms of the incident found in the grail romances of the continent imply a great deal of alteration. This in turn suggests that fundamental changes were made to the story because of the individual tastes and abilities of the grail story's authors and their patrons. The example of the corroboration between the lives of Philip and Perceval and Philip's other influences, much more restrictive than Marie, supports this conclusion. No one romance may be believed without strong complementary evidence from a source of directly Celtic provenance. The primary motive and plot of *Dysgyl* can only be guessed at through comparison to other grail versions and related material. This will be done in the next two chapters. However, the present author's hypothesis as to how the grail story was transformed into the various states found in the extant redactions is as follows:

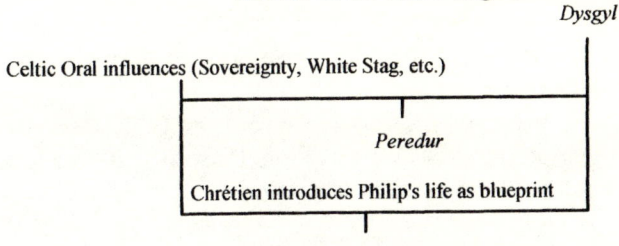

```
                                          Dysgyl
Celtic Oral influences (Sovereignty, White Stag, etc.)  |
                      |                                 |
                             Peredur
              Chrétien introduces Philip's life as blueprint
                      |
                The continental romances
```

---

[1] This object has holy qualities, though the various romances term it a chalice, platter, or rock.

[2] I am looking primarily for an explanation for the grail in these pages, though an analysis of potential sources of information will often complement this study.

[3] The dominant reading material for English speakers has been and will remain Sir Thomas Malory's *La Morte d'Arthur* (1485), a rather late version. In it the grail legend has developed to such an extent that only those who are perfect Christians may see the grail.

[4] The last prominent scholar to adhere to this theory was Professor James Douglas, in his *The Evolution of Arthurian Romance from the Beginnings Down to the Year 1300* (1923).

[5] Phrases such as "Dex vos angart"; "May God keep you", "se Dex m'amant"; "So help me God", "Cui Dex donroit si boen eür"; "If God grants him good fortune" "Dex vos saut"; May God protect you", and "Por deu"; "in the name of God", recur throughout the poem, as do set phrases for conversations such as "Par foi"; "By my faith." This reminds the reader of the centrality Christianity plays in the lives of the heroes. References to saints, such as St. Peter (ll. 2175, 4215), St. Paul (l. 49), St. Martin (l. 7252), St. David (l. 4100), and St. Richier (l. 1879) only serve to reinforce this connection. However, they are elements that are unnecessary to the pre-Chrétien plot (witness *Vita Gildae* and *Dialogue*) and could easily be imposed on an already existing story.

[6] I intend to write a more detailed article or book chapter on this subject in the near future.

[7] It is without question true that Chrétien never explicitly states that the grail is Christian, but his hero is firmly so. One can hardly imagine a poet of western Europe writing a romance for one of the most prestigious Roman Catholic families and allowing his main hero to participate in pagan rites. Those who followed Chrétien unanimously made the grail a Christian object.

[8] (Bruce 1923, 257). The lance of Chrétien's poem has no special meaning, but his First Continuator gives it a Christian quality.

[9] I find Bruce's limited examples of contrary instances in the East unsatisfying (1923, 259). Bruce's isolated examples from the East (1923, 259), are unconvincing and only serve to substantiate the belief that the overwhelming tradition of the ceremony called specifically for a temple, nothing else was appropriate for an Orthodox ceremony. First, the ceremony's identification as Christian. Second, the identification of the grail as the bearer of Christ's blood. Finally, the connection of the spear as a Christian device, most economically the Spear of Longinus.

[10] In the romances *Perlesvaus, La Queste del Saaint Graal,* and *Joseph* the grail fellowship is to consist of thirteen members in honour of Christ and his disciples. The Siege Perilous is the seat of Judas.

[11] First, the ceremony's identification as Christian. Second, the identification of the grail as the bearer of Christ's blood. Finally, the connection of the spear as a Christian device, most economically the Spear of Longinus.

[12] I find Professor Loomis' theory that the lance was based on the Spear of Luin and owned by Lug unconvincing. He uses one early but spurious text, The *First Continuation* and three extremely late versions-*Huth Merlin,* Malory, and *Demanda del Sancto Grial,* to prove the correlation. These are all less than reliable. Moreover, he evidences only one parallel to the ceremony in all of Celtic mythology (to the Spear of Lug), and that comparison is weak. It boils down to two points: Both spears are kept point down and both drip blood when held. This may be an unusual circumstance but it hardly qualifies as the water tight link Loomis believed it was (Loomis 1949, 379-82; 1956, 28-30; 1959, 283; 1963, 74-81). Nutt also called the Spear of Longinus a mutation of the Spear of Lug (Nutt 1888, 184).

[13] These claims are so consistent and valid from a territorial standpoint that Dr. Kenneth Dark has proven it is possible to mark off the boundaries of fifth and sixth century Wales using dedications to minor saints from this period (Dark 1994).

[14] It can only be a possibility that Chrétien, which means "Christian" - had Jewish training. It may be he was Jewish and wrote for Christian nobles, or that he was born a Jew and converted (hence Chrétien). He may have been Christian but had accessed and been influenced by knowledge of the Jewish religion through the fairs of Troyes.

[15] One may recall that this was Chrétien's inspiration for much of the grail castle (see Chapter IX).

[16] The Montpellier MS of *Le Conte du Graal* does state that the grail bearer was a descendent of Israel-a Jew.

[17] As she puts it, the ceremony usually involves a mourning for the departure of Spring for three to seven days, followed by a rebirth (Weston 1913, 78). This is the period from Good Friday to Easter Sunday.

[18] The concept survives in archaic phrases such as life-blood.

[19] It is necessary for Weston's argument that the grail king and the host served by the grail be two people-one the person who answers the question, the other the symbolic personification of nature. The current belief about the relationship of the grail-king and the man served by the grail is that there is indeed enough evidence to believe the two were separated at one point and that they were, indeed, originally one person.

[20] Though Professor Whitehead believes that the original wound may have been the feet. This does have parallels in other cultures. Oedipus and possibly Brân, for instance, and it is conceivable that the occasional reference to this particular wound could have some sort of Indo-European or pre Indo-European origin.

[21] (Loomis 1927, 282).

[22] When Gauvain goes to the castle and is partially successful, he sees the grail. When Lancelot is cured from his madness and when he arrives at the grail castle, he is told he is perfect in all but one regard and sees the object in its second form. Only Perceval, and in the later versions Galahad and Bors, see the grail in its final form.

[23] Professor Jackson also found the fertility myth and ritual unpalatable and thoroughly dismantled it in *The International Popular Tale*, (1961, 40-41).

[24] (Loomis 1949, ix; 1956, 51).

[25] Graves defines this as nine years without citation in context with the sending, by the Athenians, of young men and women to the island of Crete as tribute (1955, 337). In this instance it makes sense that the Cretans would have had some religious or cultural association with this period of time, and one must conclude that a definition of a great year is nine calendar years.

[26] (Villemarqué 1842). It could be argued that the idea of Irish churchmen spreading pagan Celtic rites across Europe seems unlikely, but this is exactly what happens with the *Beowulf* author. Much of what remains of pre-Christian European culture was preserved in a similar manner.

[27] As I wrote in chapters I and II, a theory for a common ancestry of most Celtic motifs and basic story structures is now the generally accepted position by current scholars beginning with O' Rahilly (1946b, 14) and followed chiefly by Mac Cana (1970, 94) and Bromwich (1974, 167-9; 1983, 51). Those who supported a theory for a specifically Irish origin wrote before this theory had been formulated.

[28] In the twelfth century the Norman world included a large part of France, England, Wales, Scotland, and Ireland.

[29] (*Culhwch ac Olwen*, l. 221; Roberts 1973, 278).

[30] (*The Welsh Triads*, trans. and ed. Bromwich 1978, 416, 555; Lloyd-Morgan 1991, 197; Sims-Williams 1991, 44).

[31] (Lejeune 1959, 396; *The Welsh Triads*, trans. and ed. Bromwich 1978), 490).

[32] Cú Chulainn and Fionn Mac Cueil (Nutt 1888, 231-4 and 158-9), respectively.

[33] Loomis believed the grail-king was Brân, therefore his nephew Pryderi must be Perceval. Another scrap of evidence he used was a further comparison; both men brought devastation to their respective countries by sitting in a perilous seat (Loomis 1959b, 281).

[34] (Hélinand de Froidmont, *Les vers de la Mort*, trans. Boyer and Santucci 1983, 11; Loomis 1959b, 277).

[35] Chrétien tells his reader that the castle of the grail was called Corbenic, which meant "Saintisme vaissel" or "most holy vessel" in the ancient Mesopotamian language of Chaldean. Since "c" and "t" were constantly mistaken for each other in manuscripts, and since the *Dutch Lancelot* gives the name of the castle as *Cambenoyt*, and a manuscript of Manassier has *Corlenot*, Loomis suspected that the original form was *Corbenoit*; in other words, the "Castle of the Blessed Horn" (Loomis 1959b, 288). He goes on to suggest the original term may also have been *Torbenoit*-the "Castle of the Blessed Bull".

[36] The one exception to this rule is *Peredur*, which quite possibly has suffered from a misunderstanding of the word per (see Appendix VIII).

[37] (Cross 1969, 199, 328, 353; Loomis 1927, 159-175, 236-241; 1949, 339; 1956, 156).

[38] Perceval, here Perlesvaus, notes the grail company is silent (Perlesvaus, ll. 275).

[39] The strong oral tradition in Wales and Brittany during the eleventh, twelfth, and thirteenth centuries attest to this. For a convenient summary of some evidence for this activity see Loomis, *Arthurian Tradition and Chrétien*, (1949, 12-24).

[40] (Vendryes 1935, 325; Sjoestedt, (trans. Dillon) 1949, 17, 31, 43, and passim; Mac Cana 1970, 48; *The Welsh Triads*, trans. and ed. Bromwich 1978, 155-6).

[41] I have not dealt with the cup of kingship aspect of the grail's functions here, but will do so in Chapter XIV.

[42] (Mac Cana 1955, 78; Appendix VI).

[43] (Piper 1892-5, II, 18; Loomis 1941, 898). I have been unable to find a *Lanzelet* in German.

[44] It is true that Christian legends have legends such as that of Brigadoon, a fairy world. These places do have this quality, but have in every case been influenced by local culture.

[45] The otherworld is probably Celtic because of the other and extensive Celtic influences, i.e. one must not fall asleep; it often vanishes and can be found only by chance; its inhabitants are incredibly long-lived.

[46] Weston believed the stag hunt was to conclude with the animal changing to a maid. This assumption was based on the late works the

Dutch Lancelot, Tyolet, and *MacPhie's Black Dog,* (1901, 30-33). Loomis (1949, 68-70), argued the tale would naturally have ended with a maiden receiving the stag's hunt. Both seem to me incongruent with what is known of Celtic myths and motifs.

[47] One more item should be noted in the Celtic argument. Loomis compared the Question Ceremony in *Le Conte* and the other grail romances to an old myth involving Conn. In it he and his descendants who were confirmed in his kingship by Lug and his wife, the Sovranty of Érin. The repetition in the scene, and the importance of Lug the bearer of a vessel and the guest form the central part of the episode, but the question "To whom shall the cup be given?" is nothing like Perceval's question "Who is served with the grail?", there is no other example of this ceremony, as it is given, in all Celtic mythology, and the grail (platter) and cup are entirely different. What is more, Loomis fails to explain how such a disparate change could have occurred and why such a change would have made it more Christian for Chrétien's audience.

[48] (Bruce 1923, 275), hit on this fact as the primary reason not to follow the theory.

[49] It would be arrogant to assume that someone of the twentieth century could know all of the intricacies of twelfth-century French thinking.

[50] Alternatively, the Ritual Theory accounts for the grail castle's proximity to the water, the Ritual and Celtic theory account for the grail king's castration, and his alternate name of Fisher King is explained by the reference to *Matthew*. It is very possible that the Nature, Christian, and Jewish aspects all represent a further degree of stratification.

[51] The comparison to the Lance is at least as tenable as the one made to Lug's Spear, whose only connection to the Spear of the Grail is that it drips blood. Even this statement is a weak one, it does so because it is put in a bowl of blood when not used.

Chapter XI: The Characters and their Roles

In the last chapter the relative importance and constitution of each of the major grail interpretations was ascertained. It was determined that the infrastructure of the tale is Celtic and that the theme of loss of sovereignty, and the Christian and Celtic motifs have been integrated into the plot successively at later stages. However, the basic nature of this Celtic infrastructure remains in doubt. The next reasonable step in better understanding the nature of the grail legend's precursor is to establish the role of all the main characters in the hypothesized original British version of the grail saga. The relative importance of the characters the grail king, Arthur, Gwalchmai, Gonemans, the hero's father, and Peredur will be examined thoroughly in this chapter.[1]

The figure of the grail king has been a mystery for centuries; he has no other function but the care of the grail. For this and other reasons Professor Roger Loomis believed that he and Perceval's father were in effect the same person, Brân, split into two characters for reasons of plot and continuity.[2] The volume and force of his arguments seem to have shut out or smothered many conflicting viewpoints. However, there is much to commend an opposing perspective.

The grail legend is a core element to this contention. No extant Welsh or Irish myth contains a royal figure who is wounded through both legs and sits waiting for the right initiate to enter his castle and ask the proper question. It would be unreasonable to believe this was ever the case, and every one involved but the eventual hero knew that the question was the key to his success. Such a scenario does not seem to be compatible to Irish or Welsh myth, either. Yet the harmony of all but one of the grail versions, *Peredur*, is perfect on this aspect of the story.[3] This presents a stumbling block, but the knowledge of the stratifying process involved in the evolution of the grail legend is the key in unraveling the Grail-king's character. First, Perceval's redundant question at the grail castle is a senseless detail in the story. There is no realism or any serious precedent for it, suggesting this detail has been modified by Wolfram von Eschenbach to suit the needs of his audience, and followed by later writers. This leads one to the conclusion that the contents here were originally Celtic, as Loomis believed seventy years ago.[4]

Second, the grail king's consistent presence in the continental romances suggests that there was some prototype to the character in the hypothetical British source *Dysgyl*. Third, the consistent tie between the grail king and the grail castle requires that the grail king was fused with this aspect of the grail story no later than the last years of the twelfth century. This was the period in which Chrétien was writing. The connection in the face of the great divergence of the grail redactions implies the combination took place sooner rather than later.

The name of the grail-king character, Pelles, was later to arrive in literature.[5] It emerges in the grail stories that probably followed Chrétien. The name is first to be found in *Perlesvaus* (ll. 38, 1080, 1645, 2928, 3572, 4989, 5198, 6108, 8674, 8669, 9821), though not in the traditional role of Grail-king.[6] In later literature the figure Pellinore (Pelle Mawr) was given grail castle affinities (Loomis 1927, 145). Another variation of the name can be seen in *Erec* as Bilis or Belin (ll. 1993-2011), and yet another was connected to a pigmy monarch of the lower hemisphere.[7] These figures have no onomastic connection to Brân, as Loomis was loath to admit. However, there is a strong literary interrelationship between Pelles, Bilis, Belin, and the legendary personage *Beli*, known later as *Beli Mawr*.

There is also a significant link here between the variations of this distinguished name and one aspect of Celtic myth that was unknown to the last great generation of grail scholars. This lack of knowledge led Professor Loomis to the conclusion that *Beli* "was a euphemerised pigmy king of the Other World" (Loomis 1949, 143). Loomis may have come along the proper line of reasoning, but his conclusions are far too simplistic. I shall here trace the line of evidence to a more educated conclusion.

As Loomis pointed out, *Beli Mawr* figures as the progenitor of many of the early medieval Welsh lineages.[8] This means that *Beli* was probably an important figure in the British pantheon. What Loomis may have been unaware of was that *Beli* was one of the pan Celtic gods; he is known to have been worshipped in France and Ireland as well as Britain. He was known as *Beli* and *Bíle*, and *Belenus*, respectively (Ellis 1992, 39-40). Professor Williams linked this *Beli* to *Belenus* (1922, 12) and Professor Rhys connected it to *Bíle*.[9] In Britain, one of the most famed resisters of Caesar's British campaign was *Cunobelinus*, which translates to "hound of *Beli*". Billingsgate in London may well evidence the popularity of a *Beli* cult in that region. Archaeological evidence shows a *Belatucudros* was one of the more prominently worshipped deities on Hadrian's Wall in the fifth century.[10]

Therefore, it seems apparent that the *Beli* Loomis assumed was a euphemerized Other World pigmy was in fact a universal character of all Celtic mythologies. The remains to be garnered from archaeological finds indicate this figure was a solar deity whose prime duties were those of fertility (Webster 1986, 74-5). *Beli*, like Cernunnos, was generally associated with horns (Ross 1967, 371).

It is unmistakable, then, that *Beli* was an euphemerized god of the British people. It should also be clearly understood that the traits that this figure exhibits are the very ones which his onomastic counterpart,[11] Pelles, has in common with him, fertility. Therefore, Pelles' literary antecedent was a fertility god whose basic functions would have revolved around the forces of birth, death, and renewal that pervade the grail persona.

However, Loomis was correct in believing Brân was to be associated with the grail king.[12] The influence was simply not a primary one. A quotation from Loomis will best point out Brân's connection to the grail literature:[13]

(1) In the *Didot Perceval* the Fisher King is called Bron.
(6) In *Perlesvaus* Gawain was present at a feast in the Fisher King's splendid castle, in company with twelve knights, "aged and grey-haired, and they did not seem to be so old as they were; for each was a hundred years old or more, and yet none seemed to be forty." Brân's followers ... passed eighty years in a great hall in the midst of abundance and joy; "none of them perceived that another was older by that time than when they came there.[14]

Further indications of Brân's presence in the grail-king are not difficult to acquire. First, Perceval and Peredur are said to have multiple brothers, yet this conforms to nothing that is known of *Beli Mawr*. On the other hand, Brân and possibly other influential characters do have brothers in Welsh myth and legend. Second, Brân's brother Manawydan and father Llyr are both sea-deities. In integrating Brân into the grail-king character it seems this element of the persona was suppressed, but evidence of it remains. It was rationalized under the influence of the Christian nature of the grail so that the grail-king may now do no more than spend his days on a lake. The reason for this association is supposedly because of a severe wound. Indeed, the addition of many of Brân's features only added to the luster and dimension of the grail legend.[15]

Unlike the grail king, Arthur is much less of a shadowy figure in the romances. He is at first glance the centerpiece of the grail narrative. His is the court to which the hero returns, it is to him that the hero comes to be made knight, and it is with his men that the hero proves his worth. One may note something else. As with all the continental romances, Arthur takes no active part in the quest for the grail castle. In *Peredur* this rule's only exception is in the curious final scene. In *Perlesvaus* his actions instigate the grail search but he does not take part.[16] Arthur is clearly an unnecessary character in the story as it can now be reconstructed. It is only if one wishes to suggest that the Peredur character has been superimposed on a role that had originally been Arthur's that his place in the story could be contemplated.[17] While this suggestion agrees with the speculation of Chapter XIII regarding Arthur as a Christianizing king, there is no complementary evidence in its favor, and some contradictory material.[18]

Gwalchmai is also an interesting character, but one who is hardly a necessary feature of the plot in the form in which we now have it.[19] In *Peredur*, Gwalchmai's only function is as a cousin and compatriot of Peredur in the destruction of a coven. This act occurs in the final scene. On the continent, Chrétien was using Gauvain as a literary contrast.[20] He was at first the perfect Christian knight against whom Perceval was judged. He was employed to show how the perfect knight was spiritually flawed, and how only a knight of God could approach perfect faith. The three scenes in which he is the protagonist -- the tournament, the encounter at his accuser's castle, and the Maiden Castle -- contain very few elements that are Celtic and none with any historical character.

On the other hand, all three scenes point out the strengths and weaknesses of the perfect knight as contrasted with the servant of God.[21] Later writers would follow Chrétien's example. One may tentatively conclude that Gwalchmai is also a character who is not imperative to *Dysgyl*.[22]

Gonemans seems to be a character specific to Perceval's youth. In Welsh literature, his only scene independent of this function is in the list of Arthur's warriors in the composite tale known as *Culhwch ac Olwen* (ed. Bromwich and Evans 1991, l. 221). Even in the very late romances of *The Vulgate Version of the Arthurian Romances* and *Le Morte d'Arthur* he is mentioned almost exclusively in relation to Perceval. The only exception to this rule is the evidently popular tradition that he was, as Gorlois (the Cornish equivalent is Gwrlois (Roberts 1973, 278), the one-time husband of Arthur's mother.[23] This adds no substantial data to his character.

Such a consistent correlation makes the traditional connection between Peredur and Gonemans a likelihood. The traditional role that he plays as Peredur's tutor and the Indo-European custom of uncles foster-raising their nephews makes this association a powerful one as well. Gonemans probably had a traditional role as the tutor of Peredur.

The role of the hero's father is not so easily understood; the evidence points away from any certainty. As noted above, Perceval is the son of an Efrawg in *Peredur*. In *Didot Perceval*, MS K of *The Continuations of Chrétien de Troyes*, *Li Chevaliers as deus espees*, and *Le Roman de Tristan en Prose* the father is an Alain.[24] In the "Prologue" to Chrétien's version, the character is named Bliocadran, while Wolfram designates him Gahmuret (*Parzival*).[25] This intimates confusion, and further study of the names warrants this initial judgment.

Welsh *Efrawg* translates as *Evrauc*, a corrupted form of the Latin for York, Ebrauc.[26] There was a chieftain in the Yorkshire area named Peredur. He lived in the last decades of the sixth century. It appears that the original *Peredur* author connected his hero to this person, whether by tradition or otherwise. The author and the author's source for this hero did not know Peredur's ancestry, though, only his region -- Latin *ab Ebrauc* "of York". This became his patronymic in the form ab Efrawg "son of Efrawg".

Alain is a common Breton name and is to be found in *Culhwch ac Olwen*, thus demonstrating an awareness of the name in British culture.[27] Sberin, son of the Breton count Alan Fergant, is also listed (ed. Bromwich and Evans 1992, l. 216), suggesting Alan Fergant may have been the inspiration for the Arthurian character.

It is conceivable, indeed the arguments which Loomis and Newstead have forwarded make it seem like a strong possibility, that Perceval's original father was the famed Brân of the *Mabinogion*. However, there are several flaws with this conclusion. Most important, the majority of the early grail stories either leave the father anonymous or names him Alain, a name that is clearly contemporary and probably a late addition to the tale (Chapter XV). The only reliable source that resists this trend is *Parzival*. This is, truly, an excellent source for information both for its Celtic connections and its date, but Loomis could only suggest the appellation there used, Gahmuret, was the epithet of Brân (Loomis 1956, 35, 173). This seems a questionable link as there is no other indication of Brân's presence in the Gahmuret character.[28] Chrétien avoided the problem by beginning his poem in Perceval's youth. He first presents Perceval as, physically, an adult.

Like Lancelot in *Le Chevalier de la Charrette* the question must be asked of Perceval, did he exist? If this question be answered in the affirmative, then when and in what capacity? Such questions are hardly necessary for the validation of *Le Conte du Graal* as a literary source for the fifth and sixth centuries. This is because the character Perceval may or may not have been superimposed on an earlier character. Nevertheless, an investigation of Perceval's historicity and chronological place seems compulsory to complete an historical study of *Le Conte du Graal*.[29]

For several reasons, Perceval has generally been identified with a Yorkshire king of the Britons in the late sixth century, Peredur ab Eliffer. First, the oral tales of any heroic age are notorious for incorporating its heroes into the literary sphere of the most famous kings -- regardless of chronology or nationality (Chadwick 1912, 350-1). Second, the late Welsh romances Gereint and Peredur assign the hero a patronymic mab Efrawg that, as generally translated, is the Welsh version of Latin ab Ebrauc, of York. Finally, the Peredur (here Parzival) of German romance is given a brother, much as the King Peredur of legend is rarely to be separated from his sibling Gwrgi.

The second two of these proofs have fundamental flaws. Medieval Welsh bards, indeed the traditions of most ancient peoples tended to associate lesser-known individuals with more famed heroes.[30] This often included connecting characters to heroes of Welsh tales haphazardly, as has probably been done regarding Perceval and his father (see above). Thus Perceval's patronymics and brother are not weighty enough evidence to satisfy a rigid examination. The only legitimate reason for following this theory is that there was a known British king in the heroic age named Peredur.

Even if this statement may seem tenable at first sight, Peredur is a name common in the North during the sixth century according to the extant records.[31] There was indeed a well-attested King Peredur of York in the mid- to late-sixth century, and certainly the patronymic mab Efrawg has something to do with him.[32] He most probably fought the pagan Germans during a large portion of his career, just as Perceval fights against pagans in *Le Conte du Graal* and other grail romances. He even has the brother whom Wolfram von Eschenbach assigned to him.[33] However, there is also a warrior Peredur Arfau dur listed among the men who fought at Catraeth (*The Gododdin of Aneirin*, ed. and trans. Koch 1997, A31). He, too, would have been in his prime toward the end of the sixth century.[34] The Welsh records also list a Peredur ab Morudd (*Early Welsh Genaeological Tracts*, ed. Bartrum 1966, 147) and Peredur ab Cadwy.[35] This gives three definite figures of the mid- to late-sixth century, with a possible fourth. Any or all of these personalities could have been the inspiration for Chrétien's Perceval.[36] So one might ask a more provocative question involving Chrétien's hero: why were at least two kings in northern Britain during the period 540-600 named Peredur? Further, why was at least one other noteworthy personage so called?

In this era, when each generation has hundreds of thousands of people with the same given name, one may find it hard to understand why four people with the same name on the same island in the same forty year span would be of importance. I must stress that it is. The pool of known individuals whose floruit was probably somewhere between 560 and 600 is approximately three hundred people. In this, four are named Peredur, a name not occurring in records before or after that for some time. After a watershed around 600, the name virtually disappears till after 1000. Someone was the inspiration for the popularity of that name, and I should like to propose that it was the Peredur who later became a romance figure.

Of course, it is also possible that conventional wisdom is correct and the Peredur of romance was not originally from Britain about 500. However, if this is so who was the source for popularity of the name Peredur in the latter half of the sixth century? The theory that there was an earlier inspiration is simply the easiest and most reasonable with the data at hand.

Did Peredur exist and was he a member of Arthur's *teulu*? It hardly matters. His mere presence symbolizes hostile military actions against non-Christians, just as a feud between the Heathobard Agnar and the Dane Bothvar in *Hrolf Kraki's Saga* represents a war between their two tribes. The political aspects of the action are important, not the people who took part in them.

It has been seen in this chapter that there are grounds for believing a Peredur may have existed as one of Arthur's *teulu*. On the other hand, the tendency of heroic age literature to move its heroes around through time and space makes it quite possible that the patronymic ab Efrawg gives away his original identification. Peredur ab Eliffer may have been the inspiration for the grail hero Peredur ab Efrawg and his continental counterparts.

From the above discussion it may also be seen that a pre 600 hero possibly named Peredur was associated with a pagan practice involving *Beli* in an historical or pseudo-historical source. In this scheme Gonemans served as the hero's tutor and Gwalchmai may have served some practical function at some point.[37] Arthur and Peredur's father were either late arrivals to the story or their roles have been altered beyond recovery. The absence of these latter two characters in the two following chapters will reinforce the theory of their absence in *Dysgyl*.

---

[1] The overall role of Cei in Welsh poetry has been discussed above (Chapter V). There is little or no reason to believe he was intended as any more than a literary device by the romance or Welsh writers. He is involved directly in no major scenes. His presence is merely used as a comic device and instructional tool; Peredur's joust with him serves both to make a mockery of Cei and to show the reward for mistreating those less fortunate.

[2] Loomis argued that both the grail king and Perceval's father were literary descendants of Brân the Blessed, a key figure in Welsh lore. He also believed that the grail legend as we now have it is a hybrid between the themes of Revenge and Bespelling. It was necessary for the father to die to incorporate the revenge element, and yet the Bespelling theme required that Perceval rescue a relative, thus the literary birth of Perceval's uncle the grail king (Loomis 1927, 178-84; 1949, 347-55; 1956, 35,173). See Appendix VII.

[3] Interestingly, *Peredur* is the romance that evidences the most primitive elements and therefore is probably closer to *Dysgyl* here as well.

[4] (Loomis 1927). His questionable form of linguistic and comparative methods, however, have been largely if not totally repudiated.

[5] In Chrétien the grail king is anonymous. However, the presence of the name Pelles slightly later in the *Arthuriana* which remains does not necessarily force the conclusion that it was a late arrival to the Arthurian world. Chrétien may well have had stylistic reasons for leaving such a mysterious figure nameless, or simply may not have had the name and worked around it by giving the grail king a further veil of Christianity by attaching a name which symbolised Christ.

[6] For a complete guide to the popularity of Pelles in French literature. See West, *An Index of Proper Names in French Arthurian Verse Romances 1150-1300*, (Toronto, 1969).

[7] This was by Giraldus Cambrensis. (Loomis 1927, 145; 1941, 922-24; 1949, 142-4).

[8] *Early Welsh Genaeological Tracts* (ed. Bartrum 1966), lists 32 genealogies of which Beli was a part. Several of these are repeated family lines, but the predominance of Beli is apparent.

[9] (Rhys 1891, 90; 1923, 41-3). O'Rahilly associated the name with the Celtic god Belgios or Bolgios in *Early Irish History and Mythology*, (1946, 67).

[10] (Ross 1967, 127; Webster 1986, 146 n. 37).

[11] Ross (1967, 128) has noted the comparability between Belenus and Belatacudros, and the Belenus/Pelles connection has been the source of agreement among Arthurian scholars for a century.

[12] I do not here intend to neglect other prominent scholars whose work has been essential to this argument, primarily *Bran the Blessed in Arthurian Romance* (1939). However, in this arena Professor Loomis' arguments are usually the most concise and lucid and therefore are the best source of understanding here.

[13] I refrain from making use of numbers two to five for the following reasons: (2 and 3) Bron is indeed mentioned in both *L'Estoire del Saint Graal* and *Joseph*. However, these two works are late and composite in nature, and are therefore generally unreliable

sources of information. (4) In Chrétien the Fisher King was wounded between the legs, while Brân was wounded in the foot. The only similarity here is a wound. (5) The Fisher King is noted for his large banquets, as is Brân. However, most famed kings and deities share this distinction.

[14] (Loomis 1927, 178-84; 1949, 347-55; 1956, 35,173).

[15] By connecting the Grail-King with the water-oriented Brân he was easily identified as a fisher and effortlessly made a Christian.

[16] This activity in *Perlesvaus* and *Peredur* could be a remnant of a Celtic tale connecting Arthur with the grail, but the two examples are incongruous with each other. It seems more likely that Arthur's adventure derives from a tradition independent of the grail.

[17] This is a common aspect of heroic age literature. Theseus often does feats that imitate Heraclian tasks, for instance.

[18] For one, the entire story would give Arthur a mother and father who are not traditional to the Welsh or continental milieu. Second, Arthur is nowhere else connected to the Great Fool motif.

[19] However, knowing the antiquity of Gwalchmai as compared to Peredur in the Arthurian milieu, his is the most logical alternative to Perceval if one were to conclude Perceval was not the original hero. See *The Legend of Sir Gawain* (Weston, 1897) for a more full discussion on the subject.

[20] In *Gauvain in Old French Literature* (1980), Keith Busby has done a masterful job of examining Gauvain's role in medieval French texts. However, he does not explore the character's historical significance, nor does he dwell on Gwalchmei's significance in Welsh literature.

[21] These are Gauvain's name and the setting in Galloway. The setting was probably more the product of the twelfth century than the sixth, however (see Chapter IX).

[22] This conclusion must be tentative because of the existence of the *Diu Crône* romance which, though generally considered to have been later than and a menagerie compilation of the earlier compositions, still contains some purely Celtic analogues. Here Perceval is absent and Gauvain is the grail hero. Such may be the result of a pure link with tradition, or simply the product of Gauvain's popularity.

[23] As Geoffrey is noted for his creative use of traditional material and characters, however, this presents no serious inconsistency with a Peredur/Gonemans link.

[24] (West 1969, 5; 1978, 10).

[25] Chrétien's collection of poems also produced a Ban or Braus de Gomeret. Loomis sought to connect the characters Bliocadran and Gahmuret through this figure. I think it more likely, however, that the opposite has here occurred and two characters where fused into one.

[26] (Pokorney 1948, 38; *The Welsh Triads*, trans. and ed. Bromwich 1978, 489).

[27] The instance of Alain in *Culhwch ac Olwen* is mab Alun Dyuet (ll. 185 and 725).

[28] (Loomis 1927, 178-84; 1949, 347-55; 1956, 35, 173).

[29] Following Pokorney, one might get some idea of where the name could have come from. He makes the observation that the word Peredur could be a corrupted, sub Romanized form of Praetor, a Roman military title ((1950), 38), found cited in *The Welsh Triads*, trans. and ed. Bromwich 1978, 489). This would explain the name's first appearance within a century after the Roman departure in 410 and allow for its Latinity, antiquity, and Christian affiliation.

[30] One conspicuous example is that of St. Germanus. By the early ninth century the exploits of a Powysian saint named Garmon had been assigned to him.

[31] The genealogies are relatively consistent here, and chronologically match the *Annales Cambriae* entry of 573, the Battle of Arfderydd. A large body of literature attests to the fact that Peredur ab Eliffer was present in this battle.

[32] His main regions are thought to have been centred about York.

[33] Though *Parzival* names him Feirfeiz and *Annales Cambriae* and *Trioedd Ynys Prydein* call him Gwrgi. There is no onomastic similarity between the two, but Feirfiz is most probably a garbled poetic nickname for a prince.

[34] Most probably he and King Peredur were not the same two men. The Peredur of *Y Gododdin* has no patronymics, the mark of royalty in this period. Further, he is not listed as a king in the poem.

[35] (*Early Welsh Genaological Tracts*, ed. Bartrum 1966, 45) though Bartrum questions its accuracy.

[36] The fame of Peredur ab Eliffer could reasonably be expected to superimpose itself on any of the others.

[37] This is because Gwalchmai assists Peredur in the final scene, and in the other romances he seems to be given space roughly equivalent to Perceval, with little or no relation to the search for the grail. It seems likely this is because his original association with the grail story has been tampered with but his prominence in the story has been retained.

Chapter XII: Literary Tools for Supplementary Material

In the previous two chapters, it has been determined that the grail story as it may be reconstructed is a Celtic story. It involves a Christian hero, the Celtic god *Beli*, Gonemans the tutor, and possibly Gwalchmai. This story was successively superimposed with elements from a wide range of Celtic motifs, Christian, and possibly Jewish influences and, finally, the contemporary references of the various men who wrote the grail romance. Chief among these men was Chrétien, whose basic plot is due to Philip's influence (see Chapter IX). His format was mimicked in all later romances. Despite all the above evidence, little has yet been determined concerning the source or sources of the grail story. The definition of this source will be the objective of this chapter.

In the pages following I shall review and discuss the independence, in part or whole, of the various early redactions of the grail story. To do so effectively I shall first review the major episodes of *Dysgyl*[1] as are found in most of the earliest and most reliable versions. This exercise will be for the purpose of giving the reader some idea of the general stock of episodes from which, presumably, the twelfth and thirteenth-century grail writers drew.[2]

The hero-to-be is raised in seclusion until he is sent to or learns of Arthur his uncle, and Arthur's court. He sets out and finds the king without difficulty. There he learns that a Red Knight has stolen a cup from Arthur and is threatening his sovereignty. The hero kills the knight and takes his armor, sending the cup back to the court and with it, apparently, restoring his uncle's honor. He himself does not return, however, but rides on and finds two more uncles who each give him advice and training in arms. Next he comes upon a besieged maiden, whom he rescues. Following this is an assortment of varied adventures, culminating in the kingship of the grail castle in the Chrétien tradition, or the destruction of its prototype in *Peredur*. Amidst this motley barrage of adventures are several episodes with little or no value as traditional. Some of the most memorable are the incident with the maiden in the tent, Cei's defeat by Peredur, and the scene with the crow's blood and snow matching his beloved's hair and face. Episodes such as these would have been used either to develop the plot or amuse an audience.

Peredur itself has been called a group of confused "reminiscences of French and Anglo-Norman texts".[3] Considering the more fluid view of the various influences on twelfth-century Arthurian literature, however, such a concrete opinion is now considered obsolete.[4]

A debate as to the year of composition of this account of the grail legend is still under way.[5] The manuscripts and the "proper" story's contents themselves remain points of contention.[6] Even the conclusion is not generally acknowledged; it is either Peredur's marriage to the empress, as in Peniarth 7, or the destruction of the witches, such as one finds in the balance of the manuscripts.[7] The textual history is so difficult that scholars have generally avoided any oblique statements regarding it, so that nothing can be learned there, either.[8] However, there are some points that are generally accepted about the tale.

There are four manuscripts containing *Peredur*. These have been dated from no later than the early fourteenth to the late fourteenth centuries. However, as Lovecy points out, *The Red Book of Hergest* (the most recent) has traces of twelfth-century orthography (Lovecy 1991, 171). This indicates both that this represents a copy of an original, and that this story has a manuscript history dating from the same century as Chrétien (1180-1191).

Until comparatively recently, Chrétien had been called the source of *Peredur* because of the romantic aspects and the general differences that all three Welsh Arthurian romances have, in contrast to the traditional stories. As Dr. Mac Cana has recently pointed out, however, such observations carry no weight.[9] There are points where the *Peredur* author does agree with Chrétien, but there are many when the *Peredur* author does not and the source for his material could not be anything but Celtic.[10] The representatives of this latter group, which contains strong Celtic affinities, are in the main to be found in sections

1b and 2 of Thurneysen's divisions.[11] The episodes involving Angharad Law Eurawg, snakes, giants, dead men rising from warm water in a tub (similar to Branwen's cauldron), sheep, an Addanc, and a grail ceremony where a man's head is featured are all to be found here. Interestingly, the majority of these themes are also to be found in the Celtic stock of motifs and oral devices.[12] These episodes are all unknown in other grail romances and in continental romances and works in general, yet are here present and occupy a large part of the story's plot in the Welsh redaction.[13] *Peredur* is, without doubt, independent of Chrétien, if it cannot be claimed to be free of continental influences.[14] To quote a recent critic "there is no indication that the redactor of *Peredur* knew these [*Le Conte* and *Didot Perceval*] works".[15]

Didot Perceval was another early redaction of the grail story. It was written between 1190 and 1212,[16] possibly by Robert de Boron.[17] The manuscript history is difficult as there are only two versions ("D" and "E"), and these are often widely divergent. However, it does imply both are degenerate versions of their common original.[18] Their customary nature of being at odds with each other is generally thought to be the result of Chrétien's influences in "D". "D" is much shorter and less coherent, indicating much of the original tale was lost in the manuscript tradition. The copyist of "E" made a rather poor attempt to resolve the conflicts between Robert's original verse and the poems of Chrétien and Wauchier. In any event, the "E" version is generally considered the less corrupt of the two.[19]

As the extant manuscripts have it, the *Didot Perceval* is a mediocre literary piece because of its consistent inconsistencies and limited creative output. As a text for better understanding Chrétien's *matière*, however, it is a stroke of good fortune. The original author was not an innovator. The fact that details and, on occasion, episodes are dependent on no known sources has led many scholars to the conclusion *Didot Perceval* had traditional sources along with Chrétien and Wauchier. In fact, at one time it was considered their source. I shall here list the main reasons for this belief.

In his monumental introduction to the *Didot Perceval*, William Roach only claimed one chapter as entirely without influences in any prior or contemporary work on the continent -- this was Episode "B" -- Perceval's childhood. Unfortunately, this section has only tenuous connections to standard Welsh themes of the twelfth century or earlier.

There are, however, several chapters that have been influenced by both Chrétien and Wauchier, and apparently a Welsh version of the Perceval story.[20]

Episode "C" describes a stone that splits and causes all the enchantments of Britain to cease. This stone is comparable to the mound Pryderi relaxes on prior to his loss of the inhabitants, animals, and all floras of his kingdom. It is found nowhere prior to this point in Arthurian literature,[21] though it did have many variants in later romances and Celtic lore (see Chapter X).

Episode "E" revolves around Perceval's visit to the Chessboard Castle, which is entirely absent from *Le Conte du Graal* and *Parzival*. This may be due to influence from Wauchier or, more probably, his source. It, and most of the scenes found therein, are largely to be found in *Peredur*.

Episode "H" describes Perceval's fight at a ford with an Urbain. Just as the hero is gaining the advantage, he is attacked by nine crows and chances to kill one. It is here that one learns the birds are his opponent's mistress and her maidens. This transformation ability has no parallel in Chrétien, Wauchier, or Wolfram, and can only be found in two other sources. These are the *Vita Merlini* (1130s), where Morgan has this ability, and *Breuddwyt Rhonabwy* (thirteenth century), where Owain and Arthur's soldiers are birds. In addition, the nine maidens and one leader sounds much like the Celtic covens discussed below and in the following chapter.

Several scenes in the abridged version of *Didot Perceval* that are extant have no continental or Insular parallels in Arthurian literature. This implies a source other than the one which Chrétien and his imitators used, or access to an oral tradition that was flowing and allowed new Celtic concepts to establish themselves into the Perceval legend. At any event, the appearance of such new themes and details in a text by Robert de Boron (or whoever wrote it) is puzzling. It suggests that the connections of these themes to the "Perceval" story were much older than the date the author wrote them down. This suggests *Didot Perceval* is a tenable source for Celtic information independent of Chrétien.

Parzival is chronologically the next version of the romance. It was begun in or after 1200 and was completed by or during 1210.[22] The poet who produced it was a man from Eschenbach named Wolfram. He was widely held by his contemporaries to have been the greatest literary mind of his era and has been called "one of the greatest poets of all time" (Wynn 1994, 187).

Wolfram von Eschenbach claims that his source was written by a Provencal named Kyôt, who found his source in an Arab manuscript. However, a survey of *Parzival* and its French precursors makes it evident that Wolfram's chief source was comparable to *Le Conte*,[23] and quite possibly that it was this poem.[24] However, there are several places where Wolfram gives what could be information directly from Welsh sources. The revenge motif, which has no continental Arthurian antecedent, appears here as Lähelin. He is introduced as the thief of Parzival's inheritance and the source of revenge (see Appendix VII).

Other details are noteworthy. The place-name *Sanguin* used by Chrétien is given a (presumably) closer rendering of *Sabîns* -- the Severn River -- by Wolfram.[25] In addition, he takes great pains to explain that Keie is a worthy man, as in *Culhwch ac Olwen* (ll. 16-297) and *Pa gur?* (l. 29), despite Chrétien's attitude toward him. In addition, the life of Gahmuret seems to be drawn from whatever source the *Peredur* author used.[26]

The clearest example of Wolfram's independence from Chrétien is Gahmuret's involvement with a dark lady of a castle. At the moment he takes her virginity, he is declared her husband and lord (*Parzival*, Book I. 44). This is an exact parallel of ancient Celtic society,[27] yet is hardly to be expected in the high society of thirteenth-century Germany. There such a relationship would be secretive, and any inheritance would be by the laws of primogeniture, not an obscure form of matrilineality.

The latter half of Book XII and the three books that followed it are without literary antecedent yet seem to finish, coherently, the poem that Chrétien did not. In these sections Gawain's episode at Castle Marvelous bears the most unmistakable signs of Celticity. There the testing bed of *Le Conte du Graal* is made to move like the bed in Cu Roi's castle (Loomis 1949, 286). Later Gawain notices a magical pillar inside the castle, much like the one to be found inside the hall of Lug (Loomis 1949, 288). The above are not isolated examples, they are part of a consistent comparison between the romances and Irish and Welsh legend that is not in Chrétien. They argue for another source independent of him.

In the last century, opinion prevailed that Kyôt was the alternative source that Wolfram employed in beginning and finishing his poem.[28] However, the thinking of scholars over the past fifty years has been a nearly unanimous disbelief in this theory. This is for several reasons. Kyôt was a Provencal, yet supposedly composed in French. He allegedly found the source in an Arab manuscript and translated it, making him trilingual. Wolfram also described Kyôt as a singer or magician, yet the source Wolfram gives for *Parzival* must have been massive and literary, not lyrical. Wolfram was clearly inventing a source. Finally, the only known Kyôt of the period seems to have been disinterested in writing a grail story. If he had, he apparently did not have the talent to write it. The Kyôt referred to in *Parzival* can not be reasonably seen as Wolfram's source, and was possibly the butt of a joke.[29]

Perlesvaus is another of the French romances which was composed in the wake of the immense popularity of the grail which Chrétien had inspired. It is a prose romance that was most probably composed between 1191 and 1212 or 1220-5.[30] The author is unknown, as is the text's relationship to the other grail versions. However, the following statements are generally regarded as truthful.

1.) The author of *Perlesvaus* begins his tale at the point Chrétien leaves off and attempts to finish much of what Chrétien began.
2.) The tendency toward brutality is not the product of an unsound mind, but one of an author aware of his audience. Its subsequent popularity supports this conclusion.
3.) The story was taken from Glastonbury, or was otherwise influenced by that church's views.
4.) It antedates the *Vulgate* version. *Perlesvaus* preserves Perceval as the hero, while *Vulgate* introduces Galahad.

These last two points are crucial. If *Vulgate* appeared before *Perlesvaus* this romance would be useless for better understanding the genesis of the Perceval story. *Vulgate* is a poor composite of previous romances (below). Second, as Glastonbury is known to have affected it, grail specialists have been very careful of the level of confidence they put into *Perlesvaus*.[31] The monastery was known to fabricate stories to further its own ends, and the probable date for this redaction would tie in well with the "discovery" of Arthur's remains in 1191. During this period the creative energy of the holy site was peaking.[32]

In addition to the author's blatant influence by Glastonbury, much of *Perlesvaus* is doubtless to be found in the pages of Chrétien and quite possibly two of his continuators.[33] However, there are hints that he had another source that was independent of Chrétien's influence.

Professor Loomis saw in one scene a parallel to the late Irish work *Fouke Fitz Warin*. In both *Perlesvaus* and *Fouke Fitz Warin* the heroes are attacked by a devil and defeat the beast with a cross on their shield. They then enter a place where a bull is worshipped.[34] Additional clues of another source abound. Guinièvre's premature death on the news of her son's demise represents an alternative tradition to earlier Arthurian tales.[35] The Grail Castle is described as a "Castle of Souls" (trans. Bryant 1978, 195), and "Castle of Four Horns" (trans. Bryant 1978, 387), one epithet for the fortress of *Preiddeu Annwn*, and the other a possible literary inspiration for Corbenic (see Chapter X).

There are also scenes the origin of which one should question in view of the Christian theme of Chrétien and the fact that Glastonbury had a strong impact on the story. One action of Perceval's ally King Gurguran is a case in point. Upon learning that his son is dead, he boils the man's body: "et quant la char de son fil fu cuite, il la fet detrenchier au plus meneument qu'il pot, et fet mander toz ses homes de sa terre, et en done a chascun tant com la char dure." (ll. 2064-2066). "And when his son's flesh was cooked, he had it cut up into the smallest pieces possible, and summoned all the people of his land and gave each one a piece until all the flesh was gone" (trans. Bryant 1978, 70).

Such actions do not sound Christian. The cooking and eating of one's son would not be invented by any sane churchman to further the holiness of Glastonbury or Perceval. It does, however, sound like a possibility in a newly or nominally converted region. It is also possible this image was intended for use as propaganda, against remote pagans of the fifth century, or against Muslims of the twelfth century.

Another scene that is not the invention of Glastonbury is one produced by Perceval's actions, one of vengeance.

Il fet aprester une grant cuve et amener emi la cort, et fet amener les xi chevalier[s], et lor fet les chiés couper en la cuve et tant saignier com il pourent rendre de sanc; et puis fet les cors oster et les chiés, si que il n'ot que le sanc tot pur en la cuve. Aprés fet desarmer le Seignor des Mores, et amener devant la cuve ou il avoit plenté de sanc. (ll. 5389-94).

He bade that a great vat be made ready and brought into the middle of the court; then he called for the eleven knights to be led forward, and had them beheaded in the vat and left to bleed as much blood as they could. Then he had their heads and bodies thrown out so that only the pure blood remained in the vat. Then he called forth the Lord of the Fens to be disarmed and led before the vat with its great fill of blood. (trans. Bryant 1978, 151).

He does this in Perceval's presence. Again, this does not represent any Christian rite, nor could it be designed for any foreseeable reason as anti-Muslim propaganda. To conclude, *Perlesvaus* shows a high level of independence from Chrétien. In at least two scenes it demonstrates an influence of which Glastonbury could not be a part.

This group represents all the grail romances believed to have been written around 1200. However, Heinrich von dem Türlin's *Diu Crône* may also be considered a part of this group even though it is usually believed to have been the last to be produced because of its conglomerate nature. Its publication date was anywhere between 1200 and 1250. Still, it is an interesting piece. To quote Spaarnay:

> On the whole, one gets the impression that Heinrich created very little out of whole cloth, that much of his material came from lost sources, but that he made his own combinations and exercised considerable freedom in the invention of detail. (Spaarnay 1959, 443)

Such invention can be seen in the various creatures that the author employs in his book. However, there are distinct elements in his romance that suggest a source other than those which had been written in the Arthurian milieu. For one, Türlin resisted the motifal personality of Cei as a boaster -- he treats him with respect. Türlin allows him control of Arthur's army (ll. 2220-1), and speaks as if to save his reputation (ll. 1521-45). Heinrich's kind words for Cei betray an antiquity to be found in the oldest Welsh poems. There is also contained in Türlin's prose a reminiscence of *Pa gur?*. One scene includes an indolent gatekeeper who plays the role of Cei and Glewlwyd, and refuses to allow Gawein into the castle that he guards (ll. 5767-5807).

Diu Crône has one more quirk in its plot which none of the earlier romances have. Instead of the hints that Gauvain was once the protagonist (see Chapter V), he is so in *Diu Crône*. This element of the romance probably antedates the other grail stories (below).

Two other redactions of the grail phenomenon should be mentioned here. The first is the four Continuations of *Le Conte du Graal*, and the other the *Vulgate*.[36] Both are later versions and are generally agreed to have drawn entirely on the previous grail redactions that are extant. The various authors simply recomposed the various motifs to be found in earlier material.[37] Specifically, the *First Continuation* (1191-1200) is primarily involved with the endeavors of Gauvain and the tying up of loose ends concerning Chrétien's poem. The use of Gauvain as the primary hero is probably more allied to *Dysgyl*. However, it is difficult to be certain the author gets this idea from a pre Chrétien source and not simply by carrying on where Chrétien began. The *First Continuation* also includes a story involving the Breton hero Caradoc.[38] The *Second Continuation* (c. 1200) provides a re emergence of Perceval as the hero. This writer uses motifs to be found in Chrétien and the *First Continuation*. The third continuator, Manassier, adds a large number of characters without British provenance (Burns 1991, 497). He uses motifs from all his predecessors and manages to conclude the tale with the hero mending the grail castle sword. He dates it to 1214x27 (Thompson 1959, 217). The Fourth Continuator (1226-30), Gerbert, takes motifs from his predecessors, inserts a Tristan redaction, and writes another conclusion. Each of the poets represent a consistently declining quality of talent (Thompson 1959, 217).

The *Vulgate* was the most widely read of the prose romances and was written between 1215 and 1230. It seems to be a combination derived from *Le Chevalier de la Charrette*, *Le Conte du Graal*, *Didot Perceval*, *Lanzelet*, Wace, *Vita Merlini*, and Robert de Boron, although it has been thought the sections that are similar to *Lanzelet* are derived from tradition (Frappier 1959, 300). The only new aspects to the legend's development one finds are the conglomeration of the various Arthurian stories, the adultery as one finds it in Malory, and the emergence of Galahad as the grail hero.

As the present state of knowledge and understanding of the grail romances stand there are six Perceval romances which show varying degrees of evidence for influence from a British source. The six contain a sort of grail ceremony that causes mourning and bears evidence that Gauvain may have been the original hero.[39] There is, then, a general idea of the pre Chrétien story. The hero is taught horsemanship, swordsmanship, and general manners by his maternal uncles according to tradition. He is sent to Arthur's court, and proves his worth through numerous victorious confrontations.

From this the separate versions diverge greatly. At one extreme is the theme of conversion and death of pagans, and the destruction of various pagan objects culminating in the murder of the nine witches at Caer Lloyw. This one finds most clearly articulated in *Peredur*. At the other end of the spectrum, represented by *Le Conte*, is the Perceval's moral development from a naïve boy to the highest standard of Christian knighthood.

The common precursor for such diverse versions must date to no later than the latter part of the eleventh century, the beginning of the crusades. In all these redactions, prominence is given to a *graal* or *dysgyl* of magical qualities. In the case of *Peredur* it contains a head. On the continent, this object takes on a Christian quality with Celtic affinities. The theme of the story, too, alters in content in the French and German versions. Instead of the theft or outright destruction of a site with Celtic connotations, those romancers from Chrétien on have superimposed a sovereignty theme.[40] Whether because it was the earlier tale or simply because it was under a stronger Celtic influence, *Peredur* contains no Christian explanation of the ceremony. It indicates no grail throne in waiting for a fully matured Peredur. It simply records a hero's *mabinogi* in several disconnected episodes, culminating in the destruction of a site of unquestionably Celtic provenance. In this respect it seems the more closely linked to a British source that had not organized Peredur's various episodes into a congruent narrative yet. It has been seen that Chrétien has formed his plot around the life of Philip here (see Chapter IX), and it would appear that later writers mimicked him in this respect. After all, the story as Chrétien had written it was an instant success and those who followed him were apparently careful to retain the basic theme of the story. In all versions the character develops slowly from naïvety to full maturity in the Christian philosophy. This was to have a profound impact on the development of the grail story; in time it would change the way the entire story was perceived.

With this in mind, one must turn to the alternate, albeit unsatisfactory, conclusion of the Perceval tale to be found in *Peredur* to find some meaning in the grail story. In light of the compromised nature of the Chrétien version this must serve as the foundation upon which to determine and compare analogous material.[41] There are two aspects of this final *Peredur* scene that are the most likely candidates, because of their peculiarity to Celtic lore, to aid in improving our understanding of the story. These are the nine witches and their destruction.

The nine witches scenario is first witnessed in a Paleolithic drawing at Cagul, "The Tablet of Larzac", and the writings of Pomponius Mela.[42] The destruction of witches or pagan priestesses directly compares to *Preiddeu Annwn*, *Pa gur?*, and the *Vitae Samsoni*. *Preiddeu Annwn* implies the maintenance of a cauldron was the central function of these women (Haycock 1984, 62, 69 n. 14). A magical cauldron is to be found in *Branwen* and *Culhwch ac Olwen*. The cauldron is most fully understood by its description in the *Tri Thlws ar Daleg Ynys Brydain* or *The Thirteen Treasures of Britain*. A brief description of each of these stories and scenes will be useful here to understand better their interrelationships and relevance to the *Peredur* scene.

The primitive art of Cagul is chronologically the first parallel. It is pre Roman in origin and portrays nine women dancing around a human-like figure with horns coming from its head (Murray 1931, 96). It is apparent from this picture that the women are showing a high degree of respect to what appears to be a pagan deity or a personification of that deity.

Further evidence, now of the Roman period, is to be found in the work of Pomponius Mela. Writing in the first century, he recorded nine witches inhabiting the island of Sena off France's coast (*Choreographia*, 3.6.48). The archaeology of Larzac, France, produces more data; a lengthy inscription buried with a woman.[43] In the infancy of study on these finds, the following items are accepted about the writings. First, that the Larzac poem is of the first century. Second, that the inscription is by people who are intimately familiar with a Celtic religion. Third, the implication is that this tablet involves at least one "coven" ("Two Gaulish Religious Inscriptions", trans. Koch 1995, 1). When the group is listed, there are ten different personal names involved in an intricate set of relationships described in familial terms. This probably represents a coven of nine sorceresses and one master.

The first British poem that contains the nine witches motif is the pseudo-Taliesin work known as *Preiddeu Annwn*. It is noteworthy that they are here described as virgin priestesses. It has been dated to between the ninth and the twelfth centuries by Dr. Marged Haycock (1984, 57), and 850-1150 by Professor Sims-Williams (1991, 54), both on purely linguistic grounds. There is no traceable plot in the work. Instead, it is a series of cryptic allusions in the Taliesin persona (Haycock 1984, 53-4, 57-8). This form of writing is immensely difficult to fathom. However, the following can be deduced about the event the poem describes. First, Arthur and his band go to a mysterious island termed Annwn. Second, the group arrives and there is a fight during which Lleog and Lleminog are instrumental and Lleminog gains an unspecified sword.[44] Finally, they depart from the island having stolen or destroyed a cauldron nurtured by nine maidens. This vessel "Ny beirw bwyl llwfyr ny ry tyghit;" "It will not boil the food of a coward, it has not been so destined" (*Preiddeu Annwn*, l. 17).

A second native British piece that has the nine witches motif is *Pa gur?*. Professor Sims-Williams dates the poem to 1100-1160 based on the language of other, dateable selections in the manuscript it is found, the *Black Book of Carmarthen*. The work is largely a monologue by Arthur to a gatekeeper -- Glewlwyd. In it is contained a list of the deeds of his band, chief of these is Cei who, the reader is told, killed the nine witches of an unidentified Ystawingun.[45]

The *vita* of Samson also has the witch destruction feature. Books XXVI-XXVII consist of the following: Samson witnesses a sorceress (*theomacha*) chasing down and wounding one of his young deacons with a trident. Samson stops her and attempts to make her repent and convert, but she says that she will never do anything but evil against God, and wishes for nothing else. She dies by Samson's prayer on the spot where she makes the refusal. Before she does, however, she tells the saint she has eight sisters and a mother who live in the forest.

The information from which this story and the book itself derives is considered to be nearly contemporary. The anonymous writer claims to have his knowledge third-hand, through the nephew of the nephew of Samson himself. It is of the seventh century, and has been dated by name-forms and a lack of ninth-century priorities to the early seventh century,[46] though all that can be certain is that it dates to no later than the ninth century.[47]

The *Branwen* tale has the cauldron motif and is the only member of this group whose characters and plot are purely mythological. The story survives in four (two partial, two in their entirety) manuscripts dateable no later than the early fifteenth and no earlier than the thirteenth centuries (Mac Cana 1992, 22). The orthography of *The Red Book of Hengerdd* redaction points to a date before 1200 (Lovecy 1991, 171). On historical grounds the dates have been quite varied, but no earlier than 1050.[48]

The plot is as follows. The heroine, Branwen, is engaged to an Irish king Matholwch by her brother Brân. However, while Matholwch is in Britain receiving her he suffers the destruction of some property by one of Brân's brothers. He is heavily recompensed and is satisfied. However, on his return, Matholwch's subjects insist he degrades his wife with chores to win back his honor. In time Brân is made to learn this. In response, he and his war-band go to rescue her. They eventually do so, but only by destroying a life-resuscitating cauldron and at the cost of Brân's life and the lives of many of his men. At Brân's request they take his still functioning head and bring it to Harddlech, where there is a feast for many years. His head is eventually buried in London. The reviving cauldron has two functions in the myth. It is one of the presents given to Matholwch as an apology for his loss of property, and it serves to rejuvenate the Irish dead when Brân and his men attack Matholwch.

Culhwch ac Olwen is a narrative concerning a wonder tale. Arthur's men help a young man obtain all the dowry needed to purchase his bride Olwen from her giant-father Yspaddaden by fulfilling all the conditions set by him. One of these tasks is the theft of a food-cooking cauldron from Ireland.

The narrative is composed of at least three tales that have been stratified one upon the other over the course of centuries. The first layer is a purely mythological recension that possibly consisted of Culhwch, Olwen, and some of the tasks.[49] Second, one that introduced historical characters from all over the Celtic world and superimposed Arthur's court on the tale (no later than the tenth century). The final addition was to the peripheries of the tale, specifically the court list and the course of the Twrch Trwyth, with additional material up through the fourteenth century.[50] These divisions are naturally not precise, but they do make the reader aware of a chief problem with the text, that of its highly composite character.[51]

The section of interest here runs as follows. Arthur and his *teulu* go by ship to Ireland and are hospitably accepted and feasted by its king. Then, Arthur and his men attack their host and proceed to carry off a magical cauldron. During the struggle a certain Lleminog plays a prominent role. *Culhwch ac Olwen* gives no more information on the subject, however another episode is of some importance here. The last task which Arthur and his men accomplish relates to our study here as well. Arthur and his band go north to kill a Black Witch (ll. 1205-29). Arthur himself does this after two pairs of his men fail to do so.

Finally, the cauldron of *The Thirteen Treasures of the Island of Britain* has much of the same characteristics as the above cauldrons (apart from Branwen). This is because it has the property of being an instrument for cooking. The Cauldron of Dyrnwch, as it is so listed, will only boil the food of a brave man (*The Welsh Triads*, trans. and ed. Bromwich 1978, 242).

More about the nature of the cauldron may be learned from the context of the list itself. First, it is worth noting that the only two qualities that are necessary to make any of *The Thirteen Treasures* function are bravery and being well-born. Second, the list's owners include primarily heroic-age kings, and no figure after the heroic age proper had ended around 650.[52] This gives some idea of the antiquity of the associations in this list, though most probably the list itself was the product of antiquarian speculation.

The early stories listed above, Pomponius' testimony, and the two archaeological remains reveal a great deal despite the limited amount of information each source gives. First, it may be determined that a group of nine maidens/witches, with a leader, is generally associated with a cult that is most likely a pan Celtic phenomenon. Second, one is told in *Preiddeu Annwn* that the nine maidens are the keepers of a magical cauldron that will not boil the food of a coward. This may or may not be a random combination of two items by the author of the poem, though there is reason to believe it was not.[53] Regardless of the provenance of both motifs and their interrelationships, the two were sufficiently linked in the *Preiddeu Annwn* poet's eyes to warrant such a blatant connection as early as the tenth century.[54] The third lesson one takes is that the cauldron as it is described in the various tales is of nearly uniform quality, it cooks food, but will not boil the food of a coward. The only exception here is *Branwen* that, as has been seen, is mythological in general content and characters. In it the cauldron is a life-giver.

A peculiarity should also be noted. The theft/destruction of the cauldron or the death of the nine sorceresses is associated solely with characters of the fifth and sixth century (Arthur and Samson, and possibly Cei?). Archaeological remains indicate this period saw great tensions between the Insular British Christians and their pagan counterparts. I shall return to this observation in the next chapter.

This comprehensive survey of the various elements of the final, largely unintelligible scene in the *Peredur* narrative explains much of what may have been the background for the story. A brief history of *Dysgyl* should serve further to clarify this literary strand of the legend.

At some time before 1200, the cauldron theft/destruction story, usually associated with Arthur or what were considered his men, was now exclusively made to do so. A series of grail tales was then written in which the character Peredur was given the primary role.[55] It is the use of Peredur as the hero, the persistent cornucopic property of the magical vessel, and the inclusion of an *enfance* of Peredur that ties this group together and argues for a common source.[56]

Dysgyl may or may not have a direct relation to the four stories in which another Arthurian hero is the more prominent figure (under the Arthur Branch). Regardless of this, the examples from this latter branch provide information about some scenes in *Dysgyl*, and appear uninfluenced by the romances. They are useful for cross-referencing and will be employed for this purpose.

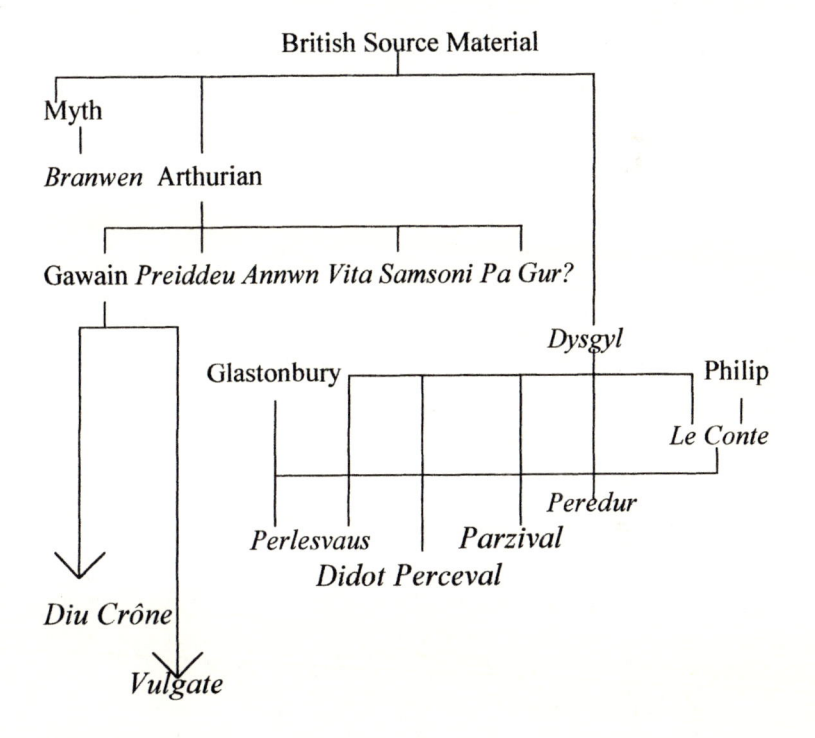

British Source Material

Myth
|
Branwen Arthurian
|
Gawain *Preiddeu Annwn Vita Samsoni Pa Gur?*

Dysgyl — Philip
Glastonbury |
                                  Le Conte
                        Peredur
      Perlesvaus   *Parzival*
           Didot Perceval

Diu Crône

Vulgate

---

[1] I use here the order by which Chrétien operates because his is the version from which the others are traditionally believed to have been drawn.

[2] *Syr Perceval* has occasionally been used in conjunction with the other grail stories to add weight to whichever argument is being posed. In agreement with the majority of scholars, however, I find that its obviously lengthy stay in an oral environment has not allowed it to retain a functional understanding of the major episodes, instead resorting to burlesque. It will not be used here.

[3] (Loomis 1963, 5), though see Lovecy (1991, 177-8), for specific examples.

[4] One theory claims a pan-Celtic origin for many motifs (Mac Cana 1970, 94; O'Rahilly 1946, 14; Bromwich 1983, 51; 1974, 167-9) and has a complementary theory that the kingdom of Henry II, including large parts of France as well as Wales, Scotland, and England, created an environment where motifs from across the Celtic and romantic worlds could flow nearly unhindered.

[5] Goetinck (1975, 304-17) and the references cited therein.

[6] The main contenders have been Dr. Williams, (1909), Dr. Lovecy, (1978, 133-46), and Dr. Lloyd-Morgan, (1981, 187-231). Professor Thurneysen has also written a landmark paper on the subject, but the only reference to it I have found is (1912, 185-189). This is a review of Mary Williams' *Essai sur la composition du roman gallois de Peredur* (1909).

[7] It is also known that the work that remains is a compilation of several previous, so that it is conceivable the episodes listed after his marriage to the empress in *Peredur* could also be placed before this event (Goetinck 1975, 21; Lovecy 1991, 177-80; Mac Cana 1992, 105-6). Keeping in mind, however, Peredur's tendency to become attached to a woman and suddenly leave, this suggestion is hardly a necessary one.

[8] (Goetinck 1975, 304-17) and references cited therein.

[9] (Mac Cana 1992, 122; Chapter XIV).

[10] For a complete comparison of the two versions, see Goetinck, (1975, 59-78).

[11] Roughly speaking, Ia is Perceval's life to the scene of the blood drops in the snow, Ib recounts the *Peredur* pursuit and attainment of Angharad's love, II ends with the fourteen year reign with the empress, and section III begins with the loathly damsel and ends with the destruction of the nine witches of Caerloyw.

[12] (Lovecy 1991, 176) notes several repeated phrases comparable to the Mabinogi collection. It should also be noted that the *enfance* of Peredur, where he is described as hunting on foot, is identical to the manner by which twelfth-century noble-youths hunted and was not intended to belittle the hero-to-be. This would have been understood by a Welsh audience, but misinterpreted by the French. The early, naïve persona Perceval is given indicates this confusion, while the *Peredur* author has significantly different scenes pertaining to Peredur's childhood and youth. This has the effect of portraying Peredur as a more matured character than Chrétien's Perceval.

[13] Though the lion reminds one of the Sword bridge episode, and the magic stone is similar to that found in *Yvain*.

[14] The most recent expert to agree with these findings is Dr. Brouland, though of course she uses different means. It is her opinion that the mythological elements in *Peredur* are what proves independence. I cannot agree with this reasoning because of the very fact that time in a Celtic oral environment would have lent itself to the borrowing of such motifs, whether or not the story was a product of Chrétien. (Brouland 1994, 59-70).

[15] (Lovecy 1991, 178). It has been noted by many key scholars that Peredur's name is Celtic, but this carries little weight as to independence from Chrétien. If the story had been borrowed or simply translated from the French, it is highly probable the translator would have used the name of a traditional figure in place of Perceval.

[16] (*Didot Perceval*, ed. Roach 1941, 125-30). However, Dr. le Gentil speculates only after 1191 and before 1202 or after 1212 (1959, 253).

[17] (*Didot Perceval*, ed. Roach 1941), 119-25). This gives a survey of the main participants in the debate and leans heavily toward the opinions of Dr. Brugger, who agrees with Robert de Boron's authorship.

[18] They are both said to be derived from an hypothetical "p".

[19] (*Didot Perceval*, trans. Nitze 1932, 152; *Didot Perceval*, ed. Roach, 1941, 5; le Gentil 1959, 258).

[20] A convenient list of the various comparisons and discrepancies can be found in Professor Roach's *Didot Perceval* (1941, 59-61).

[21] Except earlier in Robert's own composition (1927, 20).

[22] (*Parzival*, trans. Hatto 1980, 11; Wynn 1994, 185). Springer (1959, 220) believes the writing may have continued into 1212.

[23] The great many divergences from Chrétien are the poet's own creation as similar discrepancies have been noted between his Willehelm and its French source (Springer, 1959, 224).

[24] Because of Chrétien's instant fame and Wolfram's references back to him. However, his weak knowledge of French presents a problem to this theory (e.g. his translation of *graal*, if it was intended as translation).

[25] (Loomis 1949, 451, 454; Springer 1959, 239-40).

[26] Though the plot here is based either on the famed crusader Richard the Lion-heart, or is simply a recasting of Book IV according to Springer. See him for a survey of the views on this subject. (1959, 255).

[27] (Chadwick 1958b, 109; Chapter III).

[28] Indeed, he does name him in his preface and refers back to him in the book.

[29] (Springer 1959, 221). See *Parzival* (eds. Mustard and Passage 1961, xxiv-xxv) for leading scholars on both sides of the issue.

[30] (Nitze 1959, 268). This has been the source of much debate with hypotheses suggesting dates as late as 1250. For a survey of the relevant arguments see *Le Haut du Graal: Perlesvaus, A Structural Study*, (trans. Kelly 1974, 9-15).

[31] The term "Glastonbury" does not appear in the manuscript. However, it had long since been equated with "Avalon", which is mentioned several times (*Perlesvaus*, ll. 6378, 7586, 7804, 10189).

[32] Nitze, a major translator of the work, strongly believed that the book was not the product of a Glastonbury monk because of the dialect and the fact that he makes no mention of St. Philip, the man alleged by Glastonbury to have founded their monastery, supports this (*Le Haut Livre du Graal: Perlesvaus*, ed. Nitze 1937, 19 fl.). However, the references to Glastonbury are only to be found in this romance, of all those preceding 1400. This warrants the assumption of Glastonbury's influence.

[33] The author does say he received his book from the archives of Glastonbury's library.

[34] (Loomis, 1956, 44). In view of the prominence of domesticated animals in ancient societies (witness the repeated use of horse-oriented terms in Irish and Germanic personal names), this may well represent a pagan deity or place of worship. Unfortunately our present understanding of the Celtic religion is much too fragmentary to be sure.

[35] Most probably this is not of any antiquity, but the subtle method whereby the tale avoids the continental ending of Arthur's realm is definitely of Welsh provenance. Their failure to include the Tristan or Lancelot stories is some indication of this tendency to avoid embarrassing the more prominent heroes of their folklore (Lloyd-Morgan 1994, 178).

[36] For commentaries on the *Continuations* see Thompson, (1959, 206-217). For *Vulgate* see Frappier (1959, 295-318), Grimsby, (1959, 99-101), and Burns, (1991, 496-9). In the above instances I have cited only when one author has given a differing opinion.

[37] The sole exception to this rule is to be found in the description of the grail castle in the *First Continuation*, which may be more accurately Celtic than Chrétien's version. Its repeated use is an indication of the limited examples of originality in the *Continuations*.

[38] This can not be considered traditional. The entire episode of Caradoc's arm is based on a misunderstanding of the British epithet Vreichvras-strong arm. (Loomis 1965, 232-9).

[39] Classic evidence is the fact that Gauvain is given the same basic task as Perceval, yet is made to be the failure because of a flaw, as in *Le Chevalier de La Charrette*. In that poem he could not succeed in saving Guinièvre because he refused to degrade himself for love. Another weighty piece of evidence is that Gauvain is normally given as many lines as Perceval in most of the romances, yet is clearly not the intended hero. For a study on the subject, see Jessie Weston, (1897, passim).

[40] Dr. Roberts' article "Geoffrey of Monmouth and Welsh Historical Tradition" discusses the underlying theme of loss of sovereignty throughout the British world. The subsequent emergence of the sovereignty theme in twelfth century British tales can be seen as a result of this phenomenon (1976, 1-26).

[41] Chrétien is compromised in that the author was not a part of the British traditions and his patron seemed to have a very specific motive

for authorising the romances. Later romancers demonstrably followed him. British authors were not nearly so restricted.

[42] Mac Cana also compares the nine witches to the nine sisters and seven score of Imramm Brain and the nine sisters of the De Danaan who marry the nine brothers of Fionn (Mac Cana, "The Sinless Underworld of Imramm Brain", *Ériu* 65 (Dublin, 1976), 112). These are feasible connections, but have their limitations. In the first comparison, the number is not nine, or ten, but one hundred and forty-nine. In the second, the sisters have no function but to marry, and therefore generate no further comparison. However, as Ireland was a part of the Celtic world the two edited tales represent a pan Celtic theme for the nine women coven. In this respect, the nine daughters of Ægir and the nine muses establish an hypothesis for a pan European context, though it is still most fully represented in the Celtic works.

[43] To my knowledge, Professor John Koch has been the only scholar to discuss and translate the newly-discovered Gaulish writings, so I base my criticism on his translation and impressions. ("Two Gaulish Religious Inscriptions", trans. Koch 1995, 1-4).

[44] (Haycock 1984, 71). Lleminog means "The Leaping One"; this may be a personal name or an allusion to Arthur.

[45] Though Professor Sims-Williams suggests it would be in the Gloucester area. (1991, 45). In any event, the place has not been associated with the underworld.

[46] (*The Life of St. Samson of Dol*, trans. Taylor 1991, xxxix; Davies 1982, 215; Diune, 1912-13, 332-356).

[47] (Sims-Williams 1990, 80; Poulin 1977, 1-26).

[48] For historical reasons Sir Ifor Williams believed 1055-62 (1930, xl-xli), Professor Thurneysen estimated the eleventh century (1921, 24-7, 626-7, 668), Mr. Lewis said 1170-90 (1968, 230-3; 1969a, 137-42; 1969b, 185-92; 1970, 30-43), and Dr. Charles-Edwards guesses 1050-1120 (1971, 263 fl.)

[49] (*Culhwch ac Olwen*, eds. Bromwich and Evans 1992, lxxix). According to Dr. Bromwich, Culhwch definitely has mythological origins, possibly preCeltic (*Culhwch ac Olwen*, eds. Bromwich and Evans 1992, 46-7), and Olwen may have mythological associations (*Culhwch ac Olwen* eds. Bromwich and Evans 1992, 117-18). Dr.

Roberts seems to favour Olwen as a creation of the story and Culhwch as a saga figure (1991, 74).

[50] This, in all probability, would have been at one stroke, though the association of various historical characters to Arthur would have been done over some time in the past.

[51] These boundaries almost definitely do not fully represent the fluidity of this story's history.

[52] (*The Welsh Triads*, trans. and ed. Bromwich 1978, 245-250; Roberts, 1991, 86).

[53] Admittedly there are only two instances where the two are explicitly combined. However. the concept of the cauldron which only boils food for a coward is uniquely Celtic among the Indo-Europeans, and the coven of ten mortal women (nine and one leader) associated with magic is only specified in Celtic lore; it seems a neat match. It should also be pointed out that the cryptic "Taliesin" poem is the only example of British or Irish lore which represents the women in anything resembling a complimentary role. They are here referred to as "maids", MW *morwyn* (l. 14). This implies a more intimate knowledge of the subject and therefore a better understanding of its mechanisms.

[54] Dr. Haycock believes that this was made in the Taliesin persona. If this argument is a valid one, then the need to be accurate in the instances where something is clearly said would be imperative and the connection would be an unquestionable one. See Haycock's article "*Preiddeu Annwfn* and the Figure of Taliesin" (1984).

[55] Though if one will concede the cauldron which Brân's men destroy is a different type derived from a different mythological object, all other evidence points to it being the sole property of Arthur.

[56] It is highly apparent no continental source contains a scenario wherein Perceval destroys a cauldron but, as has been and will shortly be seen, this was due to Chrétien's influence. *Perlesvaus* does show some hints of the destruction feature (below).

Chapter XIII: Religion in fifth- and sixth-century Britain

The contents of the last chapters represent the sum of mainstream arguments and ideas regarding the nature of the grail and *Le Conte du Graal*'s author. Scholars have determined Chrétien was either Christian, or a Jew writing for a Christian audience. Chrétien's patron desired to see the highest Christian ideals observed, and this Chrétien catered admirably, within the limits set by the Celtic ambiance of the story. The genius in the lines is the result of the master poet himself. The grail story as Chrétien wrote it is the product of an old source. To this foundation was added a gathering of pan Celtic themes, the influence of Philip of Flanders, Christian concepts, and possibly Jewish elements. These motifs and themes were clearly integrated into the Arthurian corpus by 1200. It has also been revealed that many of the continental grail romances were influenced by a source independent of Chrétien, and that this and Chrétien's theoretical source is best represented by *Peredur*.

To gain a new and better insight into the grail, every line of thinking has been fully explored from a literary perspective.[1] Chrétien's personal tastes and professional necessities as well as the religious and political outlook of France in Chrétien's era have been amply searched. In short, the theory and accepted fact that the grail is somehow a product of the twelfth century has been fully exhausted, to no avail. The grail, its past and importance, are yet unexplained.

However, no-one has denied the Celtic elements and influence in the story, or even the grail's affinity with Celtic culture in the pre Christian past. Sadly, this concept has not been well explored, either.[2] However, there is a path to follow. Some have attempted to reconstruct certain features of a pan Celtic mythological system by finding common links in Irish, Welsh, and Gaulish tales and hypothesizing about a primary meaning and purpose. This is the key to unlocking the mystery behind the grail story. The romances themselves are not necessarily the most pertinent sources to access. One must keep in mind that the Celtic features in the grail redactions are the crystallized remains of a living religion.[3] These features have been diluted with Celtic motifs and the spiritual input of Christian and possibly some Jewish elements. The best method for providing information with which to theorize upon is by examining the historical context of 500 A.D. Britain. I shall then return to the romances for a supplementary guide to these findings.

Post Roman Celtic history has never been used to interpret the grail romances. This is presumably because no-one has previously entertained the notion that the sixth century might contain material relevant to the grail legend. However, as has been seen concerning *Le Chevalier de la Charrette*, such objections are no longer valid. With this in mind, why should one avoid making use of our knowledge of British religions in the fifth and sixth centuries to better grasp the period? Certainly there can be no harm in introducing to the grail study what is presently recognized as features of the sub-Roman Celtic politico-religious system. In doing so one can do no worse than the inconsistent explanations for all the grail or cauldron stories which literary criticism has produced.

This chapter will begin by reviewing the current thinking on the religions of Dark Age Britain. The Celtic religion was in existence in the fifth and sixth centuries. This probability will be shown first by using the negative archaeological and literary evidence. Much of Celtic Britain in the sixth century was not verifiably Christian and a great deal of the locations exhibits indications of pagan existence. Next, I shall introduce evidence for the Celtic religion's survival and eventual rebirth in the later Middle Ages as Satanic cults. Finally, I shall argue for the Celtic religion's nature and significance in the Arthurian period using comparison to the continent during this era. In accomplishing these goals I hope to validate a new look on the nature of the grail story.[4]

Christianity was not a cornerstone of British society when the legions left forever in the fifth century; it had only recently become an accepted part of society. It was not the dominant religion in 400; most British temples survived for some decades into the fifth century (Lewis 1966, 143). Further, Dr. Ross has shown that the distribution of post

Roman votive shafts, wells, and sanctuaries associated with the Celtic religion indicate a strong pagan presence in this period.[5] In 400, Christianity had not had the chance to express itself fully on this island. It would not do so for another century; it was still an uncertain dogma here.[6] Christianity's relative infertility in Britain was not unique to this island. The problem was commonplace in all of Europe during this period.[7] Many areas on the perimeter of the Roman world were pagan or partially pagan when Emperor Honorius issued his refusal to help the British people in 410. With this in mind, it is clear that locating Christianity's areas of strength is the most prudent undertaking in a study of the religious nature of the area and period.[8]

The effort of defining the areas in which Christianity was particularly strong around 500 serves several functions. First, it enables an hypothesis about and systematic enumeration of all the Christian centers in Britain. Second, the procedure allows for some understanding of how much the religion had developed geographically by the turn of the sixth century. Finally and most importantly here, the process should lend itself to an explanation about its political and social place in Britain as contrasted with the Celtic worshippers in the late-fifth century.[9]

Charles Thomas' *Christianity in Britain to 500 A.D.* (1981) is, to my knowledge, still the most up-to-date book on the extent of Christianity in the sub-Roman period.[10] It is a work by an experienced and highly regarded archaeologist in the field of sub-Roman Britain. Professor Thomas locates all the sites that may be, by way of archaeological, place-name, or textual evidence (*De Excidio Britanniae*) connected to a Christian site in the fifth century. The areas he plots incorporate much of every major British nation of the fifth century, but seem to focus on the modern counties of Cumberland, Yorkshire, Devonshire, and Wiltshire.[11] Naturally enough, these areas also represent the territories that had been most Romanised of all the states that remained in British hands till 500. Conversely, Gwynedd, Dyfed, and Lothian all show a limited number of artifacts of Christianity derivation. These nations were all on the frontier of the Roman Empire for much of its last century of rule on this island.

The observation about the geography of Christian sites in Britain is important because it signifies the social standing of the native faith. As a representation of the old, pre Roman culture, the Celtic religion was most probably seen as a symbol of Celtic tradition. As such it would have been a source of inspiration for those who continued to resist Roman power throughout the second, third, and fourth centuries.[12] During the fifth century the relationship between Christian Romanised areas and states bordering Romanised areas changed. During this period the Roman absence helped slowly diminish the hostility between those regions that had and had not been under Roman law. Many of the temples of Britain indicate that the worship of Celtic gods did continue into the fifth century, but were in disuse before 500,[13] supporting this conjecture.[14] The deterioration of these same religious sites implies a decline in the number of worshippers, or at least of persons willing to worship Celtic gods in a public setting. This in turn points to a lack of formal and socially approved practice of the Celtic religions. A brief summary of the history of Christianity will serve to further clarify why this may have been.

Historically, it is uncertain how or at what point Christianity was introduced to the island. However, the religion did exist on some scale before the year 313. Christians here suffered with the rest of the empire until Galerius issued his Edict of Toleration.[15] Thereafter its followers thrived. In 400, Christianity would not have had one century as an officially recognized religion. Within another two centuries Christianity would take a firm hold on the British psyche.

It seems logical to assume that some of the inhabitants of Britain worshipped Celtic gods for some time after 400 for three reasons. First, the circumstantial evidence of the previous chapter and the archaeological evidence in this chapter (above) supports the theory. Second, the most cited evidence for this belief is the construction of a temple for Nodens, erected in 364. Its very presence signals the continued existence of people who followed Celtic gods.[16] Finally, many of the vitae of both Welsh and Scottish saints report that their heroes did convert natives, and occasionally kings.[17] St. Uinniau (Galloway) and St. Columba (northern Pictland) served as major converters of the Britons and Picts in the next century. St. Samson, St. Cadog, and St. Brioc served a similar function in Wales. St. Kentigern (born mid-sixth century) is said to have had a semi-pagan father. St. Patrick himself hints that he may have been agnostic or a non-Christian at some point before his enslavement (*St. Patrick's Confessio*, Chapters 12 and 16). The *Life of Samson* purports that the saint had dealings with a coven of Celtic priestesses (see Chapter XI). In Wales, the druids (particularly Bwya) of David's Life imply that strong pagan beliefs persisted well into the sixth century (*The Life of St. Samson of Dol*, trans. Thomas 1988, Chapters 16-19). The outlying and least populated territories of Scotland were less definitely pagan, but these would have been the areas least directly touched by Christian missionaries. In Gaul, it was the countryside that protected the pagan religion and it would require localized Christian establishments to wipe it out completely (below). By the year 600 there are no traces, in the literature or archaeology, to indicate the overt existence of pagan cults.[18]

The politico-religious situation inside Britain in the fifth century was thus an unstable mixture of Christianity and Celtic paganism.[19] However, throughout that century and the next Christianity clearly can be seen to take the ascendancy. Patrick's mid-fifth-century letter to Coroticus is one to a fellow Christian. Moray and Caithness would resist until St. Columba himself had intimidated the druids of the Pictish king Brude.[20]

However, the worship of Celtic gods, in one form or another, continued to exist throughout the Middle Ages. The devil cults of Britain during the next few hundred years bear several resemblances to what is known of the Celtic cults.[21] In Chapter XII, it was learned that the standard coven consisted of nine priestesses and one leader. In addition, two more details of the satanic religion can be seen as specifically deriving from the Celtic religion. Archaeological remains testify to the worship of the Celtic horn-god *Cernunnos*. He survived as the "Old Hornie" of vernacular Middle English. He was worshipped by the black magic groups in the medieval period of Britain (Murray 1931, 38).

Second, the Sabbaths of the "dark religion" during the Middle Ages were identical to the ancient dates of the Celtic holidays.[22] Evidently the Celtic religion endured to become at least a part of the devil worship of the medieval period. The Celtic religion survived against the overpowering strength of Christianity in the fifth and sixth centuries, though it was eventually forced underground in the Early Medieval period.

The information above indicates that some time between 400 and the period when records of British history reappear in the last quarter of the sixth century the Christian religion gained supremacy. Those areas where the Celtic cults had been practiced ceased to leave evidence in the archaeological record.[23] The information is unanimous here. There were no active temples on these isles from the mid-sixth century on, at latest. The vitae speak of fifth- and sixth-century saints converting or destroying pagans, and the earliest Celtic poetry (late-sixth century) is at least nominally of Christian character. This data and the persistence and consistency of what medieval people termed "devil cults" imply two things. First, that the Celtic worshippers were no longer able openly to voice their religion by 600. Second, that their practices were continued underground. The questions to be posed here are a.) why were the pagans silenced; b.) how was this accomplished; c.) at what time was this most likely to have been done; d.) in what conditions were they allowed to continue worshipping (if indeed they were allowed). The answers to these questions are fundamental to the understanding of the grail story.

With the knowledge that both Christianity and the Celtic religion were in existence around 500, and that the excavated, British industrial areas were definitively Christian, one may make some general conclusions about Celtic Britain about these questions. First, the state of the worshippers in Celtic cults. There are three possibilities. The adherents of the Celtic religion could have been socially and economically inferior to their Christian contemporaries and therefore their record is nearly invisible. It is also possible that the contemporary sites were isolated. Finally, the areas in which worshippers practiced are currently areas which archaeology has not yet researched.[24]

Second, and perhaps more important, one may use the knowledge of continental history to hazard a guess that Christianity was a passive force behind the military suppression of the remaining pagan sects. This latter conclusion, its evidence, and the repercussions of its acceptance will be the basis for the next few paragraphs.

The knowledge to be garnered from France and the rest of Late Roman Europe is, as with Britain, slight and fragmented.[25] However, the *vita* of Martin is a valuable historical tool for an improved understanding of the period in religious terms. Its author, Sulpicius Severus, lived within his subject's lifetime and therefore had first-hand access to the original information (Stancliffe 1983, 71).

As is well known, Martin began his career as a military man and continued so until called by a vision from God. Equally well known is his active conversion of pagans and his destruction of pagan properties as a preacher of Christianity. Sulpicius himself lists five instances where Martin personally destroyed pagan shrines (*Vitae Martini*, 13.9, 14.1, 14.3-7, 15.1, and 15.4). Aided by western Europe's dearth of material on Christian destructions of pagan temples, Sulpicius makes his hero seem a veritable one-man demolition of the remaining pagan cults of western Europe. However, this was not the case. Several instances of other persons taking part in similar acts confirm it was not uncommon. The Eastern empire's Praetorian Prefect Cynegius (380-4) is recorded as a destroyer of pagan temples (*Pro Templis*, trans. Warmington 1969 18:15-20, 24, 50-1). It is also known that Victricius (*Vita Sancti Ambrosii*, 18.4), Martin, and his successors (Gregory of Tours, trans. Thorpe 1971, X.31) tackled the problem of rural pagan remnants by establishing village churches. It should be noted that such things were not without hazards and therefore that pagans were often martially oriented themselves. Augustine writes that the congregation of Colonia Sufetana overthrew a statue of Hercules in the face of opposition. The pagans retaliated by killing sixty of the faithful and demanding a new statue (Der Meer, trans. Brian Battershaw and G. R. Lamb 1961, 39-40). The church was thus an instrument for the eradication of many pagan cults. Individuals acting without church approval often did the destruction itself, but inevitably these actions were condoned by the church.[26]

There was one other manner by which the process of conversion to Christianity was made. In the ninth century Charlemagne would brutally enforce a campaign of Christianisation on the Saxons. In the fifth century a similar crusade took place.[27] In the 480s and 490s, Clovis of the Franks claimed Christianity as his religion and allied himself to the Roman church. In consequence, Rome gave him the authority to conquer any non-Christian or Arian nation that he chose to attack, and he made use of his blank check. He used the authority of the church to strengthen his own political and military situation by conquest. No Christian power could lift a finger against him as he rapidly captured what is modern France.[28]

According to legend, only two figures commanded equal power in fifth century Britain — Gwrtheyrn and Arthur.[29] Therefore the periods when these two were in power constitute the only times when a centralized political strength would have been able to instigate such an action. Both figures can be safely placed in the latter part of the fifth century and the early part of the sixth century.[30] This period accords well with political events on the continent. It is known that Britain and France were economically tied throughout the fifth century and culturally so with the emigrants to Brittany. It is a possibility that one of these two men made use of his broad power to strengthen his position among the British people as Clovis did with the Franks, and possibly in emulation of him.

As has been seen in Chapter XII, *Peredur* is the grail version that is the most closely linked to the "Arthur" branch, and the most ancient. It is therefore the redaction with the more ancient episodes in the "Peredur" branch. In conjunction with what has been deduced here, this clearer perception of the grail romances produces several new and puzzling questions about the grail story. What of the final scene, where Peredur, Arthur, Gwalchmai, and the rest of the *teulu* destroy the temple of the nine witches? The author of *Peredur*, it has been said, looks "as if he were throwing in his hand" at this point (Mac Cana 1992, 109). While this may be true, it could also be possible the intended audience would originally have understood the story fully given the episodes that are in *Peredur*. The three figures may well have been early associated with the destruction of pagan temples in Britain. Other romances support this theory; the *First Continuation* records Arthur warring on a Brun.[31] Both *Perlesvaus* and *Didot Perceval* list the martial accomplishments of Perceval in the precise role that has been attributed to Martin and several lesser known individuals, that of forceful converter of the unfaithful.

One might also hypothesize that the hero of the story could be or might represent a captain or chieftain who reduced pagan sanctuaries in the fifth or sixth centuries. He may have acted without the knowledge or instigation of a higher lord, as St. Martin had on the other side of the Channel. Alternatively, he may have been under the authority of a higher power such as Arthur. In any event, the *Dysgyl* conclusion can be seen as the desolation of a pagan sanctuary in literary and historical terms. Historically, it makes good sense in context with the general British trend toward Christianity in the fifth and sixth centuries. This is an idea to which I shall return.

The pagan Celts were made the focus of attention because of the current political situation or influence from the continent. One man (presumably Arthur) gained a period of ascendancy and used his power to demolish Celtic temples much like Clovis. Alternatively, the continental practice of local extermination conducted by less prominent individuals may have been brought to this island and soon became established here as well. If the anti-pagan campaign was due to Arthur's actions, it may be dated roughly between the last quarter of the fifth and first third of the sixth centuries.[32] If the activities were more vigilante in nature, they might have taken place any time between the turn of the fifth century and about the year 600. Most probably the periods of time in which such activities took place varied would have greatly from area to area. In any event, the practitioners of the Celtic religion were forced to conduct their rituals in secret after that point.

---

[1] See Chapter X and references cited therein. For the most part, these are the only sources that I would consider academically sound. There have been theories connecting the grail ceremony to the Egyptian, Babylonian, and even Cathar religions.

[2] Dr. Bromwich has often proven it is possible, however. I think, though, that her successes prove the rule. It is only when there is a plentiful supply of examples and mutations of a given motif that such instances are possible. Such is usually not the case when dealing with Celtic mythology; the early failed attempts of Professor Loomis warn the wary of the perils in this line of argument.

[3] The process by which this came about is a complex one. All mythic themes and motifs reflect society, but in the case of the British and Irish people those themes survived the common worship of the Celtic gods. These themes then crystallised after the deterioration of the Celtic religions and eventually found their way into Celtic legends and Arthurian literature.

[4] Though of course the nature of the grail itself has been explained adequately and has found a majority following (see Appendix VIII). To my knowledge the generally accepted theorem is that the origins of the grail are to be found in Celtic mythology and lore, and the alterations are to be explained through the ceremonies inherent in the Christian and Jewish religion.

[5] (Ross 1967, maps V and VII). In addition, pagans held prefectures of Italy and Rome into the 380s, and there is strong evidence for a pagan rural revival from the closing decades of the fourth century to the first years of the fifth century in this country (Lewis 1966, 144; Watts 1991, 209). The Germanic tribes of Britain were unanimously pagan during this period. They had, since their arrival, worshipped only Germanic gods and are of no interest in this study because they were not a part of the Roman world.

[6] The traditional date for St. Ninian is 400, but he may have been identical with a contemporary of Gildas named Uinniau. He would therefore be a figure of the mid- and late-sixth century (Dumville 1985,

207-214). This argument is based on textual analysis of Columbanus' *Epistle* and onomastic evidence. Dr. T. Clancy has prepared a stronger argument based on place-name evidence, though I am not aware that it has yet been published. Many Welsh and Cornish *vitae* claim their saints converted both kings and their people.

[7] It is useful here to mention the fact that 300 years later Charlemagne would spend many summers trying to enforce the conversion of the inhabitants of Saxony. The Christian saints of the fifth and sixth centuries have often been perceived as zealots and mass conversionists (e.g. David, Cadoc, Patrick). One is drawn into the possibility that these famed people were still convincing the inhabitants of their own communities about the superiority of the Christian religion. Thus post Roman Europe was very much still a community with a significant pagan population in 500 A.D.

[8] Even this avenue of research is quite daunting. The paucity of remains can be seen in Professor Thomas' attempts at defining the territories that actively practised Christianity through archaeological remains (see below).

[9] It is nearly impossible to dictate how prominent the pagan religion was because, in the words of Professor Charles Thomas: "We realise that it is not possible to map all, nor perhaps any, of the remote rural shrines far away from forts and roads where (say) the native Carvetti chose to commemorate hierophanies of Belatucadros." (1981, 98).

[10] It is, in fact, the only source which I have come across which interprets the archaeological evidence for the purpose of determining the religious preference of the various regions of British-speakers in the fifth and sixth centuries. I rely on it totally for the extent of the religion's diffusion up to the mid-sixth century.

[11] In fifth-century terms, these areas were the *dux brittanorum*'s command and the basic supply route to the North. In sixth-century terms these would have been the states of Reged or the old dux brittanorum command, British Brennych and Deur, and the territories of Glywising, Gwlad, Dubonnia, Durotriges.

[12] Archaeological remains indicate little or no Christian activity in the non Roman areas of Britain prior to 400. During the fifth and into the sixth centuries a steady increase in the number of Christian areas may be seen.

[13] (Lewis 1966, 144; Watts 1991, 209).

[14] It should be noted that the Roman-based religions, such as Mithridaism, did not long survive the Roman rule. Most of the post Roman pagan artefacts have been defined as Celtic in origin, and the rest may have been.

[15] St. Albion and other martyrs are traditionally said to have been persecuted as early as the first century, but their floruits are now usually assumed to have been in the mid-third century. (Thomas 1981, 42-50).

[16] (Williams 1912, 38; Wheeler 1932; Collingwood 1936, 10; Powell 1958, 130; Richmond 1963, 110-3; Alcock 1965, 178-81).

[17] For instance the *Vita Cadoci* claims its hero raised Caw of Prydein from the dead and converted him, and Uinniau and Columba are both said to have converted the kings of their respective regions. There is no need to believe that this means the kings involved were pagans before, but the strength of tradition inherent in the vitae implies that the saints increased the degree of their respective kings' Christianity; possibly from a nominal to a more practical form.

[18] (Rahtz 1982, 188), though Pagans Hill was roofed in the seventh century and the Wroxeter cult site was more probably a temple for a local healing deity.

[19] This is true to the extent that it is unclear which religion had the most followers in the fifth century. Apart for Volocus and possibly one early saint in the fifth century of Northumbria, there are no records of active British religious leaders before the end of the sixth century.

[20] (Adamnan, *The Life of St. Columba, Founder of Hy*, ed. and trans. William Reeves 1988, Chapters I. 37, II. 33, 34, 35). Brude is British Bridei, most probably the son of Maelgwn of Gwynedd.

[21] Margaret Murray in *The Witchcult in Western Europe*, (1921) and *The God of the Witches*, (1931) has been a particular advocate of this theory.

[22] Those dates were 2 February, 1 May, 1 August, and 1 November.

[23] The historical horizon of the *Annales Cambriae* is believed to be 573. (Miller 1975, 96-8; Dumville 1977a, 189-190).

[24] No-one, I think, would claim all potential Dark Age sites have been explored, nor that all variations of all models of artefacts have been found. However, the number of sites that have been excavated is weighty evidence for the overall conclusion that the present findings are a good representation of all the possible findings.

[25] Obviously the religions which the Christians encountered on the continent were different than those to be found in Britain; the Celts were dealing with Celtic cults, while the continent had Germanic, Mithridaic, Roman, and Jewish religions to contend with. However, the basic attitude by the priests can be assumed to have been no different. Any religion but that of Christianity was perceived as the devil's work. The Britons saw the recent mercenary Germans as God's punishment on them, and therefore showed no interest in converting them.

[26] I am aware of no record of a Christian who was punished for overzealous behavior in this period.

[27] The evidence of trade with Gaul is archaeologically based; it is to be found in the London area. The very presence of St. Germanus in Britain also represents a strong connection between Britain and Gaul in the early fifth century, as does the Breton presence. There can be no question that there were ties between Britain and Gaul in the early fifth century.

[28] It has been argued (Dark 1994, 94-5) that the entire revolt against the Roman government in the early fifth century was caused by religious motives and was fought on Martinian terms. If such a theory is not as tenable as others, it does demonstrate the degree of influence the Gallic saint is thought to have had on his contemporaries.

[29] These legends have manifested themselves in *Historia Brittonum, Historia Eccesiasticae, and Historia Regum Britanniae*. I will have much to say regarding this in a forthcoming article or chapter in a book. It seems the Gwrtheyrn generally associated with the mid-fifth century is entirely a product of a Kentish source. Kent's early history is uncertain, especially from a chronological standpoint. Gwrtheyrn's association with Kent's history is most probably a rather late addition to the legend. He may be safely discounted from fifth-century British history. He is therefore best left absent from consideration as a prominent figure in the early history of Britain.

[30] Despite the common perception, there was probably never any concept of a basic cultural or religious difference between the British and the Germans of Britain during this period, nor was there any feeling of invasion. Wars were not fought between Germans and British, but between kingdoms, regardless of ethnic dominance. British leaders like Arthur made their name as much by defeating British armies as German (*The Gododdin of Aneirin*, ed. Koch 1997, xvii-xliii). It is even

possible he never fought a German army. As to religion, Christianity at this period was a nominal religion, to be adopted alongside pagan kingship practices and cultural traditions.

[31] Which, it may be recalled, is one facet of the grail king, who is in turn a representative of the Celtic god Beli. I will have more to say on this subject in the next chapter.

[32] This is the most probable floruit for an historical Arthur.

Chapter XIV: Motifs and Details: Clues of Celtic Origins

The preceding chapters have described the main characters of *Le Conte*. Several have demonstrably well defined roles that are integral and consistent throughout the different redactions of the grail versions. Together they corroborate the theory of a stable prototype and tie together many seemingly detached fragments in the grail legend. The examination has also helped to articulate a plot with a more carefully defined objective. However, there are still elements of the romance that remain unexplained and detached from what is a consistent alignment to either classical or contemporary European literature, or Celtic myth, motifs, and themes. These vestiges are divisible into two groups. The first collection is one whose motifs and materials are congruent with both pre tenth-century British and twelfth-century French culture. Second, the purely historical elements of the poem make up a small, but highly significant portion of the poem. This chapter will survey the former of these two divisions in order to establish Chrétien's specific debt to Celtic sources in *Le Conte du Graal*.[1] In the process, it is hoped that evidence will be presented to exhibit that *Le Conte* contains many motifs and themes whose origins could be from two periods. They could be either of Chrétien's medieval world or Britain from the fifth to the ninth century. The concepts of marriage, hospitality and protection, and the dark-age hall and testing bed are all to be found in the rhymed passages of Chrétien. These are also the most conspicuous and easily definable of several instances where what seems to be contemporary continental Europe may be more safely placed in the and easily definable of several instances where what seems to be contemporary continental Europe may be more safely placed in the context of the ninth or preceding centuries of Britain. A survey of these aspects of the poem will provide a comfortable springboard for the introduction of those that have traditionally been defined as literary motifs, but are historical in nature.

The most obvious clue that something hitherto uncited lies beneath the surface of Chrétien's poem is to be found in the marital rituals in *Le Conte du Graal*.[2] However, the traits of the custom are clearer, and examples of the phenomenon more abundant, in *Le Conte*. In *La Charrette*, Gauvain is given one insinuated partner, and Lancelot several. In the grail poem, Gauvain pursues several women. A divorcee is the cause of his winning the adventure at the Castle of the Maidens (l. 7855). From another woman he receives the kindnesses of a maid in the home of a man sworn to kill him (ll. 5758-98). Perceval, too, spends an innocent evening with the Lady of Belrepaire (*Le Conte*, ll. 2034-51), and later romances give him a relationship with the Grail Maiden as well.[3] *Peredur* ties Perceval to a number of potentially intimate relations with women. Clearly multiple sexual contacts are a standard component of the world Chrétien described.

It can also be gathered that the form of temporary union that is to be found in Chrétien is strictly Celtic. Sexuality has no place in a poem portraying the intimacies of Christianity.[4] Having more than one lover at a time is in violation of the courtly love Chrétien is so careful to articulate in his Marie de Champagne poems.[5] It is known that these were the two conscious driving forces behind his *La Charrette* poem (see Chapter II), yet both are in direct contradiction with the multiple relationships of several characters. Lancelot, Gauvain, and Perceval's relationships with women indicate a form of Celtic temporary marriage that I outlined in Chapter V.

The parallels exhibited in this custom are intriguing, but the consistency between sub-Roman architecture and Chrétien's poetry provides a more striking correlation. As much as in *Le Chevalier de la Charrette*, the Grail Castle allows the careful reader some connections to the standard sixth-century hall that is described in the literature and archaeology of the British people of the sub-Roman period. Some scholars have held that the famed building is an underworld structure of Celtic myth (Nutt 1888, 191), but this cannot be. The underworld castle has a habit of spinning very rapidly, maintains a permanent

Motifs and Details: Clues of Celtic Origins 179

spring, and contains glass walls and walking dead people. Moreover, the inhabitants partake of incessant drinking. Chrétien's castle has none of these qualities. Instead, the structure that Chrétien outlines is another clue that the reader is getting a view of ancient Britain in Chrétien's pages. Chrétien describes it as:

An la sale qui fu quarree
Et autant longue come lee.
En mi la sale, sor un lit,
Un bel prodome seoir vit. (ll. 3049-52).

into the great hall, which was square in shape, as long as it was wide. In the middle of the hall he [Perceval] saw a handsome nobleman seated on a bed. (trans. Owen 1989, 415).

Later one finds the grail-king lying on one elbow:

De sesche busche cler ardant,
Et fu antre quatre colomes.
Bien poïst an quatre cenz homes
Asseoir anviron le feu,
S'aüst chascuns aeisié leu. (ll. 3060-4).

of dry logs, flaming bright between four columns. Four hundred men could easily sit around that fire, and each would have a comfortable spot. (trans. Owen 1989, 415).

This closely matches the description of the hall Heorot from *Hrolf Kraki's Saga* and the Palace of Connaught in Irish myth. In the Irish myth there is a "central fireplace, royal couch before it; four pillars of brass; and space for a large company" (Loomis 1949, 375). In contrast, there are no Celtic underworld structures of comparative frame and design.

There are further indications of antiquity in the grail castle's description. Certain innuendoes which Chrétien lets slip combine to form a consistent pattern alternative to a twelfth-century hall. As the Grail King reposes in the hall following the evening meal, he tells Perceval:

Amis,
Tant est del colchier mes anuit.
Je m'an irai, ne vos enuit,

Leanz an mes chanbres gesir;
Et quant vos vandra a pleisir,
Vos colcherez ça dehors.
Je n'ai nu pooir de mon cors,
Si covandra que l'an m'an port. (ll. 3302-9)

My good friend, it's time to retire for the night. If you don't mind, I shall go to bed into my apartment in there; and when you please you can do so outside them. I have no strength in my limbs and so shall have to be carried. (trans. Owen 1989, 418).

Chrétien is telling his reader that the grail king is to sleep in small rooms next to the hall. Perceval is to lie outside the entrance of the king's room to sleep. This suggests a form of architecture that is well described in *Hrolf Kraki's Saga* for the Danish royal hall of the Danes. It is a building with one long narrow banquet hall and a hidden sleeping chamber for the chief at one end. Archaeologists have found several examples of this type of dwelling in sub-Roman hill-forts, most conspicuously presented at Castle Dore and Yeavering.[6]

This hall was a product of the Irish, British, and Germanic heroic ages; it did not survive these heroic ages by more than a couple hundred years. The feudalisation of much of Europe, a change in the manner of entertainment, and the gradual improvements in the military and architectural sciences antiquated such structures long before the twelfth century. By Chrétien's time the dinner hall was a small part of a larger, more defensive structure.

Alternatively, the hall which Chrétien repeatedly focuses on may be only the main part of a building whose other features are not useful for his plot and therefore are not included. It could be argued that the castle that Chrétien describes could be one of a lesser nobleman in contemporary society. In the poems' halls there are features that relate more to Chrétien's period, such as the drawbridge that is raised on Perceval's departure. However, these appear to be no more than plot devices. The drawbridge is an addition by Chrétien to explain why Perceval does not re enter the grail castle, finish his test, and conclude the story. The comparisons of the Chrétien halls to the sub-Roman period are too consistent; one cannot be certain that the halls he describes are not from fifth century Britain.

There is one other scene that has a similarity to an incident in *La Charrette*, the perilous bed.[7] After entering Galloway and gaining entrance to Castle Marvelous, Gauvain is warned not to sit on a particular bed inside the castle walls. In typical Arthurian fashion, Gauvain finds the bed, sits, then lies on it. There follows a brief series of tests. First, the bed-cords give out a shrill noise and bells ring. Then, the entire hall gives out a noise and the windows fly open. Bolts and arrows follow, and many of them pierce Gauvain. The ordeal concludes with the attack of a lion, and a victory over the animal by the hero (ll. 7776-828).

No particular aspect of Gauvain's trial is a direct parallel to Lancelot's Cart Castle testing bed, and much of it is most probably invention. However, the theme, that of a bed trial, is very similar and the bed of both *Le Conte* and *La Charrette* quite possibly derive from a British inspiration. They are otherwise linked to the kingship ritual as well. The *La Charrette* scene includes only a flaming pendant attached to a lance. The *Le Conte* scene, on the other hand, does not have the pendant, but otherwise contains much more detail, and allows for slightly greater comparison to Celtic traditions and the inaugural ceremony in particular. A short description should highlight this point.

Gauvain's bed test in the Marvelous Castle is preceded by a strange noise that seems to have a direct correlation with the kingship ceremony as is currently understood by Celtic scholars. A quote from Chrétien will demonstrate the point: "Et les cor des gietent un bret, et totes quanpanes sonent, si que tot les palés estonent;" (ll. 7780-2) "the bed-cords give out a screech and all the bells ring, making the whole hall resound" (trans. Owen 1989, 477). This is the only warning the castle's inhabitants receive that Gauvain has survived the ordeal. It is effectively a vocalization of his triumph. When it is known that Gauvain has successfully braved the Marvelous Bed, he is acclaimed lord of the castle.

Such a connection -- testing feature, sovereignty, and a well-timed scream -- seems reminiscent of the mysteries surrounding *Lia Fail* (Byrne 1973, 27, 63-4). All these aspects were a part of the coronation ceremony for the rightful kings of Ireland and Scotland. It is also probable they were a part of sub-Roman British culture. At such a time of desperation one might well imagine that the British resorted to their ancient traditions in order to restore a sense of stability to society. Such customs were no doubt employed to verify the royal claims of noblemen after the long period when such offices had been vacant.

However, neither *Le Conte* nor *La Charrette* follow the passage to the conclusion of accession to a throne or precedence over a tribe. This obstacle is not a serious one, however, when it is remembered that

Chrétien probably did not understand the bed's intended function because he was not intimately familiar with British culture or pan Celtic motifs.[8]

There is one other serious problem with this theory, but it too can be easily explained. Lancelot's and Gauvain's beds are so clearly different that one would normally be wise to have some misgivings about the connection. However, both poems may well derive ultimately from the fifth or sixth century. An understanding of heroic age literature explains any objections one may have.

The evolution of heroic age literature eventually produces a clash between historical and pseudo-historical truths and myth. As the material of an heroic age develops and later bards begin to form it into epic, it is necessary to rationalize the legendary material into something that is chronologically simpler. This is often done by putting many of the culture's heroes into one or two generations.[9] This includes the process of drawing certain lesser heroes and kings into the orbit of one or more of the most revered kings of the culture. These lesser figures in time are demoted to the status of important warriors within the king's *teulu*.[10] So that this may occur, some of the adventures of each hero are adjusted to detract from any overtly royal elements in the tales. It is these stories that are retained, while those which do not adapt become extinct.

If this theory is the correct one, Gauvain and Lancelot could, at one point, have been considered sovereign characters and the two bed scenes' inauguration features. The process of these characters being drawn to Arthur's cycle would most likely have taken away any clear indication of their functions as kings. Despite the process, however, some latent hints would remain, such as the strange lance in *Le Chevalier*'s bed testing, the stone of the comb scene, and the weird noise in *Le Conte* bed test. In addition, the process of being drawn into a cycle is not a predictable one, or even one that occurs at a set pace. Therefore it should not surprise one that the end product of what is largely the same ceremony could be expected to vary widely. Thus, similar inaugurations for both Lancelot and Gauvain could have been transformed to bravery tests before Chrétien came to possess them, with only vague clues to point out their common origins. Chrétien could not have known what these unusual details meant, and might have kept them in his stories as curiosities.

On the other hand, it is possible that Chrétien knew or had heard an interpretation where either Lancelot or Gauvain, or both, assumed a

Motifs and Details: Clues of Celtic Origins   183

kingship responsibility after their test. If Chrétien had been aware that the episodes were to conclude with the accession of a new ruler he would have been forced to alter the story. Lancelot still had to be available to rescue the queen, and Gauvain was the intended point of reference for the development of the hero -- Perceval. The only acceptable role for Gauvain to play was one in which he was constantly confirmed in his bravery, marital suitability, and overall secular attractiveness. A kingship rite that focused attention on Lancelot and Gauvain and further away from Guinièvre and Perceval (respectively), would not have forwarded the plot as Marie or Philip desired it and therefore was opposed to Chrétien's intentions. On the other hand, neither Lancelot nor Gauvain could be eliminated. Lancelot was the hero, and it is safe to assume that much of Chrétien's audience desired to see Gauvain proving his superiority as a knight in *Le Conte*. So, the episodes' essentials were allowed to remain and the connotations of sovereignty were eliminated as wholly as possible.[11]

The preceding comparisons between elements of the poem and aspects of the post Roman British culture are useful for three reasons. First, they verify the poem's authenticity as a product of British source material. Second, they allow for an alternative and often better explanation of some scenes *Le Conte*. Finally, *Le Conte* contains much material that is not to be found in Chrétien's earlier works and which also resembles the Celtic stock of oral techniques and Celtic culture. Perceval's first meeting with Arthur and his troupe is a very intriguing scene from the point of view of a Celtic scholar. It makes use of the sovereignty theme with which the British were so entranced. Perceval arrives at the outskirts of Arthur's court in the last moments of an obviously dramatic scene. The Red Knight tells Perceval his story.

...Or va donc tost et si revien,
Et tant diras au malvés roi:
Se ik ne vialt tenir de moi
Sa terre, que il la me rande,
Ou il anvoit qui la desfande
Vers moi qui di que ele est moie.
Et a ces ansaignes t'an croie
Que devant lui pris orandroit
Atot le vin dont il bevoit
Ceste cope que je ci port. (*Le Conte*, ll. 868-77).

Go there quickly now, and come back again. And you can tell this good-for-nothing king [Arthur] that, if he's not willing to hold his land from me, then he must give it up to me or else send someone to defend it against me, for I declare that it's mine. Here to convince you is the evidence; for just now I seized under his very eyes the cup I'm carrying along with the wine he was drinking. (*Le Conte*, trans. Owen 1989, 386).

As the Red Knight continues, one learns that he has approached the king and taken his cup, or goblet, and now bears it as a sign of the king's dishonor (see Appendix X). In any ancient society, the theft of a royal article would be an act of unusual courage and audacity, but the Red Knight seems to have gone unpunished by Arthur's men. In fact, the Red Knight considers his political and military stature enhanced thereby, and actively seeks to fight Arthur or a champion for the sovereignty of the kingdom. He sees the cup theft as a direct challenge to Arthur and, by the tone of the court as Perceval enters it, so do the people of Arthur's retinue. The cup may easily be seen as a symbol of the kingship. Such an observation has an analogue in Irish myth.

The vessel that has a direct link to the right to rule is to be found in several analogues, most well known of which is the myth *Ecstasy of the Phantom* (O'Rahilly 1946b, 7-28). Here a legendary king of Ireland and his descendants are confirmed in the sovereignty of Ireland. According to the myth, a woman called Érin, said to be Lug's wife, repeatedly gives Conn a goblet filled with wine as Lug recites Conn's sovereign descendants. When this ritual is finished, both the woman and Lug vanish. They leave behind the cup as proof of Conn's divine selection to rule.

This version is believed to be the most fully preserved rendition of the sovereignty ritual, but there are hundreds of variants. In some versions the cup-bearer is mated to a new king. In others she is an ugly crone and regains her full beauty only after a sexual union with the new king (below). She is Sovereignty; her specific name is the name of whichever country she happens to represent in a particular region. Cumulatively, this cup-maid is the personification of the agricultural abilities of the country. Her generic name is *medb*, which translates to "cup-giver" (Mac Cana 1955, 78).

Therefore, it may be assumed that the cup that the Red Knight takes from Arthur seems to signify sovereignty in *Le Conte*, much as it does in the various other redactions of the grail story. In all grail romances the Celtic ceremony of inauguration is implied in Arthur's possession of an honour-retaining cup.[12]

From an historical standpoint, the retention of the religious aspects of the kingship in the sixth century appears reasonable. The Romans certainly adapted much Celtic ideals of sovereignty during their centuries of domination and integrated many customs into their rule of Britain; such was Roman custom. It seems probable that many of the rituals surrounding the inauguration of a king would be preserved and respected by them and their British citizens. This is for two reasons. First, the men who came to assert political authority in the fifth century can be assumed to have used every tradition in their culture and that of the Romans for the establishment of their legitimacy (above). Second, the British were not yet fully Christian in this period (see Chapter XIII), and Christianity was for many centuries after its advent flexible towards the sacral role of kingship. This policy allowed the kingship to continue its function as the divine choice of authority for the people (Chaney 1970, 247-259).

A second example of the kingship cup can be seen in Perceval's question, "For whom is the grail?" (see Appendix IV), which sounds much like the rationalization, by a later continental poet, of the Sovereignty of Ireland (Érin)'s strange query in *Ecstasy of the Phantom* "To whom shall this cup be given?" Perceval does go through the ritual, as does Conn and, like Conn, will presumably attain a kingship as a result.[13]

There is one additional Celtic element in the grail legend that is not in the Red Knight scene of *Le Conte du Graal*. Both *Peredur* and *Perlesvaus* as well as *Ecstasy of the Phantom* inform the reader that the maiden of the question ceremony can be either ugly or beautiful, depending on the state of the nation she represents. This feature may also be uniquely traced to a pan Celtic source.

The maiden who seems to possess a dual nature and has some association with the concept of kingship appears in *The Adventures of the Sons of Eochaid Mugmedón Echhtra mac n-Echnach* and *Lugaid Láigde* with both features.[14] In addition, she also appears in many other Irish tales with one or other of the two qualities.[15] She is also known in Britain under various guises. *The Weddynge of Sir Gawen and Dame Ragnell*, *The Wife of Bath's Tale* in Chaucer's *Canterbury Tales*, and *The Tale of Florent* all contain a woman with a revolting figure who, when married to the man of her choice, becomes beautiful (see Appendix VI). The Breton lais have several maidens associated with kingship. The theme is therefore confined to territories that that were predominantly Celtic as late as 400. Most likely, this theme derives from a Celtic origin.

The new king's symbolic marriage to the land in which he is to rule is evident, but only from the scraps that may be discovered in Irish law and myth. The ritual of inauguration apparently included a feast called *Banais rígi*, in which the initiate was ceremonially wedded to the country over which he was assuming authority. *The Annals of Connacht* and *The Annals of Loch Cé* give the bald association between new king and the land personified in witnessing the coronation of Feidhlim Ó Conchobhair: "ar feis d'Fedlimid ... re cóiced Connacht;" "Feidhlim's espousal to the province of Connacht." [16] In later poetry, Ireland was often described as the wife of various prominent kings of the past (O' Rahilly 1946b, 19). Such a connection between a country and person is not, to be sure, uniquely Celtic. However, the participation of a maiden with transformation characteristics in a kingship ceremony surely is. In literature, it is only to be found in the various grail romances.[17]

The Sovereignty element of *Le Conte* is so well hidden because of Chrétien. The poet clouds the kingship ethos with romance and the Christian sense of his patrons. Chrétien makes Perceval first fail like his patron and in emulation of the stereotypical Christian convert. Perceval is only allowed to become king after proving his purity by cleansing himself in true Christian fashion; this is a plot device by Chrétien. Subsequent continental romancers blindly followed this element of the grail legend. No hint of an initially unsuccessful ceremony is to be found anywhere in the purest form of the tale, *Peredur*, nor in its analogous Welsh material. Here the hero is simply witness to a strange ritual that seems to have pagan connotations.

After speaking with Perceval and boasting of his laudable theft, the Red Knight sets "la cope d'or;" "golden cup" on "un perron de roche bise;" "a slab of dark grey stone" (l. 1059). The rock sounds strangely familiar in color, anonymity, and puzzling significance. One might not be too far off the mark in seeing it as a parallel to the symbol or kingship stone encountered in *Le Chevalier de la Charrette*. Like the goblet of Arthur's dishonor, it is also a symbol of kingship, and here it is associated directly with another important object of the kingship. Once Perceval has killed the challenger and Arthur's validity has been restored, however, it disappears from the rest of the story. Chrétien has again retained a vestige of something he did not understand. The Red

Knight was directly challenging Arthur's kingship in a subtle manner that would have been unfamiliar to Chrétien.

Another link to the Celtic way of life can be seen in Cei, whose character is heroic. However, to do so one must cleanse his character of Chrétien's motives and the misunderstandings of progressive generations of storytellers to apprehend better Cei's office and function at Arthur's court. There are some assurances this process of deconstruction is the path to be taken. Chrétien himself says something complimentary about the most troublesome knight of Arthur's court: "N'ot plus bel chevalier el mont;" (l. 2794) "There was no more handsome knight in the world" (trans. Owen 1989, 411).

The traditional role of Cei in the conventional Arthurian romance is a very clearly defined one that broadens slightly over the intervening centuries between Chrétien's poems and the prose of Sir Thomas Malory.[18] He is a merciless wit to newcomers. Eschenbach put it best:

Ich gihe von im der mære,
er was ein merkære.
er tet vil rûhes willen schîn
ze scherme dem hêrren sîn:
partierre und valsche diet,
von den werden er die schiet:
er was ir fuore ein strenger hagel,
noch scherpfer dan der bîn ir zagel. (*Parzival* Book VI. 297).

I own that Keie was a critical observer. In order to protect his lord he displayed much asperity, sorting out imposters and dishonest folk from the honest -- he came down on their behaviour like a hailstorm, with a sting sharper than a bee's. (*Parzival*, ed. and trans. Hatto 1980, 155).

If one may, for a moment, forget the normal supplementary quality of Cei's constant verbal outbreaks, one might see an alternative primary role for the hero. This other role would align better with the character of *Pa gur?*, *Culhwch ac Olwen*, and *Ymddiddan Gwenhwyfar ac Arthur*. He was Arthur's porter, the man at the gate to the hall whose duty it was to screen unworthies from the king's presence. This obligation often included being critical of newcomer warriors and forcing them to prove themselves mentally or through their physical prowess before entrance to the hall was allowed. Such is the situation Arthur finds himself in with the porter Glewlwyd in *Pa gur?*, as Melwas finds himself with Cai in *Ymddiddan*.[19]

To the uninitiated, the passages contained in these works seem uncouth in the extreme, but the participants, indeed the original audiences, would have perceived Cai's actions as no more than fulfilled duties. It is believed Cai's obligations to his lord were misunderstood against the changing world of the twelfth century. Dr. Gowans has noted two of Cei's qualities and two verbal exchanges in the remaining literature where Cei's nature would be questionable to a twelfth-century Frenchman. The characteristics would be perfectly discernible, however, to one who lived in an Insular or Breton community. These four are Cei's boastful nature in the early Welsh tales, his magical qualities, his handling of the knowledge that an unknown is at the hall's gate, and his great offense at the englyn Arthur gives him upon delivering Dillus' beard in *Culhwch ac Olwen*.[20] A brief summary of all four will elucidate Cei's responses and the mental and cultural disposition behind them.

Cei's brazen character in *Pa gur?* is strictly of the heroic age in nature. Arthur boasts that Cei entreated his enemies as he killed them (trans. Roberts 1992, ll. 31 and 35). This is generally agreed to have been an accepted part of heroic age society. As demonstrated in Chapter V, the boast and personal pride were necessary ingredients in the disposition of the heroic age hero.

Cei's magical qualities also link him to heroic age society. In *Culhwch ac Olwen* the reader learns that Cei's father gave him the peculiarities of always having cold hands, of bearing fire and water better than anyone, of being peerless as a servant and officer, and of being able to hide any burden that he happened to be carrying. Later the story introduces further abilities: To be nine days and nights without water, to be of great height when he chose, to kill an opponent with every landed blow, his hands to be a source of great heat when needed. *Pa gur?* adds that he can drink enough from a buffalo horn for four men (trans. Roberts 1992, ll. 70-1).

Most of the above listed attributes have clear analogues in the Celtic spectrum of early literature. The cold hands demonstrate a nervelessness that is an integral component to any hero's repertoire. Many Irish heroes are said to have had heated hands.[21] Cei's ability to withstand cold and heat is one he shares with the Cormac of Irish myth. His greatness as a servant or officer is something that bears similarity to Cú Chulainn and other Ulster heroes. The statement that no man wounded from his sword will live resembles similar statements regarding Fionn and Cú Chulainn.

In *Pa gur?*, the reader also learns that Cei is associated with both *Y Hen Ogled* and northern Wales. This duality of location is consistent with Welsh heroic age figures such as Urien Reged, Llywarch Hen, and possibly Arthur himself.[22] This places Cei in the deepest folds of Arthurian literature, to a period prior to the mid-seventh century.

The third instance where Cei's actions would be readily misinterpreted is to be found in *Culhwch ac Olwen*. Culhwch approaches the gate of Arthur's hall and is advised the evening meal has begun. He is also told the law of the court is that no one may enter the hall after the meal is in progress but prince or craftsman. He does not say he is either but insists nevertheless on his entrance. Glewlwyd proceeds to tell Arthur of a stranger at the entrance who seems of beautiful stature. Cei reminds his lord of the hall's custom and with it the need to keep one's honor. Arthur, however, overrides him. He decides that the renown of being generous is the greater principle to keep. Cei is not in this instance rude. He is instead protecting his king's honor and person. Later, when Culhwch announces his request, Cei is the first to offer his aid (ll. 381-3).

The fourth instance where Cei's behavior seems antisocial takes place following the episode where Cei has tricked the giant Dillus son of Eurei, shaved his beard, and killed him. Arthur greets him with verse. "Kynllyuan a oruc Kei/ O uaryf Dillus uab Eurei/ Pei iach dy angheu uydei;" (*Culhwch ac Olwen*, ll. 978-80). "Cei made a leash from Dillus' beard, son of Eurei. Were he alive, thy death he'd be" (*Mabinogion*, trans. Jones and Jones 1974, 128). In today's society, such a welcome might be pardonable; one wonders why Cei is so upset. However, to quote Dr. Gowans:

Something which is conveyed very strongly in the stories of the Irish heroes is a horror of being satirised. Cú Chulainn is prepared to expend the last of his weapons to prevent it, and the power of the spoken word to cause more than mental harm is strongly attested in Medieval Wales, as well as an influential factor in the beliefs and folklore of cultures far beyond in the beliefs and folklore of cultures far beyond Celtic lands. The suggestion that Cei might have met his match would alone cause great offence, but in addition, the border between satire and what would now be seen as prophecy or curse is an indistinct one. In any society such a casual and flippant reference to the possibility of a leading warrior's death (especially a reference in verse) would be very foolish, and put Cei to shame in a far more subtle and dangerous way than the mid-river transformation of a herd of cattle. (1988, 22).

Cei was not a feeble wit to the Welsh. He was instead a character whose personality has been misunderstood over the centuries because he responds to situations in a manner consistent with heroic age behavior and is often described in terms that are heroic age in character. In the courtly society of twelfth-century Europe, such characteristics must have seemed awkward and undesirable, and the portrayal of Cei suffered accordingly with Chrétien and those who followed him. The great champion was immediately made a foil to Chrétien's heroes and a parody of his Welsh predecessor.[23]

Structures and kingship paraphernalia aside, the romance's basic composition carries some fundamental similarities to the post Roman period. For one, there is a very specific method and reason why Arthur's recruits are often unrelated and always unknown in Chrétien's world. The phenomenon has little to do with the society of medieval France in general, or Philip in particular. Generations of knights were commonly a part of the same household in twelfth-century Europe; men would have known each other and other knights throughout a large breadth of territories. However, such was not the case in heroic age society, which has been seen as a culture that reorders civilization away from the traditional blood-ties and orients a man's sympathies toward a *teulu*. H.M. Chadwick observed that it was: "At one time a regular custom for young princes to set out from their homes, on reaching manhood, and to seek the court of some foreign king with a view to marrying his daughter and thereby acquiring a share in the sovereignty" (1912, 351). This form of society was a highly mobile one.

There would have been other reasons why young men would be unrecognized by a *teulu* such as Arthur's. A blood feud or *ronin* (to transpose a Japanese term) status would bring lesser men into a household from afar.[24] A local peasant of unusual size might be enlisted and retained. Professor Chadwick explained it succinctly: "Most frequently perhaps the men who sought service abroad were those who had either lost their lords or had to leave their homes through vendetta" (1912, 350). If Arthur was as famed a warrior in his time as our current records indicate, he would have been the most attractive lord in Britain around 500. Therefore, the number of foreigners who were his men would have been higher than the norm.

It should also be self-apparent that any new member of Arthur's court is not allowed much respect in either romance or legend, with the notable exception of Arthur's nephew, Culhwch.[25] This, too, was a part of the heroic age and Celtic tradition. A novitiate served a sort of probation during which he was not only expected to learn to fight and survive the battlefield, but to prove his loyalty to his new lord. The Irish called the youthful man's status *fer midboth*. This term was applied to males of a royal household aged fourteen to twenty. It was intended legally for an unproved boy of man's strength. Chadwick believes that a king in heroic age society was generally expected to give land to the young of his *teulu* once they reached the age of twenty-four or twenty-five. That is, the king granted land after they had legally reached manhood status and proven themselves (1912, 349). In Irish law a person not attached to the royal household attained full adult status only after he had inherited his father's lands.[26]

The heroic age customs and legal texts help explain much of Arthurian society. They explain why the knights Gauvain, Lancelot, and Perceval are landless and wandering men yet are attached to Arthur's household; they are youths attempting to prove themselves.[27] They also explain why accomplished and older men such as Gornemanz of Gohort acknowledge they are Arthur's men and act accordingly, yet have land of their own.

On the other hand, one might side with Dr. Köhler in seeing the Arthurian knights in Chrétien's poems as reaffirming the now-crumbling medieval institutions of Feudalism and courtlife by envisioning a compromise between what had been and what was happening (1956, 5-36). In this, both king and knight had additional responsibilities. The king must preserve the customs of the past as best he could and, naturally, try to protect those who had most loyally served him. It was a knight's duty to retain that loyalty. However, the author sees two problems with this theory. First, if Chrétien has created this aspect of his own world in his poems, why would the Welsh equivalents have them as well? The only reasonable way would be to assume that the Welsh romances came later, and as a result of, Chrétien. This is a leap I think many scholars would like to avoid.

Second, I have read nowhere of Marie de Champagne's interest in Feudalism, or the kingship. In fact, as has been seen in the chapters above, Marie found herself in a male-dominated world and despised it. All the romances which she commissioned to the Troyes poet deal with romance, and in all the woman plays a key role. In these, Arthur is portrayed as a weak man. This is clear enough a picture to weaken Dr. Köhler's argument.

The careful reader can see other comparisons between Chrétien and the British world. Among them is the observation that Arthur's heroes are continually sending men of worth to their king to become part of his household. It is a habit consistent with captains in the sub-Roman world and inharmonious with that of twelfth-century culture. Hostage-giving was a sort of promise of good behavior in ancient society; the Romans were most successful with this form of surety. Emperors often educated the sons of important allied or subservient chiefs inside the walls of Rome, allowing them to attain a high status in the Roman armies. The presence of the chieftains' children was designed to act as a deterrent against attacking Italy. The Romans hoped that a young man educated in their culture would seek to preserve it once he had inherited a barbarian throne. Such hopes were not in vain. Many Germanic kings sought titles of Imperial authority and readily protected the Roman way of life from less respectful peoples. In this regard the system prospered and similar measures were repeated by the kings of post Roman western European nations.

Perceval appears to be following this Roman custom of hostages as well, though here again Chrétien has apparently modified the content to fit into his needs. Chrétien had his own agenda to follow; he needed to perpetuate the fantasy that he had created in his earlier romances. Consequently, hostages of a newly conquered region became instead the victims of innocent jousts. However, he retained a hint of what may have been the original. Arthur always accepts the captured men as permanent members of his *teulu*, just as the Romans and the Germanic heroic age tribes, and probably as Celtic heroic age nations did.[28] In contrast, medieval society saw hostages as the personal defeat of a warrior in battle, a joust or duel. A medieval hostage's person was no more than a temporary surety for money or a promised act. He generally had no hope or desire of joining his captor's entourage in any other capacity.

This aspect of the Arthurian world has not been noted previously because of the nature of *Le Chevalier de la Charrette*'s plot. In *La Charrette*, the hero is on a mission with a single purpose, to regain the queen. It is a detailed story of one week that chronicles all Lancelot's contacts and relationships. During this journey, Lancelot goes through mainly friendly territory and therefore finds few hostile warriors to send to Arthur until he comes to Gorre. His only enemy there is Meleagant, whom he kills. In contrast, *Le Conte* allows one to witness Perceval's life for several years. An Engygeron is defeated by Perceval and sent to Arthur where he is kept "et s'estoit a cot retenuz Et de mesniee et de conseil;" (l. 2761) as a member of the household and as counsellor" (trans. Owens 1989, 413). His lord Clamadeu is also sent (l. 2780), and eventually marries a lady of the court. The reader is told Peredur sent many others to Arthur, but nothing is said of their fate there. Roland does not send Charlemagne prisoners in the medieval tales, and Cú Chulainn makes it a point to bring trophies, not people back to Conchobar's hall. The act has no literary precedent to my knowledge. It was a product of Roman culture and is uncritically reiterated by Chrétien. It may be assumed the hostages of *Le Conte* represent political conquests.[29]

Another example of Chrétien's reluctance to deal with war can be found in the "tournament" and "joust". It is the backdrop of one scene each in both *Le Chevalier* and *Le Conte*. One may safely assume that the knightly exercise that Chrétien describes did not take place in sixth-century Britain,[30] indicating Chrétien is modernizing this element of the tale. This transition is almost complete in *Le Conte*, where the narrator explains "Qui gaaing i fait, si l'an porte/La ou mialz le cuide avoir sauf;" (*Le Conte*, ll. 5078-9) "Those who win booty carry it off to where they think it will be safest" (trans. Owen 1989, 442).

Chrétien does not say the knights who participate win *rançon* or *chevals*, ransom or horses. In a tournament of the twelfth century, both would have been indications that one party was having a good tournament and both would be symbols of honor and valor. These items would be returned to their owner in the evening, or at the end of the tournament, in return for the proper amount of currency. No person of twelfth-century Europe would disguise these things. Such objects were the very measure of knightly prowess. However, in place of this Chrétien implies there is plunder, or at least more to be gained than prestige. The word he writes is *gaaing*, as Owen translates it "booty", which points to a battle.[31] He possibly adapted the original description of a hotly contested battle to his needs. In contrast to the internecine, bitter, and bloody struggles of post Roman Britain, he made them more friendly in nature by changing battle to tournament.

He would have had several reasons for doing so. A pseudo-historical battle in which literary characters traditionally associated with Arthur's court were opposed to and often fought against each other would simply be unpalatable to an audience that accounted Arthur the most chivalrous king of the medieval world. All that which could be known of perfect knighthood was to be found in books like *Historia Regum Britanniae* and these works had no factionalism. The tournament allowed Chrétien both a contest between two Arthurian heroes and the opportunity to praise the protagonist's martial virtues. It allowed him to pit one Arthurian knight against each other on terms his audience could both understand and respect. It was the perfect solution. In the words of Dr. Ker:

> This collision of blind forces, this tournament at random, takes the place, in the French romances, of the older form of combat. In the older kind the parties have always good reasons of their own for fighting; they do not go into it with the same sort of readiness as the wandering champions of romance. (Ker 1896, 212).

and also

> The change of temper and fashion represented by the appearance and the vogue of the medieval French romances is a change involving the whole world, and going far beyond the compass of literature and literary history. It meant the final surrender of the old ideas, independent of Christendom, which had been enough for the Germanic nations in their earlier days; it was the close of their heroic age. (Ker 1896, 6).

Other instances in which this conversion has been partially made are also evident. In *Peredur*: "of Efrawc and his first six sons it is said that they followed the tournaments, battles, and wars", "ac nyt oed oet ydaw gyrchu brwydyr;"[32] "And as often befalls him who follows the wars, he was slain, both he and his six sons".[33]

Chrétien unknowingly describes several Celtic customs, but he also gives one interesting physical picture of a character, a squire. Chrétien's words will best serve to show his Celtic affinities. "Ses chevox or merlez et ros, Roides et contremont dreciez Come pors qui est hericiez;" (*Le Conte*, ll. 6946-8) "He had tousled red hair that stood stiffly on end like an angry porcupine's" (*Le Conte*, trans. Owens 1989, 466).

Red hair has never been confined to Britain, though many red-haired people do come from that region. However the quality of this man's locks, that of standing "stiffly" on end, is most unusual. To my knowledge, the bristling hair relates only to the Celts, who traditionally covered their hair with lye before battle so that they would appear more fearsome to their foe. Such a tactic is congruent with both pre and post Roman Britain, but not in medieval France.[34] In fact, it was apparently a little revolting to Chrétien's audience, and he understood and made use of that. Chrétien uses this description to generate hostility to the character, who thereafter performs a dubious role in the plot.

In addition, there is one social aspect of the Arthurian world which has been conventionally associated with twelfth-century invention. However, one can easily see a potential British original, or more accurately a British inspiration through the *troubadours*. Such is the case with the adventure quests in Chrétien's romances.

Both Ernest Renan and Proinsias Mac Cana have noted that the adventure quest is an ancient, pre Celtic topos (Mac Cana 1992, 122). One may find it in the voyages of the Celtic saints, the folk-tales regarding Fionn MacCueil, and the Breton lais. Their first instance in Arthuriana is to be found in the ancient and pre Galfridic poems *Preiddeu Annwn* and *Pa gur?*, not the poems of Marie de France and Chrétien de Troyes.[35]

The vague topography and otherworldliness that characterizes *Arthuriana* are also not French per se. It is found in the Fionn and occasionally the Ulster cycle (Mac Cana 1992, 120-2). If the general thinking in modern Irish scholarship is accurate, most of Ireland's mythic and legendary characters were set to historic dates and given a rough chronology many centuries after their legends were established.[36] This suggests a great deal of Irish lore also had an obscure quality to it at an early stage of development and that it began with the same qualities that distinguish Arthurian literature.

This concludes my survey of Celtic motifs in *Le Conte du Graal* that also have counterparts in the twelfth century. It has been seen that *Le Conte du Graal* contains many elements that have been borrowed from the pan Celtic pool of motifs either directly or through the *troubadours* and *trouvères*. It should be restated that this should in no way limit one's estimation of Chrétien's ability. On the contrary, artists of the Middle Ages were judged on their ability to recraft the same stories. The barrage of sources and the obvious talent Chrétien has used in disguising them attest to his ability within the constraints of his period. He did not recreate the Matter of Britain in the image of Geoffrey of Monmouth, but instead took the material he had access to and successfully recompiled it into a beautiful romance. What more could Chrétien have desired than entertainment and the lucidity of a conglomerate romance poem consisting of such diverse elements as those found in the British heroic age and twelfth-century France?

In seeing the debt to both Celtic and continental sources in this chapter, however, one must be aware that not one of the above subjects are definitely Celtic. These items are even less likely to have been created from situations in the ninth century or earlier. On the other hand, all the components surveyed here could have been Celtic and pre-tenth century just as easily as they could be twelfth-century French. In addition, certain features generally favor the Celtic argument and the pre tenth-century dating. An extension of these observations will be forthcoming.

---

[1] This has been done in Chapter X, but only in that the source for his plot was Celtic. I hope to demonstrate here both that this source was probably written, and the possibility that Chrétien's source has some historical value.

[2] The origins and Celticity of the rituals were established and are more lucidly demonstrated in the chapters of this book pertaining to *Le Chevalier de La Charrette*.

[3] The nature of his relationship with this lady and the fact that he has a relationship only with this lady in the Chrétien poem should not lead one astray. It should be remembered that Philip of Flanders wanted the portrayal of a saintly figure, not a womanizer. Any extra-marital relationships would have been expressly forbidden Chrétien's poem and therefore Perceval cannot be expected to have more than one romantic interest in *Le Conte*.

[4] This is not necessarily the case with *La Charrette*, but is most definitely with *Le Conte*.

[5] These are *Erec*, *Cligès*, *Le Chevalier au Lion*, and *Le Chevalier de La Charrette*, and possibly a Tristan romance.

[6] (Radford 1951; Colvin 1963, 2-4), summarized in Alcock (1995, 31).

[7] Loomis (1949, 205-6), believed the bed scene was originally like that in *The Vulgate Version of the Arthurian Romances*. However, this source is not trustworthy. The *Vulgate* was produced between 1215 and 1230, well into the age of grail story writing. It is also known the *Vulgate* redaction is an untrustworthy tale. See Chapter XI.

[8] I cannot accept Professor Loomis' statement, derived from the later and less authentic *L'Atre Perilloux*, that Chrétien in both cases inverted the outcome and the hero's entrance to the castle. Such handling of sources was not Chrétien's nature.

[9] A good example of this is the Greek myths, where there are two great generations of heroes. The first includes Heracles, the Argonauts, and the Epigoni, while the second make up the Greek army at Troy and the early part of the Oedipus cycle. Before Heracles, heroes such as Cadmus and Perseus behave as culture heroes who rely on divine intervention, while after Oedipus begins to rule Thebes no more mythic or semi-mythic figures are known.

[10] (Chadwick 1912); the classic example is *Nibelungenlied* which incorporates Attila, Theodoric the Great, and several Burgundian kings from dates as widespread as the early fifth to the second half of the sixth century.

[11] This connection is the most compelling. However, there is another to be found in Celtic literature. The lightning bolt/lance test has a vague analogue in Celtic lore with *Fled Bricrend*. Here the three heroes of the story are also being tested for their bravery. One test involves standing watch, one night per warrior. At one point during each man's sentinel, they are attacked by a giant who hurls trees at them while they are in the seat of watch (*Fled Bricrenn; Bricriu's Feast*, trans. Henderson 1899, 101-15). This may also have a hint of the sovereignty motif.

[12] (O' Rahilly Dublin, 1946b, 17). O' Rahilly's belief that Gwenhwyfar represents a medb is untenable with the current knowledge of Late Celtic Britain. No region from which the name Gwenhwyfar could have derived is known to have existed.

[13] Though what this may be is uncertain. My speculation on the subject would be that this element is one which has been superimposed by Celtic bards at some point in the tale's Celtic development on the continent.

[14] She has both dual appearance and is linked to kingship.

[15] Mac Cana (1955, 76-114) gives a series of later versions of the sovereignty theme in Irish literature and Mac Cana (1955, 356-413), gives historical analogies.

[16] (*The Annals of Connacht*, RC li, 107 fl.; *The Annals of Loch Cé*, i 554).

[17] Thompson (1955-8, 732), gives one alternate, and that in northern Rhodesia.

[18] French *Keu*, later German *Keie* or English *Kay*.

[19] A witty dialogue of insults about the opponent's shortcomings, lack of ability and other such degrading language was evidently used by two heroic contestants to infuriate themselves to a degree where any restraints based on friendship and familial ties could be severed. Cú Chúlainn is involved in a number of them and his responses are of fascinating depth and humour, along the lines of the samurai haiku. For a selection of haiku see Yasuda (1957).

[20] An *englyn* is the oldest known Welsh metrical form; it was in existence by 900. The style is characterised by a unique brevity and integral intricacy which lends itself to impromptu composition. There are a variety of different forms (Stephens 1986, 178).

[21] In fact the mutually exclusive properties of having both cold and hot hands suggests these qualities were borrowed ad hoc from Irish stories.

[22] (*The Welsh Triads*, trans. and ed. Bromwich 1978, 274; 1976, 180-1; Jones, trans. Morgan 1963, 6, 15-16).

[23] For a full narrative and chronological development of Cei's character in literature see Gowans (1988).

[24] *Ronin* is a samurai whose lord has died before him, a masterless warrior.

[25] It seems reasonable to conclude near relatives could avoid the hazing used to prove one's worth. The subtlety of narrative and the author's willingness to belittle traditional scenes also allows for the possibility that he deliberately eliminated this aspect of the story.

[26] (Kelly 1988, 82-3). It should be noted, however that if, as seems likely, Dr. Miller was correct and a great majority of people in this period did not live to age fifty but to the late forties (1970, 118-160), this would make the average age of a new landowner 20-25.

[27] Though if the kingship ceremonies have been properly identified, we have some witness to Lancelot and Gauvain's eventual promotion to adult status.

[28] The older and less well preserved *Nibelungenlied* is probably the most famous of the many Germanic legends which contains this custom.

[29] As a British theme it would be unique; no other group of heroes send men back to their king alive. It is very possible the troubadours and trouvères may have used the idea of captives, but one must ask what the inspiration most probably was for this. Again, the only likely literary or historical source it could be derived from is the sub Roman period.

[30] Jousting and tournaments were little more than a century or two old when Chrétien wrote (Loomis 1949, 117.)

[31] *Gaaing* is French for "gain". In light of the context of the sentence the translation "booty" makes good sense.

[32] (*White Book of Rhydderch*, 286.5).

[33] (*Mabinogion*, trans. Jones and Jones 1974, 183). It is a fact that tournaments were dangerous, but that an *Yarll* (earl) and his six children would die in them seems unlikely. More probable would be their death in war.

[34] It could be argued that Philip's court had heard of the Celtic customs informally and unintentionally through reports of the English wars in Scotland. Scotland was allied to France in this period.

[35] No scholar has dated the poems at any period concurrent with the development of the Arthurian romances. Guesses have ranged from 800 to 1050.

[36] O' Rahilly assumed this as a premise to his book *Early Irish History and Mythology*, (1946, vi). To my knowledge, this has never been overturned.

Chapter XV: The Sixth Century in Chrétien

While Chrétien's patron may have changed because of money, death, a fallen relationship or otherwise, the material Chrétien uses in *Le Conte* does have some similarities to his earlier romance, *Le Chevalier de la Charrette*. As has been seen, *Le Conte du Graal*, much like *Le Chevalier*, has several instances that correspond to pre eleventh and possibly pre tenth-century British culture. This is particularly so in the named places, the nine maidens of *Dysgyl*, and the presence of the pan Celtic god *Beli*.

In Chapter XIV, the elements of the pre-ninth century to be found in *Le Conte du Graal* were discussed and the manner by which they found their way into Chrétien's poem theorized upon. There were also components that had no Norman connection and yet indicated a location of Scotland. Gauvain's association with Galloway is one of these, and the location there of his female relatives (ll. 8691-8714), suggests a traditional bond to that region for this character. This is indeed curious, and one should be well rewarded by asking oneself how Chrétien could have come across the designation.

There were only two periods during which northern British history was officially collected for the purpose of recording. Therefore, there was only two periods when such things would have been "in the news" for the nobility of England, Scotland and France. The first period was early ninth-century Strathclyde, and the data compiled then was largely brought to Gwynedd and used in the *Historia Brittonum*, *Annales Cambriae*, and *Y Gododdin* texts. The second occasion, and the more likely here, was in 1114 at the behest of David, Earl of Cumbria, for the purpose of establishing the claims of the Glasgow bishopric. It is said that he collected all the information from the sources of the Kentigern

Life and *Historia Brittonum*. In addition, he added all the traditions that the elders of Cumbria could verify to establish his Earldom's validity and antiquity as a religious domain in its own right (Ritchie 1954, 153). Unfortunately, no documents from those proceedings have come down to us.[1] However, it is apparent he must have accessed sources that dated back to the seventh century, at the least.[2] This means that the source from which Chrétien obtained the name Gauvain also contained information that dated to the seventh century and possibly earlier.

A second historical element was more difficult to see, but once observed was obvious. A study of the influences of Chrétien's plot revealed it was based on Philip's life, and a study of the direct analogues revealed the consistent influence Chrétien had on his contemporaries. Only *Peredur* did not follow this pattern, and for that its plot assumed primacy among the grail romances (see Chapter XII). Instead of a grail ceremony there was a platter with a head on it. Instead of the hero being destined to be the new grail-king, he was to take part in the destruction of witches. A study of similar motifs in Celtic myths, legends, and vitae revealed there was a further pattern among tales in which there occurred the slaying of one or nine sisters of non-Christian character. The heroes of *Pa gur?*, *The Life of Samson*, and *Peredur* all seem to date around 500 and none may be located to a period later than the sixth century. This was a peculiar trend and in itself suggested a recurrent historical pattern in one short period rather than a motif ulilized over centuries.

It was not far to see that this was an accurate appraisal of the tendency. In Chapter XIII, it was seen that Celtic cults not only survived the Christian onslaught, they revived later in the Middle Ages as witchcraft after an apparent event or policy that relegated the cult to a socially and politically unacceptable group. The logical conclusion was that the Celtic religion was openly active in the period 400-550, despite the dearth of archaeological evidence.[3] The general character of fifth- and sixth-century British archaeology, however, makes clear that Christianity was dominant. Specific references to Arthur as Christian in the vitae and as a prominent political leader in the *Historia Brittonum* suggest that the British hero was Christian also. By deduction he would have had an ideological conflict with the pagan sects, or regions, in the British nations. This difference could have been used by him as a political vehicle. All the admittedly little evidence there is fits neatly together if the Christians of c. 500 were destroying pagan communities, whether under the command of a single king or in isolated instances.

Again, this is not in Chrétien's version. Count Philip had not been taught the art of war by women. Certainly he would not have been associated with any story that allowed a Christian man to be taught by them; such material would be inappropriate. Second, the killing of women in combat, witches or no, was simply unthinkable in western Europe. When one turns again to the pages of Perceval's visit with his uncle, Gonemans, one is reminded of how short his training is (two days) and the reason for his departure (to find his mother, which he never does). These are two loose ends in the story that suggest Chrétien has here done some editing of motifs and plot.

It has also been seen that a *Bile/Beli* incarnate was early associated with the grail. This *Beli/Belatucadrus* was a fertility deity; he had the same quality any grail-king can be expected to have had and thus was probably an early component of the grail story. The Celtic god *Beli*, in the embodiment of *Belatucadrus*, was also linked with horns (a fertility symbol) and was the prototype of the chief god of the satanic cults during the Middle Ages.

In Chapter XIII it was noted that the nine maidens drawn in the Cagul mural were worshipping or otherwise paying respect to a man with horns. The Gaulish inscription which Professor John Koch has translated indicated ten individuals. The two together imply a typical coven consisted of nine women and one man who presumably wore horns as a living substitute to a god during ceremonies. This man was probably a surrogate for a fertility god such as *Beli*. This explains three things:

1. *Beli*, as a cognate of the grail-king, is a persistent fixture in the grail romances. However, he never handles the grail. The grail-maiden does this. This seeming anomaly was a serious obstacle for forming a strong Christian or Jewish theory of the grail's origins, but as a Celtic story this detail makes good sense. *Preiddeu Annwn* clearly states it was the maidens' duty to care for the grail (l. 14).

2. The grail/cauldron has the original property of a cornucopia. This identifies it as an agricultural item and ties it, too, to the maidens and *Beli*.

3. The waste land is obviously a symbol for the last season in the regeneration of nature. Similarly, the expected death of the grail-king is the personified death of the old year in expectation of the renewed life of spring. This is a basic component of fertility rites.

It also explains the copper bull that is being worshipped in *Fouke Fitz Warin*, and *Perlesvaus*,[4] where Perceval discontinues its worship.[5] It also explains a scene that occurs the night before Lancelot's crossing of the Sword Bridge in *Le Chevalier de la Charrette*. Here the hero is forced to fight a duel with a knight metaphorically associated with a bull.[6] Upon his defeat, Jandrée appears and insists on his death. No reason is given for Jandrée's request, nor does this scene seem to cause any consternation to the participants. Apparently Chrétien has here again attempted to cover up the destruction of something pagan. He could not have known, he should not have understood, and he did not care to know the truth.

The internal evidence of *Le Conte du Graal* is intriguing and, as in *Le Chevalier de la Charrette*, again points to an origin before 900. Chrétien has reformed data that was current with elements of much greater antiquity: He has omitted the scenes with the nine sisters because of Philip's aesthetic needs. He probably did not know what they represented, and did not care. Feminine villains were not a part of Chrétien's style. He has altered, borrowed, misunderstood, and recreated the story in the image of his patron. He has also retained enough of the ancient material for there to be a hint of its origins.

---

[1] There is, however, an unofficial and considerably later document that records the witnesses called (Ritchie 1954, 152).

[2] This is because of the specific British names to be found in the birth and childhood episodes of the two *vitae*. See Chapter III. One must assume the source of the two versions would have contained more of this traditional material.

[3] If the cults were a rural phenomenon to begin with, however, the lack of sites in the archaeological record is easily explicable. Rahtz (1982, 188) has found evidence of paganism in Cadbury-Congresbury during the sixth century.

[4] (*Perlesvaus*, ll. 5917-65). According to Professor Nitze, the best manuscript gives *le tor*, while MS Br reads *le torel*, bull calf. Variations are many and often obscure.

[5] Remember, even the pessimistic Dr. Brown could find no literary antecedent for it (1966, 125).

[6] (*La Charrette*, l. 2568). The bull was the animal most associated with Beli; the destruction of a copper bull or a man resembling one would symbolically constitute the destruction of the cult.

Chapter XVI: Conclusion

Chrétien de Troyes' *Le Conte du Graal* is an intriguing document. Many of the details seem historical and the plot is indisputably an interpretation of Philip of Flanders' life, but the question remains: Is the poem's base a romanced version of an historical event, or a series of oral motifs joined loosely together? The latter has popular opinion and a well-treaded argument for support. However, evidence has been produced to show it is quite probable that *Le Conte* is in some way historical, though its reliability is yet questionable. One must keep in mind that the records Chrétien was using were, at best, the product of an age without the rigid concept of objective history which modern scholars have developed. However, the following is certain or probable about *Le Conte du Graal* and its analogues:

1. The plot itself is twelfth century. The chronology, familial relationships and actions, and overall development of the main character are demonstrably a reconstruction of Philip of Flanders' life up to his departure for the crusades.

2. The grail and the ceremony surrounding it are very much Celtic, indicating this was the grail's original nature. The Christian and Jewish details of the ceremony were superimposed for Philip of Flanders' benefit and Chrétien's personal taste. The prominence of the grail over the blood of Christ, its cornucopian properties in Chrétien, and the recurring theme of nine maidens/witches/sisters and Pelles/Pellinore/Beli in *Peredur* and its cognates support this theory.

3. The customs and etiquette that the characters of *Le Conte* adhere to are often demonstrably of British origin. In the few instances in which some of these elements of the romance can be dated, these pieces can be shown to pertain to the ninth century or before.

3. The customs and etiquette that the characters of *Le Conte* adhere to are often demonstrably of British origin. In the few instances in which some of these elements of the romance can be dated, these pieces can be shown to pertain to the ninth century or before.

4. One can hardly be made to believe that a young man of the proper lineage was called upon to make a simple query that any curious visitor would have asked. It seems hardly more believable that this question would cure his grandfather and qualify himself to become a king. Such things have no parallels in Celtic legend. They are bizarre in a traditional environment, yet fit comfortably with Chrétien's style and purpose. This element is therefore a twelfth-century accretion.

5. The chief actor, Perceval, is without dispute the French version of Welsh Peredur. There is some evidence that a renowned man of that name lived in early sixth-century Britain. It is also possible that the York king Peredur mab Efrawg has been plucked from the late-sixth century to replace an original Arthurian character, possibly Gwalchmai/Gauvain.

6. In conjunction with certain other grail romances, a prototype of much greater historical value is visible.

7. There is evidence derived from *Pa gur?*, *Preiddeu Annwn*, *Le Conte*, *Perlesvaus*, *Didot Perceval*, *Diu Crône*, *Vitae Samsoni* and *Peredur* to show the fifth- and sixth-century characters Cei, Peredur, Gwalchmai, Samson, and Arthur as destroyers of paganism. This is despite the general dearth of oral and literary records in Welsh or Latin regarding this period of British history.

The following is a reconstruction of the original dynamics of *Dysgyl*'s historical subject and its history before being written down by Chrétien.[1] During the fifth and sixth centuries, individual local leaders of Britain, both religious and secular, took an active part in the extermination of pagan Celtic cults.[2] These activities were erratically recorded and many of the records of these crusades have not survived to the present. These stories were written down relatively soon after they had occurred, as happened with the *Life of Samson*, and possibly *Peredur*.[3] Alternatively, the actions may have been remembered in a strictly oral environment, as has apparently happened in *Pa gur?*. Those of the figures Cei, St. Samson, and Peredur have for various reasons endured.[4] The story involving Peredur was cultivated by Chrétien and his predecessors because of the etymology of his name.

Conclusion

The Celtic cults were simply formed; there were nine female members and a leader, presumably male, in each coven.[5] They were agricultural in nature and worshipped the bull-oriented god *Beli*. Like all agriculturally based religions, their god ceremonially died every year. He was replaced with his own reborn self. With the widespread anti-pagan movement that apparently happened in the fifth and sixth centuries, the remaining sects were forced underground, only to reemerge in a mutated form in the later Middle Ages.

For the grail story to be suitable to a romance format, certain changes were introduced. First, the murder of women by the hero was not acceptable, so the witches of Gloucester to be found in *Peredur* vanished in the continental romances, changing the make-up of the story drastically. Second, Philip's influence made it necessary to describe a foreign castle in terms similar to Jerusalem, and *Beli*'s hall was the most readily available. This change also forced an alteration in *Beli*'s personality; he had to represent the flower of Christianity as the story's version of the Christian king in Jerusalem. Nevertheless, clues of this modification remained. The grail is still a Celtic object. His proximity to a lake and his nickname, Fisher-King, are the vestiges of his role as an agricultural deity.

```
                    Cadegr
                      |
                    Dysgyl
          _____|_____
          |        |            |         |
          Preiddeu Annwn Vita Samsoni Pa Gur?
                                          | Peredur
 Philip                              Gwalchmai
   |                                      |
 Le Conte                             ____|____
   |_____          |         |
          |        |       Glastonbury
          |        |        |
 Didot Perceval Parzival Perlesvaus   ?     Diu Crône
                                      |
                                   Vulgate
Continuations
```

One might ask why there is no better record of the event than *Le Conte*, *Perlesvaus*, *Peredur*, and later romances, and why this base of information itself is flawed and conflicts in so many ways. The answers are familiar to those who have studied the gray areas of world history. There is little surviving information of any validity for the period and it, too, often conflicts. The fifth century was a time of tribal movements and insecurity of life, kingdoms, and values. On the continent, where Roman historians did keep better records of happenings and peoples, there are only the sketchiest and haphazard clues about the lives of both major and minor kings. Bloodlines are often impossible to trace. Even the very tribes are often misnamed or culturally misplaced by the Latin historians. In Britain, the manuscripts were unable to survive in the wet climate. Because of this obstacle, comparatively less was remembered accurately. There is only one chronologically based version of the

Conclusion

Arthurian period (Geoffrey of Monmouth), and this was written several hundred years later and is pseudo-historical in the extreme.

The solution that Chrétien reconstructed what was apparently a tale of destruction with Philip's life as an outline seems more likely than the traditional one. Namely, that Chrétien inherited a weird and unique plot that was soon imitated and added to by dozens of other authors. Too often the details in the romances, and *Le Conte* and *Peredur* in particular, make more sense in a pre-tenth century context. This makes it unlikely the story was the invention of a man with a twelfth-century French background.

All the details to be found in *Le Conte du Graal* and the other grail romances which show original Celtic material make sense together. The names of the heroes belong to the proper era, and the plot -- stripped of all its patron- and author-driven stimuli, belong only in fifth- and sixth-century Britain. How far can *Le Conte* be used as history? The writer's purpose, to create a religious hero and place him in Arthur's court, must necessarily leave the reader skeptical. However, in conjunction with other romances and the knowledge to be had of the period, one can potentially see through the biases of a single writer, culture, or period (see Chapter VI). The fact that the men who wrote the romances were not historical authorities should not impede the scholar, either. *The Bible*, *Iliad*, and *De Excidio Britanniae* had religious motives, yet they have all been used to establish historical fact.

One must visualize the two stories of the abduction and the grail as something more than literature. They can be added to the list of primary sources for the Arthurian period. The fifth and sixth centuries did indeed have more sources than the traditional Gildas, St. Patrick, and archaeology. The Welsh, Irish, and Gallic annals, Procopius, and many continental historians verify several chronological sequences. The genealogies help with bloodlines and the locations of princes. Saints' Lives have been used in conjunction with each other and other sources for locating kings and battles, pinpointing customs and materials. They, too, have been used to help build chronological sequences.[6] The Arthurian corpus contains similar sources, among them *Le Chevalier de la Charrette* and *Le Conte du Graal* or more accurately, *Glas* and *Dysgyl*. Like the histories, annals, genealogies, and vitae, the motives are often suspect, but the works are valuable sources of information and must be used as such if one is to unravel the Arthurian labyrinth. I believe this investigation is a step to attain that goal. However, the sources must first be evaluated as historical documents.

In looking at the historicity of a literary work, there are three aspects that must be scrutinized; external validation, historical context, and transmission (Dumville 1988, 1). Through the revelation of evidence that proved the antiquity of the poem, one might use these criteria for *Glas* and *Dysgyl*. I shall analyze each source separately. External validation and historical context are, as in the case of *Y Gododdin*, not viable options for *Glas* (Dumville 1988, 1-4). Since all the extant versions of the abduction are from the same viewpoint, they must be regarded as variations of one source, whether directly or indirectly so. Unfortunately, no account of Meleagant's version of the story survives.[7] The romances are therefore invalid for affirming *Glas*'s historicity. Historical context, too, is very difficult. The customs and social mores for the century and a half between the departure of the Romans and the rise of Urien are unknown. Because of this, only hypotheses can be made from comparison with early Irish laws and the codex of Hywel Dda. There may have been a Meleagant, Arthur, and Guinièvre and an abduction could have taken place, but no more can be said with any certainty.

The transmission theories surveyed in Chapter II have not been useful, either. To reiterate, the Arthurian tales could have originated in any area that was in British hands around 500. They could have developed in Scotland, Wales, Cornwall, Cumberland, Yorkshire, or Brittany. Such evidence does not allow room for much optimism. However, with the additional evidence from Chapter II here summarized, one might hazard more specificity as to the age of the forerunner of Chrétien's poem:

I. The knowledge that Caradoc of Llancarfan composed the first known and solidly dateable abduction of Guinièvre allows one to hypothesize that the story was known before 1100.[8]

II. The historical evidence to be found in the poem included three non-motifal examples from a period before 900, the same century as that of the elder manuscript version of *Y Gododdin*.

III. Charles Thomas is the most recent and prolific expert on Pictish stones, and he claims a fifth or sixth-century date for the chariot in Meigle.

Dysgyl also lacks any form of external validation except by way of comparison. However, Chapter XIII has allowed some basis for historical context. There is reason to believe that pagan cults were actively suppressed between 400 and the 570s, as on the continent. It has also been seen to be most reasonable to assume a central authority instigated this island-wide purge, as Clovis did in France.

Transmission of the poem is clearly much too complex to unravel with our present body of knowledge. However, it is possible to date the poem's origins to well before Geoffrey of Monmouth's *Historia Regum Britanniae*, as the following demonstrates.

I. The theme of the abduction of Arthur's queen arises in the literary record rather suddenly in three widely variant romances in the years after 1190. This phenomenon allows one to assume the story, in basic form, was at least several decades old by the time these stories were written.

II. The reference to Perceval as a grail hero in the troubadour poetry around 1160 suggests this date as a *terminus post quem* for the birthdate of the Perceval character.

III. It has been demonstrated that some geographic details of *Le Conte du Graal*, particularly the Gauvain-Galloway tie, hint at an older source. This in turn may have extended back to the seventh century and King David's early twelfth-century collection of historical materials.

IV. The presence in the grail romances and analogues of *Beli*, nine witches, a magical cauldron/grail, and the grail king's expected death lead to the conclusion that there was here a pagan agricultural ritual. In turn this rite may be placed in Britain and identified with a Celtic religious practice, no later that 600 when the Celtic cults seem to have gone underground.

V. The material analogous to *Peredur* (the most Celtic version of the grail romance) contains stories wherein Cei, Arthur, Gwalchmai, and St. Samson are all witch-fighters. These are all fifth- or sixth-century figures, and Samson's *vitae* dates to the early-seventh century. II. Again, this implies that both proposed historical events were taking place no later than the sixth century. Unfortunately, it is impossible (yet) to determine exactly what happened to both tales between say 600 and 1100, when both stories appear to have been given new life through a variety of factors.[9] Before this time we have only hints; there is general evidence that historical and pseudo-historical material about Arthur and other heroes of the British heroic age did exist in manuscript form at an early period. These materials were from the *Northern Memoranda* or a related text. This has been seen in Chapter III. To reiterate:Two of Professor Jackson's *Northern Memoranda* observations point to a date in the sixth century. First, the linguistic evidence in the names of the cities of *Historia Brittonum*, particularly *Din Guoaroy*, *Medcaut*, and *Gai*.[10] Second, of the five poets mentioned by Ninnius, only two have poems extant in the collection of Welsh literature. The other three are virtually anonymous. This implies that their poetry was lost relatively early in the literary tradition. Any memory of these people would have come from a contemporary or near contemporary source.

It is known that other records were being kept in Scotland before the eleventh century, though the only evidence that remains is to be found in the vitae of Ninian and Kentigern. The *Life of Ninian* is generally accepted as taken from a seventh century source. Professor Jackson would only postulate a tenth-century source for Kentigern's *Vita*, but later critics have placed it in the seventh century as well.

This means that some version of both the abduction and grail episodes were in existence before 900, and tentatively as early as the fifth and sixth centuries. The nature of the source from which such material could have come is apparent, the *Northern Memoranda* or a document of similar historical value.

It is not claimed, however, that *Le Chevalier de la Charrette* and *Le Conte du Graal*, or *Glas and Dysgyl*, are historical documents. Such literatures for the sixth century are like the cries of ghosts -- always howling but never seen. What is claimed is that the poem is useful for historians, and possibly contains historical elements.

How much importance should be given these historical elements? Analogies alone can answer this. The *Iliad* has very little strictly historical information, and yet Schliemann was able to find Troy from only the lines of the poem and a very basic grasp of the concept of archaeology. In the sub-Roman period of Britain, the authentic Taliesin poetry has been used to outline Urien's kingdom and locate several other personalities. It has also aided in improving the understanding of the political color and chronology of the late-sixth century. *Y Gododdin* is used as a sounding board by archaeologists against which they compare their own finds. What I am suggesting in this thesis is that *Glas* and *Dysgyl*, as may be recovered from Chrétien, the Welsh and continental authors, can also serve historians as a source of information about the fifth and sixth centuries.[11] Surely the luxury of having another literary source for the period can only enhance the understanding of the era. Similarly *Iliad*, the Taliesin and Aneirin poetry have done in the above instances, and a number of other examples.[12]

Conclusion

The historical importance of *Le Chevalier de la Charrette* and *Le Conte du Graal* does not rest on the merits of the two works being poetic versions of historic events. In passages, scenes, and objects, the twelfth-century romance author gives a glimpse into the culture of sixth-century Britain, and for that it deserves attention. The stories, with Chrétien's known continental sources cut and the misinterpretations accounted for, could have happened in sixth-century Britain. In the study of any period this information would be of interest. However, when dealing with the limited textual and artefactual evidence of the Arthurian era, this revelation should command the further attention of experts in the fields of history and archaeology.

---

[1] Again, this original could only be determined from a study of Peredur and its Welsh analogues.

[2] The reasoning behind my belief that Arthur was not the political figure who enacted these religious wars is that Arthur is not associated with St. David, and Cei's extermination of the witches at *Ystawingun* is not made in conjunction with the king. Also, Arthur's relationship with Perceval seems generally detached, even in Peredur. I would theorise this aspect of the grail story has been superimposed. However, Arthur was at one point directly associated with the destruction of pagan centres, as his encounter in *Culhwch ac Olwen* proves.

[3] I would argue that the many different connections to be made between the various romances and fifth and sixth century culture support such a claim.

[4] In my estimation, the brief reference in *Pa gur?* is due to Cei's early relationship with Arthur. Without it, no record of Cei would exist. *The Life of St. Samson* contains the reference because of the near-contemporary nature of its author. Perceval's story seems to have survived because of the popularity of Chrétien's romance.

[5] The painting at Cagul indicates this. Based on this evidence, it is also possible that a female leader could have been made to look like the male god Beli, but this is only speculation

[6] (Morris 1976). I believe Professor Morris was right in principle; the use of two or more literary sources of different origins that have been written for different reasons is a viable historical tool. However, I must side with the weight of scholarly opinion and agree that here Morris took the use of his sources of information too far.

[7] Unless one would care to postulate *Yonec* is such a version; but this raises more questions than it answers.

[8] *Ymddiddan Gwenhwyfar ac Arthur* and the Modena Archivolt are, one may recall, of widely disputed dates. See Chapter III.

[9] The political landscape of Britain and most of France under Henry II, the development of the troubadours, and the power and linguistic abilities of the Bretons.

[10] Jackson also uses *Atbret* for his proof, but this may be an orthographic error (Dumville 1977b, 347).

[11] In listing Chrétien first I acknowledge his own reputation in the Middle Ages and recognise that any further study in this field cannot be done without a thorough understanding of the motives of him and his patrons. In many respects, he forged the mould by which later authors would write their romances.

[12] Such as *Hrolf Kraki's Saga*; this story has been used to reconstruct a Danish hall in the pre-Viking period. Other literary sources of importance have been the Polynesian myths and legends; they have been used to forward a theory about the method of and the political context behind the eventual migration across much of the Pacific islands of the Polynesian people. Finally, the Gilgamesh Cycle, which supports the idea that the dominance of city-states in Babylonia was of a temporary nature and has led to the hypothesis that this area had an heroic period of its own in the mid- to late-third milennium.

Appendices

I. The ceremonial chariot, or cart found on the Meigle stone is not an Irish or pre Roman model for three major reasons. First, it has open sides, with two pole shafts to serve as railings. The reconstruction of Irish heroic-age chariots by David Greene has two closed side boards (1972, 69). The carving shows three people -- a driver and two passengers side by side, unlike Greene's construct. Also, the wheels have twelve spokes, presumably stronger than the eight from Ireland (1972, 65).

Second, there is no archaeological evidence for awnings or chariots designed for more than two people in pre Roman Britain (Laing 1985, 278), or in the Irish literary evidence. This means that this picture of three is probably not representative of pre Caesar British culture.

II. Chrétien's "Bed" scene, like the Sword Bridge and the *charrette* as found in his poem, has no parallel in Celtic myth. This implies one of two things. Either he has invented the scene or he has misunderstood or reinterpreted something that was British in the material he had at hand. The "Bed" of Diarmid and Grainne of Ireland offers a potential reason for the latter belief. Irish folklore in the Medieval period called the unusual stone monuments, found there and in Britain, France, and Spain the "Bed of Diarmid and Grainne". That is, local legend had it they were places where the two famous lovers slept together while trying to escape Fionn macCumhail.

The other option, that Chrétien invented the material, is most definitely possible, but unlikely in view of his usual tendency to borrow wholesale from a classical author or Celtic source.

III. There is one potential Angus held within the body of Celtic Arthurian lore. *Pa gur?* contains an *Anguas Edeinauc* (*Culhwch ac Olwen,* eds. Bromwich and Evans 1992, xxxv), alternatively *Anwas Edeinauc.*[1] Of course, a belief that this example is the Lancelot of romances forces a further leap of faith. If this is indeed the literary precursor of Lancelot, it would be nearly impossible to prove. It adds another language through which the name must be rationalized, and the theoretical linguistic changes are anything but perfect. Even if this particular reading of the word and its components are recognized, Arthurian linguistics are notoriously difficult and cannot be thought of as certain. Still, the existence of the name does add weight to the suggestion that Lancelot did originally have some sort of pre Chrétien counterpart.

IV.   Dr. Bromwich believes the cup-spilling incident was in origin another version of Guinièvre's abduction, with Gereint in the role of rescuer (*The Welsh Triads,* trans. and ed. Bromwich 1978, 385). The problems with this supposition are numerous. Foremost, this Gereint is a late addition to the Arthurian arena. He appears to have been a sixth-century ruler in Brittany and is nowhere recorded in Arthurian romance before Chrétien (Bromwich 1961, 464). If Dr. Bromwich's hypothesis was true, both abductor and rescuer would then have four incarnations in the various Welsh and continental versions (Cei/Gwnhwyfar, Lancelot/Ginover, Erec/Ginover, Gereint/wenhvyfar -- whose counterpart is also Arthur's wife), plus another romance character -- Gauvein. This seems strange considering the consistency with which this particular tale has made Arthur's wife the abducted party.[2]

V.   Professor Loomis and Professor Nutt have also used the fact that Perceval kills the Red Knight in every redaction to further a theory about a blood feud between Gauvain and Perceval's clans.[3] This, too, has its flaws. For one, colored armor is undoubtedly a product of Chrétien's pen. If it is not, the Red Knight stands as a symbol of the underworld. This would mean Perceval was fighting the King of Annwfn; fortunately, the conclusion has no precedence. Second, Loomis believed the family with which Perceval was feuding was Gawain's, yet the two are quite amiable when they first meet outside Arthur's court.[4] Later, even though Perceval has finished dismounting two dozen of Arthur's men, he asks for Gauvain's friendship. There is no display of enmity between the two men in the poem, except towards the very end of *Le Conte*, where Loomis says they have come to a mutual agreement. Here they joust in anonymous combat first. If it is to be held that this is a romance writer's cover up of a premeditated fight, as Loomis did, there are other options than a feud. Impromptu fights over petty matters were commonplace in Celtic heroic warrior society. Brawls over precedence or unintentional slights were frequent. A feud, on the other hand, would be used to further one's honor and should therefore be made quite open before the violence began. So, even if the combat in *Le Conte* was a more extended conflict, it hardly needs to have been a clue that there was a war between the two families. Furthermore, if the mysterious cup that the Red Knight steals is a kingship cup, which I believe, it has no place in the hands of any sibling of Gauvain. Such an act of treason is unknown among that family in every Arthurian history and romance of which I am aware.

VI. The form of the story that is extant in the English versions has clearly been muddled and the connection to sovereignty forgotten or deliberately suppressed.[5] I say this because *The Wife of Bath's Tale*, *The Weddynge of Sir Gawen*, and *Dame Ragnell* all have one thing in common -- the Arthurian hero Gawen is the protagonist. It is generally regarded that as a royal cycle matures, the adventures of the king are given to chief heroes to keep the king at home. It would be ridiculous to any writer of the Middle Ages to allow Gwalchmai/Gauvain a kingship. This explains the absence of the sovereignty facet of the story and the consequent plot dearth, which was easily filled with a morality theme. *The Tale of Sir Florent* is much later than the Arthurian tales and probably based upon them.

VII. The Unspelling Quest is a long-established and important element in the *Le Conte du Graal*. An understanding of it is essential for a comprehensive grasp of the grail persona. A brief outline of the theme based on Alfred Nutt's essay will serve to explain the phenomena (1888, 195-203).

The Unspelling Quest involves the disenchantment of an under- or otherworld abode by a mortal visitor. In it, a mortal visitor is asked, cajoled or summoned to an under- or otherworld region. Here he is well fed and happily entertained in hopes that he will free the inhabitants of the place from their magical punishment by either asking or refraining from asking an obvious question. Professor Nutt believed the prototype to this tale was to be found in the swan maids' prohibitions of not being asked to be with their visitors (here plural) in rising or going to bed. Here the probation lasts one year. Alternatively, the inhabitants of this otherworld may be freed by an act. The Potter Thompson of folklore could have liberated Arthur and his men from their magical sleep in a cave by blowing a horn that was hanging nearby.[6]

Apparently at some preliterary stage of development the unspelling theme was incorporated into the grail corpus. This may or may not have been in conjunction with the addition of the *Brân* figure.[7] In any event, the motif was most probably used to Christianize the grail and produce the mandatory plot alterations that this change produced.

VIII. The nature of the grail has been the subject of some debate since Chrétien first described it with the word *graal* (*Le Conte*, l. 3191), OF deep, wide dish. The next major continental grail writer was Wolfram von Eschenbach, who called it a small stone. Later romancers termed it a cup or goblet. Clearly there was some confusion in translating the original word used to describe it. Alfred Nutt only showed the extent of the problem with his revelation that OW *per* was basin, and Peredur can be translated as "basin-seeker" (1888, 97). The latter was either a bard's pun or the man's title or kenning. The only commonality in all the romances is that they are liquid containers. This leaves the door open for the grail being either the kingship cup of *Ecstasy of the Phantom*, or the cauldron of *Culhwch ac Olwen* and *Preiddeu Annwn*. As was seen in Chapter X, the grail's qualities more resemble the variations of the magical cauldron than the Cup of Sovereignty the Red Knight stole.

IX. While it may be true that Pellinore is a creation later than Chrétien, he is strongly linked with the grail. Further, his name is close linguistically to the grail king -- Pelles -- who is in most of the continental grail redactions. It is quite likely he is a later regeneration of the grail king under the corruption *Beli Mawr* < Pelli + nore, though his independent link to *Beli Mawr* is not beyond question (Loomis 1927, 145). Regardless, as a name linguistically compatible to the grail king, he deserves attention and anything consistently linked to him has earned serious scrutiny.

X. In *Arthurian Tradition and Chrétien de Troyes*, Professor Loomis stated his belief that the cup-spilling incident in *Le Conte* was "a condensed and modified version of the first adventure of Gauvain in *L'Atre Perilleux*, where Guinevere is kidnapped".[8] However, there are two obstacles to this explanation. First, *L'Atre Perilleux* dates to the mid-twelfth century, though this is not necessarily a problem in Arthurian studies. Second, *L'Atre Perilleux* is otherwise bereft of any original material. This is a serious argument against preferring it over Chrétien's scene, in terms of priority.

Dr. Brouland has conjectured that the Guinevere/Gwenhwyfar character was in fact a sovereignty figure, and is supported in Professor O'Rahilly's article (1946b, 7-28). She also claims that the plot of *La Charrette* is that two men are trying to win her, and therefore the sovereignty of Arthur's kingdom. Her argument is a complex one, but simplified is as follows:

1. In *Le Conte*, Arthur is insulted through her when the Red Knight spills wine on her dress and taunts him about having stolen from her a cup which somehow symbolizes kingship.
2. She humiliates Lancelot as the fairy sovereign figure humiliates her lover Lanval in *Lanval*.
3. Étain and Medb, both sovereignty figures, are said in myth to have been born three times, Gwenhwyfar is said to have been three women and three wives of Arthur.
4. Medb provokes *Tain Bo Cuailgne* as Gwenhwyfar provokes Camlann.
5. In *La Charrette*, Gauvain, Lancelot, Keu, and Meleagant are the only men who attempt to possess her. Since Arthur's court is much larger than three men, there must be some more powerful reason why only they are chasing her (Brouland 1995, 77-85).

These arguments are reflective of a limited knowledge of the Celtic culture. Three appears repeatedly in many forms throughout, as it does in many cultures. The humiliation motif was one of French derivation and was a product of the romantic literature movement of the twelfth century.

---

[1] (Sims-Williams 1991, 40). In *Culhwch ac Olwen* it is Anwas Edeinavc, in *The White Book of Rhydderch* he is named Henwas Edeinavc mab Erim.

[2] Lancelot's presence is easy to explain; his name means servant making him the perfect vehicle of courtly love.

[3] (Loomis 1949, 398-401; Nutt 1888, 169).

[4] (*Le Conte*, ll. 4401-71). All such rationale which is based solely on the romances and not the social and economic reasons behind them are doomed to be unsupportable. Chrétien is as likely to have invented the combat as he is to have civilized an actual account. As has been seen, those who followed him were only too happy to continue his legacy.

[5] Much of the original lore on this island concerning the sovereignty figure was no doubt submerged in the Roman period and possibly lost or modernised in the centuries of oral telling.

[6] (Nutt 1888, 198). This was apparently first printed by Nutt in *Folk-Lore Journal*, Vol. I, 193. I have been unable to find this periodical.

[7] It is presumably because of Brân's influence that the extreme age element of the Grail-King is present.

[8] (Loomis 1949, 356-7; *Le Conte*, ll. 122-374, *L'Atre Perilloux*, ll. 2070-2462).

Bibliography

Primary Sources

The Anglo-Saxon Chronicle. trans. G. N. Garmonsway. (London, 1986).
  -"*The Anglo-Saxon Chronicle MS A*". ed. J. Bately. *The Anglo-Saxon Chronicle: A Collective Edition.* eds. David Dumville and S. Keynes. (Cambridge, 1986).
L'Atre périlleux. ed. Brian Woledge. (Paris, 1936).
Beowulf. trans. Kevin Crossley-Holland. (Oxford, 1982).
"The Boyhood Deeds of Finn", trans. John Carey. *The Celtic Heroic Age: Literary Sources for Ancient Celtic Europe and Early Ireland and Wales.* eds. John Koch and John Carey. (Malden, 1994), 183-90.
"Co(i)mpert Conchobuir [maic Nessa]: The Conception of Conchobar son of Nes", trans. John Carey. *The Celtic Heroic Age: Literary Sources for Ancient Celtic Europe and Early Ireland and Wales.* eds. John Koch and John Carey. (Malden, 1994), 48-51.
"Conall Corc and the Corco Luigde", trans. Vernam Hull. *PMLA* 62 (Menasha, 1943), 887-909.
Críth Gablach. ed. D. A. Binchy. (Oxford, 1970).
Culhwch ac Olwen: An Edition and Study of the Earliest Arthurian Tale. eds. Rachel Bromwich and D. Simon Evans. (Cardiff, 1992).
"The Death of Diarmait mac Cerbaill", trans. John Carey, *The Celtic Heroic Age: Literary Sources for Ancient Celtic Europe and Early Ireland and Wales.* ed. John Koch and John Carey. (Malden, 1994), 200-3.
Didot Perceval. trans. William A. Nitze. (Chicago, 1932-7).
  -*The Didot Perceval, according to the Manuscript of Modena and Paris.* trans. William Roach. (Philadelphia, 1941).
Duanaire Finn English and Irish. 3 vols. vol. 1 ed. Eoin MacNeill. (Dublin, 1908).
  -vols. 2 and 3 ed. Gerard Murphy. (Dublin, 1936-53).
Early Welsh Genealogical Tracts. ed. P.C. Bartrum. (Cardiff, 1966).
Fingal Rónáin and other Stories. ed. David Greene. (Dublin, 1955).
"Fled Bricrenn; Bricriu's Feast", *Irish Text Society vol. 2.* ed. and trans. George Henderson. (Dublin, 1899), rev. 1995, *The Celtic*

"Fled Bricrenn; Bricriu's Feast", *Irish Text Society vol. 2*. ed. and trans. George Henderson. (Dublin, 1899), rev. 1995, *The Celtic Heroic Age*. eds. John Koch and John Carey. (Malden, 1994), 64-95.

The Four Ancient Books of Wales. trans. William F. Skene. (Edinburgh, 1868).

Le Haut Livre du Graal: Perlesvaus. ed. William Nitze. (Totowa, 1937).

-*Le Haut du Graal: Perlesvaus, A Structural Study*. trans. Thomas E. Kelly. (Genève, 1974).

-*Perlesvaus Prose English, The High Book of the Grail: A Translation of the Thirteenth Century Romance of Perlesvaus*. trans. Nigel Bryant. (Ipswich, 1978).

Historia Brittnonum. trans. John Morris. (Chichester, 1978).

-*The Vatican Recension of the 'Historia Brittonum'*. ed. David Dumville. (Cambridge, 1985).

Hrolf Kraki's Saga. trans. Poul Anderson. (New York, 1988).

The Law of Hywel Dda. trans. and ed. by Dafydd Jenkins. (Llandysul, 1986).

"Lebor Gabála Érenn: The Book of Invasions", trans. John Carey. *The Celtic Heroic Age: Literary Sources for Ancient Celtic Europe and Early Ireland and Wales*. eds. John Koch and John Carey. (Malden, 1994), 213-66.

Liber Landavensis: The Book of Llandaf. ed. J. Rhys and J. G. Evans. (Oxford, 1883).

-*The Llandaff Charters*. ed. Wendy Davies. (Cardiff, 1979).

Mabinogion. trans. Charlotte Guest. (London, 1877).

-trans. Gwyn Jones and Thomas Jones. (London, 1974).

-trans. Sir Ifor Williams. (Cardiff, 1930).

"Marwnad Cynddylan", ed. Sir Ifor Williams. *B* 6 (Oxford, 1933), 134-140.

-trans. John T. Koch. *The Celtic Heroic Age: Literary Sources for Ancient Celtic Europe and Early Ireland and Wales*. eds. John Koch and John Carey. (Malden, 1994), 360-2.

"Mesca Ulad: Intoxication of the Ulstermen", trans. J. Carmichael Watson. *The Celtic Heroic Age: Literary Sources for Ancient Celtic Europe and Early Ireland and Wales*. eds. John Koch and John Carey. (Malden, 1994), 95-117.

Nennius: The Historia Brittonum. ed. John Morris. (Totowa, 1980).

-The Vatican Recension of the 'Historia Brittonum'. ed. David Dumville. (Cambridge, 1985).

"Pa gur", trans. Brinley Roberts. eds. Rachel Bromwich and D. Simon Evans. *Culhwch ac Olwen: An Edition and Study of the Earliest Arthurian Tale*. (Cardiff, 1992).

" 'Preiddeu Annwn' and the figure of Taliesin", ed. and trans. Marged Haycock. *SC* 14/15. (Cardiff, 1984), 52-77.

Sir Perceval of Gales. eds. J. Campion and F. Hothausen. (New York, 1913).

Táin Bó Cuailnge. trans. Thomas Kinsella. (Oxford, 1969).

"Togail Bruidne Da Derga: The Destruction of Da Derga's Hostel", trans. Whitley Stokes, John Koch and John Carey. *The Celtic Heroic Age: Literary Sources for Ancient Celtic Europe and Early Ireland and Wales*. (Malden, 1994), 155-74.

The Welsh Triads (Trioedd ynys Prydein). trans. and ed. Rachel Bromwich. (Cardiff, rev. 1978).

Tóruigheacht Dhiarmada agus Ghráinne: The Pursuit of Diarmid and Gráinne. trans. Ness Ní Shéaghdha. Irish Text Society 48 (Dublin, 1967).

The Tripartite Life of Patrick, with other documents relating to that saint. trans. Whitley Stokes. (London, 1887).

"Two Gaulish Religious Inscriptions", trans. John T. Koch. *The Celtic Heroic Age: Literary Sources for Ancient Celtic Europe and Early Ireland and Wales*. eds. John Koch and John Carey. (Malden, 1994), 1-4.

The Life of St. David. trans. Ernest Rhys. (Newtown, 1927).

The Life of St. Samson of Dol. trans. Thomas Taylor. (Llanerch, rep. 1991).

The *Vulgate Version of the Arthurian Romance: edited from Manuscripts in the British Museum*. 8 vols. trans. Henry Oskar Sommer. (Washington, 1909-16).

The White Book: Welsh Tales and Romance Reproduced from the Peniarth Manuscripts. ed. J Gwenogary Evans. (Private Press, 1907).

"An Early Ritual Poem in Welsh" ("Ymddiddan Gwenhwyfar ac Arthur"), ed. Mary Williams. *S* 13 (Cambridge, 1938), 38-51.

Adamnan. *The Life of St. Columba, Founder of Hy*. ed. and trans. William Reeves. (Llanerch, rep. 1988).

Andrew of Wyntoun. *The Original Chronicle of Andrew of Wyntoun*. 4 vols. ed. F. J. Amours. (Edinburgh, 1906).

Aneirin. *The Gododdin: The Oldest Scottish Poem.* trans. Kenneth Hurlstone Jackson. (Edinburgh, 1969).
-*Aneirin: Y Gododdin, Britain's Oldest Poem.* trans. Alfred Owen Hughes Jarman. (Llandysul, 1990).
-*Aneirin: The Gododdin.* trans. Steve Short. (Llanerch, rep. 1994).
-*The Gododdin of Aneirin: Text and Context for Dark Age North Britain.* ed. and trans. John T. Koch. (Cardiff, 1997).
Aue, Hartmann von. *Iwein.* trans. Patrick M. McConeghy. (New York, 1984).
Bede. *A History of the English Church and People.* trans. Leo Sherley-Price. rev. R. E. Lathan. (London, 1978).
Caesar, Julius Gaius. *The Gallic Wars.* trans. S. A. Handford. (Baltimore, 1951).
Capellanus, Andreas. *The Art of Courtly Love.* trans. John Jay Parry. (New York, 1959).
-*De Amore: Libri Tres.* ed. E. Trojel. (Munich, 1972).
Chrétien de Troyes. *Les chansons courtoises de Chrétien de Troyes.* ed. Marie Claire Zai. (Lang, 1974).
-trans. D.D.R. Owen. *Arthurian Romances.* (London, 1989).
Dio Cassius. *Dio's Roman History.* trans. Earnest Cary. 9 vols. (London, 1914).
Diodorus Siculus. *The Bibliotheca Historia of Diodorus Siculus.* trans. John Skelton. ed. F. M. Salter and H. L. K. Edward. (Oxford, 1968-71).
Eschenbach, Wolfram von. *Wolfram von Eschenbach: Parzival.* ed. Gottfried Weber. (Darmstadt, 1963).
-*Parzival.* trans. Arthur Thomas Hatto. (Baltimore, 1980).
-*Parzival.* trans. Helen M. Mustard and Charles E. Passage. (New York, 1961).
Florence of Worcester. *Chronicle of Florence of Worcester.* trans. Thomas Forester. (London, 1854).
Four Ancient Books of Wales. trans. William Forbes Skenes. 2 vols. (Edinburgh, 1868)
Freculf, Bishop of Lisieux. *Chronicorum libri Dvo.* ed. E. Grunauer as *De Fontibus historiae Freculfi.* (Winterthur, 1864).
Geoffrey of Monmouth. *The History of the Kings of Britain.* trans. Lewis G. M. Thorpe (New York, 1966).
-*The Historia Regum Britanniae of Geoffrey of Monmouth.* eds. Acton Griscom and Robert Ellis Jones. (London, 1929).

Geoffrey de Vinsauf. *Documentum de modo et arte dictandi et versificandi.* trans. Robert P. Parr. (Milwaukee, 1968).

Gildas. *The Ruin of Britain.* trans. Michael Winterbottom. (London, 1978).

Grafenburg, Wirnt von. *Wigalois.* trans. J. W. Thomas. (London, 1977).

Gregory of Tours. *The History of the Franks.* trans. Lewis G.M. Thorpe. (Baltimore, 1971).

Hélinand de Froidmont. *Les vers de la Mort.* trans. Michel Boyer and Monique Santucci. (Paris, 1983).

Herodotus. *The Historia.* trans. Aubrey de Sélincourt. (London, 1954 rev. 1972).

Libanius. *Selected Orations.* 2 vols. ed. E. H. Warmington. (New York, 1968).

Livy. *Ab Urbe condita.* vols. 1-10. eds. Carol Flamstead Walters and Robert Seymour Conway. (Oxford, 1914-65).

Malory, Sir Thomas. *Caxton's Malory.* ed. James W. Spisak. (Berkeley, 1983).

Marie de France. *The Lais of Marie de France.* trans. Glyn S. Burgess and Keith Busby (London, 1986).

A Monk of Rhuys and Caradoc of Llancarfan. *Two Lives of Gildas.* trans. Hugh Williams. (Llanerch, rep. 1990).

Paulinus of Milan. *Vita Sancti Ambrosii, mediolensis episcopi, a paulino eius notario ad beatum Augustinum conscripta.* trans. Mary Simplicia Kaniecka. (Washington D. C., 1928).

Polybius. *The Histories.* 6 vols. ed. G. P. Goold. (Cambridge, 1975).

Robert de Boron. *Robert de Boron: Le Roman de L' Estoire dou Graal.* trans. William Roach. (Paris, 1927).

-*Robert de Boron: Merlin Roman du XIIIe siécle.* trans. Alexandre Micha. (Genève, 1974).

Silius Italicus, Tiberius Cato. *Punica.* trans. James Duff Duff. 2 vols. (Cambridge, 1934).

Strabo. *The Geography.* 8 vols. trans. Horace Leonard Jones. (New York, 1923).

Tacitus, Cornelius. *The Agricola and the Germania.* trans. H. Mattingly. rev. S. A. Handford. (Middlesex, 1970).

-*Canu Taliesin: gyda Rhagymadrodd a Nodiadau.* ed. Sir Ifor Williams. (Cardiff, 1960).

Türlin, Heinrich von dem. *The Crown (Diu Crône).* trans. John Wesley Thomas. (Lincoln, 1989).

Wauchier de Denain. *Continuations of the Old French Perceval of Chrétien de Troyes: The First Continuation.* trans. and ed. William Roach. (Philadelphia, 1949).

William of Malmesbury. *De Antiquitate Glastonie Ecclesie.* ed. and trans. John Scott. (Woodbridge, 1981).

-*De Rebus Gestis Regum Anglorum.* ed. William Stubbs. (London, 1889).

Zatzikhoven, Ulrich von. *Lanzelet.* trans. Kenneth G.T. Webster, ed. Roger S. Loomis. (New York, 1951).

Secondary Sources

Abrams, Leslie and James P. Carley. (eds.) *The Archaeology and History of Glastonbury Abbey. Essays in Honour of the Ninetieth birthday of C.A. Ralegh Radford.* (Woodbridge, 1991).

Addymein, P. V. *Anglian York.* 7 Council for British Archaeology series, (London, 1973-81).

Adolf, Helen. "A Historical Background to Chrétien's *Perceval*", *PMLA* 58 (Menasha, 1943), 597-620.

Alcock, Leslie. *Dinas Powys.* (Cardiff, 1963).
-"Wales in the Fifth and Seventh centuries A.D.: Archaeological Evidence", *Prehistoric and Early Wales.* eds. Idris Llewelyn Foster and Glyn Edmund Daniel. (London, 1965), 177-212.
-"Was there an Irish Sea Culture-Province in the Dark Ages", *The Irish Sea Province.* ed. Donald Moore. Cambrian Archaeological Association, (Cardiff, 1970), 55-64.
-*Arthur's Britain.* (New York, 1971).
-"Reconnaissance excavations on early historic fortifications and other royal sites in Scotland, 1974-84. 4: Excavations at Alt Clut, Clyde Rock, Strathclyde, 1974-75", *PSAS* 120 (Edinburgh, 1990), 95-149.
-*Economy, Society and Warfare among the Britons and Saxons.* (Cardiff, 1987).
-*Cadbury Castle, Somerset: The Early Medieval Archaeology.* (Cardiff, 1995).

Anderson, Marjorie O. *Kings and Kingship in Early Scotland.* (Edinburgh, 1973).

Anglade, Joseph. *Anthologie des Troubadours.* (Paris, 1929).

Arbois de Jubainville, Henri de. *Le Cycle Mythologique irlandais et la mythologie celtiques.* (Paris, 1884).

Ashe, Geoffrey (ed.) *Quest for Arthur's Britain.* (London, 1967).

Balcou, Jean et al. *Histoire littéraire et culturelle de la Bretagne.* (Paris, 1987).

Bannerman, John. *Studies in the History of Dalriada.* (Edinburgh, 1974).

Barber, Richard. *King Arthur: Hero and Legend.* (New York, 1986).

Barley, Maurice Willmore and Rich Patick Crosland Hansen (eds.) *Christianity in Britain, 300-570.* (*"From the Conference on Christianity in Roman and Sub-Roman Britain April 17-20, 1967"*). (Leicester, 1968).

Barrow, Geoffrey Walls Steuart. *Glasgow Cathedral: King David and the Church of Glasgow.* (Glasgow, 1995).

Barrow, Geoffrey Walls Steuart. *Glasgow Cathedral: King David and the Church of Glasgow*. (Glasgow, 1995).

Bartrum, Peter C. *A Welsh Classical Dictionary: People in History and Legend up to about 1000 A.D.* (Cardiff, 1993).

Binchy, David A. "Celtic and Anglo-Saxon Kingship", May 23-4, *O'Donnell Lectures Publications*. (Oxford, 1970).

Bromwich, Rachel. "Celtic Dynastic Themes and Breton Lays". *EC* 9 (Paris, 1961), 439-474.

-"Dwy Chwedl a Thair Rhamant". *Y Traddodiad Rhyddiaithyn yr Oesoedd Canol*. ed. Geraint Bowen. (Llandysul, 1974), 143-175.

-"Concepts of Arthur", *SC* 10/11 (Cardiff, 1976), 163-181.

-"Celtic Elements in Arthurian Romance: A General Survey", *The Legend of Arthur in the Middle Ages*. eds. P. B. Grout et al. (Cambridge, 1983), 41-55.

-a "The Tristan of the Welsh", *The Arthur of the Welsh*. eds. Rachel Bromwich et al. (Cardiff, 1991), 209-228.

-b "First Transmission to England and France", *The Arthur of the Welsh*. eds. Rachel Bromwich et al. (Cardiff, 1991), 273-298.

Bromwich, Rachel and R. Brinley Roberts. (eds.) *Astudiaethau ar yr Hengerdd: Studies in Old Welsh Poetry*. (Cardiff, 1978).

- Brynley F. Roberts and Alfred Owen Hughes Jarman. *The Arthur of the Welsh: The Arthurian Legend in Medieval Welsh Literature*. (Cardiff, 1991).

Brouland, Marie Thérèse. "Peredur ab Efrawg", *Perceval-Parzival; Hier et Aujourdhui*. ", eds. Danielle Buschinger and Wolfgang Spiewok. (Reineke, 1994), 59-70.

-"La souveraineté de Gwenhwyfar-Guenièvre", *Lancelot-Lanzelet; Hier et Aujourdhui*. eds. Danielle Buschinger and Michel Zink. (Reineke, 1995), 53-64.

Brown, Arthur C. L. *The Origin of the Grail Legend*. (New York, 1966).

Bruce, James Douglas. *The Evolution of Arthurian Romance from the Beginnings Down to the Year 1300*. (Gottingen, 1923).

Bruford, Alan. *Gaelic Folktales and Medieval Romances*. (Dublin, 1966).

Brusegan, Rosanna. "L' autre monde et *Le Chevalier de la Charrette*", eds. Danielle Buschinger and Michel Zink. *Lancelot-Lanzelet; Hier et Aujourdhui* (Reineke, 1995), 53-64.

Bullock-Davies, Constance. *Professional Interpreters and the Matter of Britain*. (Cardiff, 1966).

Burns, E. Jane. "*Vulgate Cycle*", *The New Arthurian Encyclopedia.* ed. Norris J. Lacy. (London, 1991), 496-498.

Busby, Keith. *Gauvain in Old French Literature.* (Amsterdam, 1980).

Buschinger, Danielle and Michel Zink (eds.) *Lancelot-Lanzelet; Hier et Aujourdhui.* (Reineke, 1995), 53-64.

Byrne, John Francis. *Irish Kings and high-Kings.* (London, 1973).

Campbell, John Francis. *More West Highland tales.* (Edinburgh, 1840-1860).

Carney, James. *Studies in Irish Literature and History.* Dublin Institute for Advanced Studies Series, (Dublin, 1955).

Chadwick, Hector Munro. *The Heroic Age.* (Cambridge, 1912).

Chadwick, Hector Munro and Nora Kershaw. *The Growth of Oral Literature.* 3 vols. (Cambridge, 1932, 1936, 1940).

Chadwick, Nora Kershaw. ed. *Studies in Early British History.* (Cambridge, 1954).

-*Studies in the Early British Church.* (Cambridge, 1958).

-*Celt and Saxon: Studies in the Early British Border.* (Cambridge, 1963).

Chadwick, Nora Kershaw. "Early Culture and Learning in North Wales", ed. Nora Chadwick. *Studies in the Early British Church.* (Cambridge, 1958), 29-120.

-b "Pictish and Celtic Marriage in Early Literary Tradition", *Scottish Gaelic Studies* 8 (Edinburgh, 1958), 56-115.

-*The Age of the Saints in the Early Celtic Church.* Riddell Memorial Lectures given March 22-24, 1960. (London, 1961).

-*Celtic Britain.* (London, 1964).

-*Early Brittany.* (Cardiff, 1969).

-"Early Literary Contacts Between Wales and Ireland", ed. Donald Moore. *The Irish Sea Province.* Cambrian Archaeological Association. (Cardiff, 1970).

-*The British Heroic Age: The Welsh and the Men of the North.* (Cardiff, 1976).

Chambers, Edmund Kerchever. *Arthur of Britain.* (London, 1927).

Chaney, William A. *The Cult of Kingship in Anglo-Saxon England: the transition from paganism to Christianity.* (Manchester, 1970).

Charles-Edwards, Thomas M. "The Date of the Four Branches of the Mabinogi", *THSC* (London, 1971), 263-298.

-"The Authenticity of the Gododdin: An Historian's View", *Astudiaethau ar yr Hengerdd.* eds. Rachel Bromwich and R. Brinley Jones. (Cardiff, 1978), 44-71.

-"The Arthur of History", *The Arthur of the Welsh*. eds. Rachel Bromwich et al. (Cardiff, 1991), 15-32.

Clancy, Thomas. Personal interview, 1996.

Collingwood, Roger George and John Nowell Linton Myres. *Roman Britain and the English Settlement*. (Oxford, 1936).

Colvin, H. M. "The king's works before the Norman conquest", *The History of the king's works, The Middle Ages*. eds. R. A. Brown and Howard Montagu Colvin. (London, 1963), 1-17.

Crick, Julia. "The Marshalling of Antiquity: Glastonbury's Historical Dossier", *The Archaeology and History of Glastonbury Abbey. Essays in Honour of the Ninetieth Birthday of C.A. Ralegh Radford*. eds. Lesley Abrams and James P. Carley. (Woodbridge, 1991), 163-190.

Cross, Tom Peete and William Albert Nitze. *Motif-Index of Early Irish Literature*. (Chicago, 1952).
-*Lancelot and Guinevere: A Study on the Origins of Courtly Love*. (New York, 1930).

Cross, Tom Peete and Clark Harris Slover. *Ancient Irish Tales*. (Dublin, rep. 1969).

Curle, Alexander Ormiston. "Report on the Excavation, in September 1913, of a Vitrified Fort at Rockcliffe, Dalbeattie, known as the Mote of Mark", *PSAS* 12, 4th series. (Edinburgh, 1914), 125-169.

Dark, Kenneth Rainsbury. "A Sub-Roman Defence of Hadrian's Wall", *Brit* 18 (London, 1992), 111-120.
-*Civitas to Kingdom: British Political Continuity 300-800*. (Leicester, 1994).

Darrah, John. *Paganism in Arthurian Romance*. (Woodbridge, 1994).

Davies, Wendy. "Property Rights and Property Claims in Welsh "Vitae" of the Eleventh Century", *Hagiographie, cultures et sociétés ive-xiie sieclés*. ed. P. Riché. (Paris, 1981), 515-533.

Der Meer, F. van. *Augustine the Bishop: the life and work of a father of the church*. trans. Brian Battershaw and G. R. Lamb. (London, 1961).

Diune, Francoise. "La vie de S. Samson, à propos d'un ouvrage récent", *Annales de Bretagne* 28 (1912-13), 332-356.

Diverres, Armel Hughes. "The Grail and the Third Crusade: Thoughts on *Le Conte du Graal* by Chrétien de Troyes", *Arthurian Literature X*. ed. Richard Barber. (Cambridge, 1990), 13-109.

Dumville, David. "Some Aspects of the Chronology of the *Historia Brittonum*", *BBCS* 25 (Cardiff, 1974), 439-445.

- "Nennius and the *Historia Brittonum*", *SC* 10/11 (Cardiff, 1976), 78-95.
- "The Anglian Collection of Royal Genealogies and Regnal Lists", *ASE* 5 (Cambridge, 1976), 23-50.
- "Sub-Roman Britain: history and legend", *History* 42 no. 205 (London, 1977), 173-192.
- "On the North British section of the *Historia Brittonum*", *WHR* 8 (Cardiff, 1977), 345-354.
- *Ireland in Early Mediaeval Europe studies in memory of Kathleen Hughes.* (Cambridge, 1982).
- "The Chronology of *De Excidio Britanniae*, Book I", eds. Michael Lapidge and David Dumville. *Gildas: New Approaches.* (Dover, 1984), 61-84.
- "Gildas and Uinniau", eds. Michael Lapidge and David Dumville. *Gildas: New Approaches.* (Dover, 1984), 207-214.
- "Early Welsh Poetry: Problems of Historicity", ed. Brynley F. Roberts. *Early Welsh Poetry: Studies in the Book of Aneirin.* (Aberystwyth, 1988), 1-16.
- *St. Patrick, A. D. 493-1993.* (Cambridge, 1993).

Ellis, Peter Berresford. *Dictionary of Celtic Mythology.* (London, 1992).

Evison, Vera I. ed. *Angles, Jutes, and Saxons.* (Oxford, 1981).

"Distribution Map of England in the first two phases", *Angles, Jutes, and Saxons.* ed. Vera I. Evison. (Oxford, 1981).

Faral, Edmond. "Ovide et quelques autres *Roman d'Éneas*", *Romania* 40 (Paris, 1911), 161-234.

Fletcher, Robert Huntington. *Studies and Notes in Philology and Literature: vol. X. The Arthurian Material in the Chronicles, Especially those of Britain and France.* (Boston, 1906).

Finberg, "St. Patrick and Glastonbury", *The Irish Ecclesiastical Record* 107 (Dublin, 1967).

Foot, Sarah. "Glastonbury's Early Abbots", *The Archaeology and History of Glastonbury Abbey: Essays in Honour of the Ninetieth Birthday of C.A. Ralegh Radford.* eds. Lesley Abrams and James P. Carley. (Woodbridge, 1991), 163-90.

Frappier, Jean. "Chrétien de Troyes", *Arthurian Literature in the Middle Ages.* ed. Roger Sherman Loomis. (Oxford, 1959), 157-91.
- "The Vulgate Cycle", *Arthurian Literature in the Middle Ages.* ed. Roger Sherman Loomis. (Oxford, 1959), 295-318.

Fulford, Michael. "Roman Britain: New Perspectives and Directions", *Dalrymple Lectures Series*. Feb. 13-16, 1996.
Goetinck, Glenys. *Peredur: a study of Welsh tradition in the grail legends*. (Cardiff, 1975).
Goodrich, Norma Lorre. *King Arthur*. (Philadelphia, 1986).
Goodwin, Thomas. *A Latin-English Dictionary*. (London, 1855).
Gove, Philip Babcock. ed. *Webster's Third New International Dictionary of the English Language Unabridged*. (London, 1961).
Gowans, Linda. *Cei and the Arthurian Legend*. (Cambridge, 1988).
Graves, Robert. *The Greek Myths*. 2 vols. (Baltimore, 1955).
Greene, David. "The Chariot as described in Irish Literature", *The Iron Age in the Irish Sea Province*. ed. Charles Thomas. (London, 1972), 59-73.
Grimsby, John L. "The Continuations of Chrétien de Troyes", *The New Arthurian Encyclopedia*. ed. Norris J. Lacy. (London, 1991), 99-101.
Griscom, Acton. *The 'Historia Regum Britanniae' of Geoffrey of Monmouth, with contributions to the study of its place in early British history by Acton Griscom, M.A.* (London, 1929).
Grout, P. B. et al. *Arthurian Studies VII: The Legend of King Arthur in the Middle Ages*. (Cambridge, 1983).
Guyer, Foster, E. *Dissertation: The Influence of Ovid on Chréstien de Troyes*. (Chicago, 1921).
Hanson, R. P. C. *Saint Patrick: His Origins and Career*. (Oxford, 1968).
Harbison, Peter. *Guide to the National Monuments of Ireland*. (London, 1970).
Henderson, Jane Frances Anne. "A Critical Edition of Evrat's *Genesis: Creation to the Flood*", unpublished D.Phil. thesis, Toronto, 1977.
Hicks, Edward. *Sir Thomas Malory: His Turbulent Career*. (Cambridge, 1928).
Higham, Nicholas. *The English Conquest: Gildas and Britain in the fifth century*. (Leicester, 1994).
Hooke, Della. *Anglo-Saxon Settlements*. (Oxford, 1988).
Hope-Taylor, Brian. *Yeavering: An Anglo-British Centre of Early Northumbria*. HMSO, (London, 1977).
Hughes, Kathleen. *The Church in Early Irish Society*. (Cambridge, 1966).
-"The Welsh Latin Chronicles: *Annales Cambriae* and related texts", *PBA* 59 (London, 1975), 233-259.

-*Celtic Britain in the Early Middle Ages; studies in Welsh and Scottish sources.* ed. David Dumville. (Cambridge, 1980).
-*Church and Society in Ireland, A.D. 400-1200.* ed. David Dumville. (Cambridge, 1980).

Hunt, Tony. "The Prologue to Chrestien's *Li contes del graal*", *Romania* 92 (Paris, 1971), 359-379.
-"Chrétien's Prologues Reconsidered. Medieval Studies in Honor of Douglas Kelly", Keith Busby and Norris Lacy. *Faux Titre: Études de Langue et Litterature Francaises.* (Amsterdam, 1994), 153-168.

Jackson, Anthony. *The Symbol Stones of Scotland.* (Stromness, 1984).

Jackson, Kenneth Hurlstone. "Again Arthur's Battles", *MP* 43 (Chicago, 1946), 44-57.
-*Language and History in Early Britain: A Chronological Survey of the Brittonic Languages 1st to 12th c. A.D.* (Edinburgh, 1953).
-"The British Language during the Period of English Settlement", *Studies in Early British History.* ed. Nora Kershaw Chadwick. (Cambridge, 1954), 61-82.
-"The Britons in Southern Scotland", *A* 29 (Gloucester, 1955), 77-88.
-"The Sources for the Life of St. Kentigern", *Studies in the Early British Church.* ed. Nora Kershaw Chadwick. (Cambridge, 1958), 273-358.
-"The Arthur of History", *Arthurian Literature in the Middle Ages.* ed. Roger Sherman Loomis. (Oxford, 1959), 1-11.
-*The International Popular Tale and Early Welsh Tradition.* (Cardiff, 1961).
-"On the Northern British Section in Nennius", *Celt and Saxon: Studies in the Early British Border.* ed. Nora Kershaw Chadwick. (Cambridge, 1963), 20-62.

Jackson, Sidney. *Celtic and Other Stone Heads.* (Shipley, 1973).
-*The Pictish Trail: A traveller's Guide to the Old Pictish Kingdoms.* (St. Ola, 1989).

Jarman, Alfred Owen Hughes and Gwillym Rees Jones (eds.) *A Guide to Early Welsh Literature.* 4 vols. (Cardiff, 1976).

Johnston, James B. *Place-Names of Scotland.* (London, 1934).

Jones, Gwynn T. "Some Arthurian Material in Keltic", *Aberystwyth Studies* 14 (Aberystwyth, 1936), 37-93.

Jones, Robert M. "Y Rhamantau Cymraeg a'u Cysylltiad a'r Rhamantau Ffrangeg", *LlC* 4 (Cardiff, 1957), 208-227.

Jones, Thomas. "Datblygiadau Cynnar Chwedl Arthur", trans. Gerald Morgan. "The Early Evolution of Arthur", *NMS* 8 (Nottingam, 1964), 3-21.

Kelly, Anne. *Eleanor of Aquitaine and the Four Kings.* (Cambridge, 1950).

Kelly, Fergus. ed. *A Guide to Early Irish Law.* vol. 3 of *Early Irish Law Series.* Dublin Institute for Advanced Studies, (Dublin, 1988).

Kenyon, John R. *Medieval Fortifications.* (Leicester, 1990).

Ker, William P. *Epic and Romance: Essays on Medieval Literature.* (Dover, 1896).

Kittredge, George Lyman. *A Study of Gawain and the Green Knight.* (Harvard, 1916).

Koch, John T. and John Carey, eds. *The Celtic Heroic Age: Literary Sources for Ancient Celtic Europe and Early Ireland and Wales.* (Malden, 1994).

Köhler, Erich. "Ideal und Wirklichkeit in der Höfischen Epik: Studien zur form der Frühen Artus-und Graldichtung", *Zeitschrift fur Romanische Philologie* 97 (Tübingen, 1956).

Krey, A. C. "William of Tyre", *S* 16 (Cambridge, 1941), 149-66.

Laing, Lloyd and Jennifer. "Timber Halls in Dark Age Britain-Some Problems", *TDGNAHS* 3rd Series 46. (Dumfries, 1969).
-*The Archaeology of Late Celtic Britain and Ireland.* (London, 1975).
-"Archaeological Notes on Some Scottish Early Christian Stones", *PSAS* 114 (Darking, 1985), 277-287.

Lapidge, Michael and David Dumville. *Gildas: New Approaches.* (Dover, 1984).

Laurie, Helen C. R. *Two Studies in Chrétien de Troyes.* (Genève, 1972).

le Gentil, Pierre. "The Work of Robert de Boron and the *Didot Perceval*, *Arthurian Literature in the Middle Ages.* ed. Roger Sherman Loomis. (Oxford, 1959), 251-262.

Lejeune, Rita. "The *Troubadours*", *Arthurian Literature in the Middle Ages.* ed. Roger Sherman Loomis. (Oxford, 1959), 393-399.

Lewis, Ceri. "The Historical Background of Early Welsh Verse", *A Guide to Early Welsh Literature.* vol. 1. eds. Alfred Owen Hughes Jarman and Gwillym Rees Jones. (Cardiff, 1976), 11-50.

Lewis, Michael Jonathan Taunton. *Temples in Roman Britain.* (Cambridge, 1966).

Lewis, Saunders. "Pwyll Pen Annwfn", *LlC* 9 (Cardiff, 1967), 230-233.
-"Branwen", *LlC* 10 (Cardiff, 1968), 230-3.
-"Branwen", *Y Traethodydd* (Cardiff, 1969a), 137-42.
-"Branwen", *Y Traethodydd* (Cardiff, 1969b), 185-92.
-"*Branwen*", *Ysgrifau Beirniadol* 5 (Gwag gee, 1970), 30-43.
Lloyd-Morgan, Ceridwen. "Narrative Structure in *Peredur*", *ZCP* 38 (Berlin, 1981), 187-231.
-"Breuddwyd Rhonabwy and Later Arthurian Literature", *The Arthur of the Welsh.* eds. Rachel Bromwich et al. (Cardiff, 1991), 183-208.
-"Lancelot in Wales", *Shifts and Transpositions in Medieval Literature.* ed. Karen Pratt. (Cambridge, 1994), 169-179.
Loomis, Laura Hibbard. "The Sword Bridge of Chrétien de Troyes and its Celtic Original", *PMLA* 4 (Columbia, 1913), 166-190.
Loomis, Roger Sherman (ed.) *Arthurian Literature in the Middle Ages.* (Oxford, 1959).
Loomis, Roger Sherman. *Celtic Myth and Arthurian Romance.* (New York, 1927).
-"The Date of the Arthurian Sculpture at Modena", *Medieval Studies in Memory of Gertrude Schoepperle Loomis.* ed. Roger Sherman Loomis. (New York, 1927), 209-228.
-"Discussions: Cause or Coincidence, a Reply to Monsieur Ferdinand Lot", *Romania* 54 (Paris, 1928), 515-526.
-"Calogrenanz and Crestien's Originality", *MLN* 43 (Baltimore, 1928), 215-222.
-"By What Route did the Romantic Tradition of Arthur Reach the French?", *MP* 33, 3. (Chicago, 1936), 225-238.
-"The Spoils of Annwfn: An Early Arthurian Poem", *PMLA* 56 (Menasha, 1941), 887-936.
-*Arthurian Tradition and Chrétien de Troyes.* (New York, 1949).
-"Edward I, Arthurian Admirer", *S* 28 (Cambridge, 1953), 114-127.
-*Wales and the Arthurian Legend.* (Cardiff, 1956).
-"The Oral Diffusion of the Arthurian Legend", *Arthurian Literature in the Middle Ages.* ed. Roger Sherman Loomis. (Oxford, 1959), 52-64.
-b "The Origins of the Grail Legends", *Arthurian Literature in the Middle Ages.* ed. Roger Sherman Loomis. (Oxford, 1959), 274-294.
-*The Grail: From Celtic Myth to Christian Symbol.* (Cardiff, 1963).

-"The Strange History of Caradoc of Vannes", *Franciplegius: Medieval Studies in Honor of Francis Peabody Magoun, Jr.* eds. Jess B. Bessinger and Robert P. Creed. (New York, 1965), 232-9.
Lot, Ferdinand. *Nennius et l' Historia Brittonum. Étude critique suivie d' une édition de diverses versions de ce texte.* 2 vols. (Paris, 1934).
Lovecy, Ian. "The Celtic Sovereignty Theme and the Structure of *Peredur*", *SC* 12-13 (Cardiff, 1978), 133-46.
-"Historia Peredur ab Efrawg", *The Arthur of the Welsh.* eds. Rachel Bromwich et al. (Cardiff, 1991), 171-182.
Macalister, R. A. Stewart. *Studies in Irish Epigraphy pt. III.* (London, 1907).
Mac Cana, Proinsias. "Aspects of the Theme of the King and Goddess", *EC* 5 (Paris, 1955), 76-114.
-"Aspects of the Theme of the King and Goddess", *EC* 6 (Paris, 1956), 356-413.
-*Branwen daughter of Llyr.* (Cardiff, 1958).
-*Celtic Mythology.* (Hamlyn, 1970).
-"The Sinless Underworld of *Immram Brain*", *Ériu* 65. Royal Irish Academy, (Dublin, 1976), 73-94.
Mac Cana, Proinsias, Meic Stephens and R. Brinley Jones. (eds.). *The Mabinogi.* (Cardiff, 1992).
MacQueen, John. "Yvain, Ewen, and Owein ap Urien", *TDGNAHS*, 3rd Series 33. Council of the Society, (Dumfries, 1956), 107-131.
-"A Reply to Professor Jackson", *TDGNAHS*, 3rd Series 36, (Dumfries, 1959), 175-84.
Mallory, J.P. et al (eds.) *Aspects of the Táin.* (Belfast, 1992).
-"The World of Cú Chulainn: The Archaeology of *Taín Bo Cuailgne*", eds. J.P. Mallory et al. *Aspects of the Táin.* (Belfast, 1992), 103-53.
Mason, J. F. A. "The 'Honour of Richmond' in 1086", *EHR* 78. (London, 1963), 703-4.
McCash, June Hall. "Marie de Champagne's 'Cuer d'ome et cors de Fame': Aspects of Feminism and Misogyny in the Twelfth Century", *The Spirit of the Court: Selected Proceedings of the Fourth Congress of the International Courtly Literature Society.* eds. Glyn S. Burgess and Robert A. Taylor. (Toronto, 1985), 234-245.
Middleton, Roger. "Chwedl Geraint ab Erbin", *The Arthur of the Welsh.* eds. Rachel Bromwich et al. (Cardiff, 1991), 147-158.
Miller, Molly. *Sicilian Colony Dates.* (New York, 1970).

-"The Commanders at Arthuret", *TCWAAS* 75 (Kendall, 1975), 96-118.

-"Historicity and the Pedigrees of the North countrymen", *B* 26 (Cardiff, 1976), 255-280.

-"Date-guessing and Pedigrees", *SC* 10 (Cardiff, 1976), 78-95.

Moore, Donald et al (eds.) *The Irish Sea Province in Archaeology and History*. Cambrian Archaeological Association, (Cardiff, 1970).

Morris, John. *The Age of Arthur*. (London, 1973).

-*Arthurian Period Sources, vol. 3: Persons.* (Shopwyke Manor Barn, 1995).

Murray, James A. H. et al (eds.) *The Oxford English Dictionary*. vol. 3. (Oxford, 1961).

Murray, Margaret Alice. *The Witchcult in Western Europe*. (London, 1921).

-*The God of the Witches*. (London, 1931).

Newell, William W. "Arthurian Notes", *MLN* 17 (Baltimore, 1902), 277-8.

Newstead, Helen. *Brân the Blessed in Arthurian Romance*. (New York, rep. 1966).

Nitze, William Albert. "*Sens et Matière* dans les Oeuvres de Chrétien de Troyes", *Romania* 44 (Paris, 1915-17), 14-36.

-"Arthurian Names: Arthur", *PMLA* 64 (Menasha, 1949), 585-596.

-"*Perlesvaus*", *Arthurian Literature in the Middle Ages*. ed. Roger Sherman Loomis. (Oxford, 1959), 263-273.

Noble, Peter S. *Love and Marriage in Chrétien de Troyes*. (Cardiff, 1982).

Nutt, Alfred. *Studies on the Legend of the Holy Grail*. (London, 1888).

Oinas, Felix J. et al. *Heroic Epic and Saga: An Introduction to the World's Great Folk Epics*. (London, 1978).

The Old French Arthurian Vulgate and Post-Vulgate. vols. 1-5. trans. Norris J. Lacy. (New York, 1993).

O' Hogain, Daithi. *Fionn macCumhail. Images of the Celtic Hero*. (Dublin, 1988).

O' Rahilly, Cecile. *Ireland and Wales: Their Historical and Literary Traditions*. (New York, 1924).

O'Rahilly, Thomas F. *Early Irish History and Mythology*. (Dublin, 1946).

-"On the Origin of the Names Érainn and Ériu", *Ériu* 35 (Dublin, 1946), 7-28.

Owen, D.D.R. "Chrétien and the *Roland*", *An Arthurian Tapestry: Essays in Memory of Lewis Thorpe.* eds. Kenneth Varty et al. (Glasgow, 1981), 139-49.
-*The Evolution of the Grail Legend.* (Edinburgh, 1968).
Padel, O. J. "The Cornish Background of the Tristan Stories", *CMCS* 1 (Cambridge, 1982), 53-82.
-"Geoffrey of Monmouth and Cornwall", *CMCS* 9 (Cambridge, 1984), 1-28.
-"The Nature of Arthur", *CMCS* 27 (Cambridge, 1994), 1-32.
Paris, Gaston. "Études sur les Romans de la Table Ronde: Lancelot du Lac", *Romania* 19 (Paris, 1883), 459-534.
Paton, Lucy Allen. *Fairy Mythology in Arthurian Romance.* (New York, 1960).
Peebles, Rose J. *Legend of Longinus in Ecclesiastical Tradition and in English Literature.* (Baltimore, 1911).
Pelan, Margaret. *L' influence du Brut de Wace sur les romanciers francais de son temps.* (Genève, rep. 1974).
Piggott, Stuart. "The Sources of Geoffrey of Monmouth I: The Pre Roman King List", *A* 15 (Gloucester, 1941), 269-286.
Piper, Paul Hermann Eduard. *Höfisches Epik* 2 (Stuttgart, 1892-5).
Pokorny, Julius. "Der cymrische Sagenheld Peredur", *Beiträge zur Namenforsung* 1 (Berlin, 1948), 38.
Pope, Mildred Katharine. *From Latin to Modern French with Especial Consideration of Anglo-Norman*; phonology and morphology. (Manchester, rev. 1952).
Poulin, J.C. "Hagiographie et Politique. La première vie de S. Samson de Dol", *Francia* 5 (Paris, 1977), 1-26.
Powell, Thomas George Eyre. *The Celts.* (London, 1958).
Radford, Courtenay Arthur Ralegh. "Report on the excavations at Castle Dore", *The Journal of the Royal Institute of Cornwall.* (Truro, 1951).
Raftery, Barry. "Irish hill-forts", *The Iron Age in the Irish Sea-Province.* ed. Charles Thomas. (Dublin, 1972), 79-98.
Rahtz, Philip A. "Celtic Society in Somerset A. D. 400-700", *B* 30 (Cardiff, 1982), 176-200.
Rankin, H. D. *Celts and the Classical World.* (London, 1987).
Remy. "Graal", *The Catholic Encyclopedia: an international work of reference on the constitution, doctrine, and history of the Catholic Church.* eds. Charles G. Herbermann et al. (London, 1907).
Rhys, Sir John. *Studies in the Arthurian Legend.* (Oxford, 1891).

-"Notes on the Hunting of the Twrch Trwyth", *THSC* (London, 1896).
-*Celtic Folklore: Welsh and Manx.* (Oxford, 1901).
-and David Brynmor-Jones. *The Welsh People: Chapters on their Origin, History, and Laws, Language, Literature, and Characteristics.* (London, 1923).
Richmond, Sir Ian Archibald. *Roman Britain.* (Baltimore, 1963).
Rider, Jeff. "Arthur and the Saints", *King Arthur through the Ages.* (London, 1990), 3-21.
Ritchie, Graham. *Chrétien de Troyes and Scotland.* (Oxford, 1952).
-*The Normans in Scotland.* (Edinburgh, 1954).
Roberts, Brynley F. "The Welsh Romance of the Lady of the Fountain", *Arthurian Literature in the Middle Ages.* ed. Roger Sherman Loomis. (Oxford, 1959), 170-182.
-"The Treatment of Personal Names in the Early Welsh Versions of *Historia Regum Britanniae*", *B* 25 (Cardiff, 1973), 274-290.
-"Geoffrey of Monmouth and Welsh Historical Tradition", *NMS* 20 (Nottingham, 1976), 1-26.
-"*Culhwch ac Olwen, The Triads*, and Saints' Lives", *The Arthur of the Welsh.* eds. Rachel Bromwich et al. (Cardiff, 1991), 73-96.
Roberts, Brynley F. (ed.) *Early Welsh Poetry: Studies in the Book of Aneirin.* (Aberystwth, 1988).
Ross, Anne. *Pagan Celtic Britain.* (London, 1967).
Rychner, J. "Le prologue du *Chevalier de la Charrette*", *Vox Romanica* 26 (Paris, 1967), 1-23.
Selkirk, A. "Birdoswald. Dark Age Walls in a Roman Fort", *Current Archaeology* 116 (London, 1990), 288-291.
Sims-Williams, Patrick. *Religion and Literature in Western England, 600-800.* (Cambridge, 1990).
-"The Early Welsh Arthurian Poems", *The Arthur of the Welsh.* eds. Rachel Bromwich et al. (Cardiff, 1991), 33-72.
Sjoestedt, Marie Louise. trans. Myles Dillon. *Gods and Heroes of the Celts.* (London, 1949).
Spaarnay, Hendricus. "Hartmann von Aue and his Successors", *Arthurian Literature in the Middle Ages.* eds. Roger Sherman Loomis. (Oxford, 1959), 430-443.
Springer, Otto. "Wolfram's *Parzival*", *Arthurian Literature in the Middle Ages.* eds. Roger Sherman Loomis. (Oxford, 1959), 218-250.

Stancliffe, Clare. *St. Martin and his Hagiographer: History and Miracle in Sulpicius Severus.* (Oxford, 1983).

Stenton, Sir Frank Merry. *The First Century of English Feudalism 1066-1166.* (London, 1932).

Stephens, Meic. ed. *The Oxford Companion the Literature of Wales.* (Oxford, 1986).

Tatlock, John Strong Perry. *The Legendary History of Britain: Geoffrey of Monmouth's Historia Regum Britanniae and Its Early Vernacular Versions.* (Berkeley, 1950).

Thomas, Charles. *Britain and Ireland in Early Christian Times: A.D. 440-800.* (London, 1971).

-*The Iron Age in the Irish Sea Province from papers given at a CBA conference held at Cardiff January 3 to 5, 1969.* Council for British Archaeology, (London, 1972).

-*Christianity in Roman Britain to A.D. 500.* (London, 1981).

-*English Heritage Book of Tintagel.* (London, 1993).

Thompson, Albert Wilder. "The Additions to Chrétien's *Perceval*", *Arthurian Literature in the Middle Ages.* ed. Roger Sherman Loomis. (Oxford, 1959), 206-217.

Thompson, E. A. *St. Germanus and the End of Roman Britain.* (Woodbridge, 1984).

Thomson, R. L. *Owain, or Chwedl Iarlles y Ffynnon.* (Dublin, 1955).

-"Owain: Chwedl Iarles y Ffynnon", *The Arthur of the Welsh.* eds. Rachel Bromwich et al. (Cardiff, 1991), 159-170.

Thompson, Stith. *Motif-Index of Folk-Literature: a classification of narrative elements in folktales, ballads, myths, fables, mediaeval romances, exempla, fabliaux, jestbooks, and local legends.* 6 vols. (Copenhagen, 1955-8).

Thurneysen, Rudolf. "Zimmer, Nennius vindicatus". *ZDP* 28 (Halle, 1896), 80-113.

-*Die Irisch Helden-und Königsage bis zum siebzehnten Jahrhundert.* (Halle, 1921).

Varty, Kenneth et al. *An Arthurian Tapestry: Essays in Memory of Lewis Thorpe.* (Glasgow, 1981).

Vendryes, John. "L'Unité en trois personnes chez les Celtes", *Compte-rendus de l'Academie des Inscriptions et des Belles Lettres.* (Paris, 1935).

Vigneras. "Chrétien de Troyes rediscovered", *MP* 32 (Paris, 1934-5), 341-2.

Villemarqué, Viscount Hersart de la. *Les Romans de la Table Ronde et les Contes des anciens Bretons.* (Paris, 1842).
Vinaver, Eugene. *The Works of Thomas Malory.* (Oxford, 1947).
Voresch, Karl. *Introduction to the Study of Old French Literature.* trans. Francis M. duMont. (New York, 1931).
Warren, F.M. "On the Latin sources of *Thèbes* and *Énéas*", *PMLA* 16 (Menasha, 1901), 375-384.
Watts, Dorothy. *Christians and Pagans in Roman Britain.* (New York, 1991).
Webster, Graham. *The British Celts and their Gods under Rome.* (London, 1986).
Webster, Kenneth Grant Tremayne. "Arthur and Charlemagne", *Englische Studien; Zeitschrift für Englische Philologie* 36 (Leipzig, 1906), 340-51.
-"Ulrich von Zatzikhoven's 'Welsches Buoch", *Harvard Studies and Notes in Philology and Literature* 16 (Harvard, 1934), 203-28.
Weinraub, Eugene J. *Chrétien's Jewish Grail: A New Investigation of the Imagery and Significance of Chrétien de Troyes's Grail Episode Based Upon Medieval Hebraic Sources.* (Chapel Hill, 1976).
West, Geoffrey D. *An Index of Proper Names in French Arthurian Verse Romances 1150-1300.* (Toronto, 1969).
-*An Index of Proper Names in French Arthurian Prose Romances.* (Toronto, 1978).
Weston, Jessie L. *The Legend of Sir Gawain: Studies Upon its Original Scope and Significance.* (London, 1897).
-*The Legend of Lancelot du Lac.* (London, 1901).
-*The Legend of Sir Perceval: Studies upon its Origin, Development, and Position in the Arthurian Cycle.* 2 vols. (London, 1906 and 1909).
-*The Quest of the Holy Grail.* (London, 1913).
-*From Ritual to Romance.* (London, 1920).
Wheeler, Robert Eric Mortimer. *Report on the Excavation of the Prehistoric, Roman, and post Roman site in Lydney Park, Gloucestershire.* (Oxford, 1932).
Williams, Hugh. *Christianity in Early Britain.* (Oxford, 1912).
Williams, Sir Ifor. *Cyfranc Lludd a Llevelys.* (Bangor, 1922).
-*Pedeir Keinc y Mabinogi.* (Cardiff, 1930).
-*Lectures on Old Welsh Poetry.* (Dublin, 1944).
Williams, Mary. *Essai sur la composition du roman gallois de Peredur.* (Paris, 1909).

Wynn, Marianne. "Wolfram von Eschenbach", *Dictionary of Literary Biography vol. 138: German Writers and Works of the High Middle Ages: 1170-1280.* eds. James Hardy and Will Hasty. (London, 1994), 185-206.

Yasuda, Kenneth. *The Japanese Haiku: its essential nature, history, and possibilities in English: with selected examples.* (Tuttle, 1957).

Zaddy, Zara Patrick. *Chrétien Studies: Problems of Form and Meaning in 'Erec', 'Yvain', 'Cligés' and 'the Charrete'.* (Glasgow, 1973).

Index

Adamnan, 69, 173
Addanc, 143
Adonis, 112
Aesir, 43
Agricola, 80
Alcock, Leslie, 3, 7, 56, 76, 173, 196
Alexander the Great, 117
Alexander King of Scotland, 101
Alexander, 24, 31, 63, 73
Andrew of Wyntoun, 74
Angharad Law Eurawg, 143
Annales Cambriae, xii, xvi, 13, 14, 15, 16, 139, 173, 201
Annals of Connacht, 186, 197
Annals of Loch Cé, 186, 197
Anubis, 76
Arawn, 76
Armes Prydein, 120
Atbret, 215
Babylonia, 83, 112, 215
Bademagus, 6, 9, 48, 49, 64, 65, 66, 76
Bartrum, Peter, 2, 140, 223
Bede, xi
Belatacudros, 4, 137
Beli, 4, 94, 116, 130, 131, 132, 136, 137, 141, 175, 201, 203, 205, 207, 208, 209, 212, 215, 220
Beowulf, 42, 56, 73, 74, 126
Black Book of Carmarthen, 38, 152
Brân, 57, 76, 116, 118, 125, 126, 129, 130, 131, 132, 134, 136, 138, 152, 161, 220, 222
Branwen, 143, 151, 152, 153, 154, 237

Breton, 1, 14, 21, 31, 43, 78, 102, 119, 120, 133, 149, 174, 185, 188, 195
Breuddwyt Rhonabwy, 144
Brittany, 21, 40, 120, 127, 169, 211, 218
Bromwich, Rachel, vii, xvi, xvii, 1, 2, 3, 7, 12, 13, 16, 17, 29, 30, 34, 37, 38, 39, 40, 41, 42, 43, 53, 72, 78, 90, 102, 118, 119, 120, 126, 127, 139, 153, 156, 160, 161, 171, 198, 218
Bron, 29, 116, 131, 137
Brun, 170
Bushido, 82
Bwya, 166

Cadegr, xv, 5
Caer Lloyw, 149
Caesar, Julius, 24, 58, 80, 86, 117, 131, 217
Caithness, 167
Canu Taliesin, 64
Capellanus, 22, 23, 25, 26, 32, 59, 61, 79, 85
Caradoc, 45, 46, 47, 52, 54, 116, 149, 159, 212
Caradoc of Llancarfan, 47, 212
Carlisle, 14, 100
Caw, 173
Cei, 35, 46, 47, 48, 91, 95, 116, 136, 142, 148, 152, 154, 186, 187, 188, 189, 198, 208, 213, 214, 215, 218
Cernunnos, 131, 167
Chadwick, 2, 15, 29, 30, 36, 43, 74, 75, 76, 134, 158, 190, 197

Chariot, v xvii, 80, 81, 82, 86, 212, 217
Charlemagne, 24, 117, 169, 172, 192
Chaucer, 63, 90, 185
Cicero, 25
Clamadeu, 192
Cligès, 21, 22, 23, 24, 25, 31, 32, 35, 63, 64, 196
Clovis, 169, 170, 212
Coel, 30
Conchobar, 63, 84, 193
Conn, 77, 128, 184, 185
Corbenic, 117, 127, 147
Cornwall, 3, 14, 21, 211, 240
Coroticus, 167
Cotouatre, 100, 102
Críth Gablach, 58, 59, 64, 65, 223
Crockett, Davy, 36
Cú Chúlainn, 74, 75, 197
Culhwch, 13, 29, 34, 35, 38, 41, 58, 67, 70, 116, 126, 133, 139, 145, 151, 153, 160, 187, 188, 189, 190, 214, 218, 220, 221
Culhwch ac Olwen, 13, 29, 34, 35, 38, 41, 58, 67, 70, 116, 126, 133, 139, 145, 151, 153, 160, 187, 188, 189, 214, 218, 220, 221
Cumbria, 29, 30, 201
Cumbric, 13, 29, 36
Dagda, 118
Dame Ragnell, 185, 219
Davies, Wendy, 8, 18, 20, 52
De Amore, 23, 26
De Antiquitate Glastonie Ecclesie, 105
De Bello Gallica, 58, 86

De Excidio Britanniae, xii, xv, 165, 210
Diarmid, 217
Dido, 24
Didot Perceval, 52, 108, 119, 131, 133, 143, 144, 149, 157, 170, 208
Dillus, 188, 189
Dio Cassius, 58
Dio's Roman History, 58
Diodorus Siculus, 66, 226
Diu Crône, 33, 50, 51, 77, 84, 119, 138, 148, 208
Documentum de modo et arte dictandi et versificandi, 73
Drust, 14, 43
Dumville, David, xii, xv, 2, 7, 14, 29, 30, 90, 171, 173, 211, 215
Dyfed, 165
Dyrnwch, 153
Dysgyl, 5, 8, 16, 95, 122, 130, 133, 136, 137, 141, 149, 154, 155, 170, 201, 208, 211, 212, 213, 214

Ecstasy of the Phantom, 185, 220
Efrawg, 133, 134, 135, 136, 208
Engygeron, 192
Enlil, 106
Erec, xiii, 11, 22, 23, 24, 25, 32, 37, 41, 43, 64, 70, 83, 90, 117, 120, 130, 196, 218
Erec et Enide, 11, 22, 25, 70, 120
Escoce Watre, 100, 102

Fergus, 2, 100

Fionn, 67, 106, 109, 116, 126, 160, 188, 195, 217
First Continuation, 124, 148, 159, 170
Fled Bricrenn, 197
Fouke Fitz Warin, 147, 204
Frappier, Jean, 31, 149, 159
Freculf, 105

Galerius, 166
Galloway, vii, 14, 71, 100, 101, 138, 166, 180, 201, 212
Gauvain, 6, 7, 11, 14, 24, 32, 33, 35, 41, 55, 59, 60, 64, 66, 70, 71, 75, 77, 80, 82, 85, 91, 95, 100, 101, 116, 125, 132, 138, 148, 149, 159, 178, 180, 181, 182, 191, 198, 201, 202, 208, 212, 218, 219, 221
Gawain, 101, 131, 138, 145, 218
Genesis, 26
Geoffrey of Monmouth, xi, 18, 23, 34, 35, 47, 54, 159, 195, 210, 212
Geography, 58
Gerbert, 149
Gereint, 134, 218
Germanus, 139, 174
Gilgamesh, 53, 215
Glas, 5, 8, 16, 40, 55, 73, 79, 85, 89, 93, 211, 213, 214
Glastonbury, 45, 46, 47, 52, 53, 105, 146, 147, 148, 158
Glewlwyd, 148, 152, 187, 189
Gonemans, 29, 116, 129, 133, 136, 139, 141, 203
Gorlois, 133

Gorre, 6, 25, 66, 68, 69, 70, 71, 76, 80, 82, 83, 192
Gottfried von Strassbourg, 90
Graelant, 119, 120
Grainne, 217
Greece, 83, 112
Gregory of Tours, 69, 169
Guinevere, 8, 221
Guinièvre, 6, 21, 22, 25, 27, 33, 34, 35, 40, 41, 45, 46, 47, 48, 50, 51, 59, 61, 66, 70, 71, 79, 82, 83, 84, 85, 86, 95, 147, 159, 183, 211, 212, 218
Gwalchmai, 91, 129, 132, 136, 138, 140, 141, 170, 208, 213, 219
Gwenhwyfar, 34, 35, 42, 46, 47, 51, 72, 77, 187, 197, 215, 221
Gwrtheyrn, 169, 174
Gwynedd, 15, 18, 30, 165, 173, 201

Hades, 76, 119
Hadrian's Wall, 131
Hafgan, 76
Hartmann von Aue, 50, 70, 77
Heinrich von dem Türlin, 50, 148
Hélinand de Froidmont, 116, 126
Henry I, xi, 21, 25, 90, 100, 156, 215
Henry II, xi, 21, 25, 90, 100, 156, 215
Heracles, 68, 76, 196
Hercules, 58, 169
Herodotus, 57, 58
Heroic Age, ix, 7, 8, 75

Historia, xi, xii, xv, xvi, 14, 15, 16, 27, 30, 35, 41, 48, 53, 67, 120, 174, 193, 201, 202, 212, 213

Historia Brittonum, xii, xv, xvi, 14, 15, 16, 30, 120, 174, 201, 202, 213

Historia Regum Britanniae, xi, 27, 35, 41, 48, 53, 121, 174, 193, 212

Histories, 57, 58

Hrolf Kraki's Saga, 56, 64, 73, 136, 179, 180, 215

Hugh de Morville, 48, 49

Hughes, Kathleen, xii, 2, 7, 14, 29, 30, 90

Iliad, 8, 63, 210, 213

Irish Law, 58

Iwein, 35, 50, 54

Jackson, Kenneth Hurlstone, xii, xv, 2, 7, 13, 15, 16, 29, 30, 90, 126, 213, 215

Jandrée, 9, 57, 61, 204

Jason, 25

Keii, 49, 50, 91

Keu, 32, 33, 35, 49, 197, 221

Kingship, 53, 84, 85, 105, 111, 119, 127, 128, 142, 175, 181, 182, 183, 184, 185, 186, 190, 191, 197, 198, 219, 221, 220, 221

Koch, John, xvi, 30, 64, 67, 75, 151, 160, 174, 203

Laing, Lloyd, 3, 56, 86

Lancelot, xiii, 6, 7, 21, 22, 25, 27, 33, 35, 36, 37, 38, 39, 40, 42, 53, 55, 56, 57, 59, 60, 61, 62, 64, 65, 66, 67, 69, 70, 71, 73, 76, 77, 79, 80, 81, 82, 83, 84, 85, 86, 90, 91, 125, 127, 128, 134, 159, 178, 181, 182, 191, 192, 198, 204, 218, 221

Lanval, 86, 221

Lanzelet, v, 33, 35, 37, 40, 43, 48, 49, 51, 53, 62, 83, 84, 119, 127, 149

Latimari, 3, 20, 67, 118

Latin, 21, 31, 32, 39, 43, 133, 134, 208, 210

Law of Hywel Dda, 67, 74, 75

Lewis, 29, 160

Lia Fail, 181

Livy, 57

Llacheu, 116

Lladmerydd, 8

Llywarch Hen, 91, 188

Loholt, 116

London, 121, 131, 153, 174

Loomis, ix, 1, 2, 7, 13, 14, 17, 18, 29, 36, 37, 38, 40, 43, 48, 49, 52, 53, 69, 70, 76, 77, 83, 84, 90, 109, 116, 121, 122, 124, 125, 126, 127, 128, 129, 130, 131, 134, 136, 137, 138, 139, 145, 147, 156, 158, 159, 171, 179, 196, 198, 218, 220, 221, 222

Lothian, 14, 31, 39, 165

Lucan, 25

Lucretius, 24

Lug, 37, 38, 124, 128, 145, 184

Mabinogi, 157

Mabinogion, 2, 36, 57, 58, 70, 76, 84, 118, 134, 189, 199
Mabon, 17
Mac Cana, Proinsias, 1, 126, 127, 142, 152, 156, 160, 170, 184, 195, 197
Mahabharata, 8, 53, 63
Mallory, Sir Thomas, 41
Manawydan, 132
Marie de Champagne, ix, xiv, 4, 11, 25, 27, 32, 35, 61, 81, 85, 89, 90, 93, 94, 101, 178, 191
Marie de France, 84, 86, 195
Matholwch, 152
Medb, 62, 75, 119, 221
Medea, 25
Medrawt, 43, 53
Meleagant, 6, 22, 33, 57, 61, 66, 71, 192, 211, 221
Melwas, 17, 32, 33, 35, 40, 41, 43, 46, 47, 53, 71, 91, 187
Mesca Ulad, 63
Middle Welsh, 2, 37, 50, 116
Miller, Molly, 2, 173, 198
Modena Archivolt, 34, 46, 51, 215
Modred, 14, 23, 43, 47, 48, 53
Moray, 39, 42, 43, 167
Le Morte d'Arthur, 41, 123, 133
Moses, 110

Nature Ritual, 105, 113, 114
Nibelungenlied, 41, 42, 53, 197, 198
Ninnius, 15, 16, 29, 91, 213
Nitze, William, 2, 28, 29, 52, 108, 157, 158, 204
Northern History, 30

Northumbria, 15, 173

Orpheus, 68, 76
Ovid, 21, 22, 23, 25, 79
Owain, 14, 29, 43, 47, 53, 144,

Pa gur?, 29, 35, 38, 50, 145, 148, 150, 152, 187, 188, 195, 202, 208, 215, 218
Padel, Oliver, 7, 14
Parzival, 133, 134, 139, 144, 145, 146, 157, 158, 187
Pelles, 4, 116, 130, 131, 137, 207, 220
Pellinore, 121, 130, 207, 220
Penda, 16
Peniarth 7, 142
Perceval, 14, 20, 43, 52, 59, 61, 63, 64, 67, 90, 95, 99, 100, 102, 105, 106, 107, 108, 109, 110, 111, 113, 115, 116, 117, 119, 120, 121, 122, 125, 126, 127, 128, 129, 130, 131, 132, 133, 134, 135, 136, 138, 140, 143, 144, 146, 147, 148, 149, 150, 156, 157, 159, 161, 170, 178, 179, 180, 183, 184, 185, 186, 191, 192, 196, 203, 204, 208, 212, 214, 215, 218
Peredur, 2, 14, 43, 57, 101, 116, 119, 127, 129, 130, 132, 133, 134, 135, 136, 137, 138, 139, 140, 142, 144, 145, 149, 150, 151, 154, 156, 157, 163, 170, 178, 185, 186, 192, 194, 202, 207, 208, 209, 210, 213, 214, 220

Perlesvaus, 46, 117, 118, 119, 121, 124, 127, 130, 131, 132, 138, 146, 147, 148, 158, 161, 170, 185, 204, 208, 210

Philip of Flanders, iii, ix, xiv, 4, 26, 93, 94, 97, 98, 99, 100, 101, 102, 105, 106, 107, 122, 141, 150, 158, 163, 183, 190, 196, 199, 202, 203, 204, 207, 209, 210

Philip Augustus, 26, 98, 99

Plato, 25

Pomponius Mela, 150, 151

Pont evage, 77

Powys, 18, 29, 56, 74

Preiddeu Annwn, 13, 36, 38, 147, 150, 151, 152, 154, 195, 203, 208, 220

Procopius, 211

Propertius, 24

Pryderi, 116, 126, 144

Pwyll, 76, 237

Quintilian, 25

Red Book of Hengerdd, 152

Red Knight, 95, 141, 183, 184, 185, 186, 218, 220, 221

Rhydderch Hael, 30

Rhys, Sir John, 1, 2, 5, 9, 79, 121, 131, 137

Richard, xviii, 27, 48, 158

Robert de Boron, 143, 144, 149, 157

Roberts, Brynley, 2, 31, 52, 121, 126, 133, 159, 161, 188

Roland, 23, 24, 31, 32, 62, 67, 192

Sabîns, 145

St. Augustine, 25, 169

St. Brioc, 166

St. Cadoc, 172

St. Columba, 81, 82, 166, 167, 173

St. David, xii, xvii, 2, 86, 100, 123, 166, 172, 201, 212, 214, 217

St. Kentigern, 14, 16, 58, 166, 201, 213

St. Martin, 123, 168, 170

St. Ninian, 171, 213

St. Patrick, 2, 7, 59, 166, 167, 172, 211

St. Samson, 152, 154, 160, 166, 167, 202, 208, 213, 215

Sanguin, 145

Scáthach, 68, 74

Second Continuation, 149

Sigurd, 58

Somerset, 14, 56

Sovereignty, 184, 185, 186, 220

Strathclyde, 16, 29, 30, 201

Tale of Sir Florent, 219

Taliesin, 15, 29, 64, 151, 161, 214

Tammuz, 112

The Bibliotheca Historia of Diodorus Siculus, 67

Thirteen Treasures of Britain, 118, 151

Thurneysen, Rudolf, xiii, 14, 16, 29, 30, 143, 156, 160

Tochmarc Emere, 58, 69
Trioedd Ynys Prydein, vii, 13, 29, 37, 38, 39, 41, 42, 53, 118, 126, 127, 139, 153, 161, 198, 218
Tristan, 14, 20, 22, 24, 25, 35, 43, 133, 149, 159, 196
Troubadour, xi, 20, 67, 75, 118, 195, 198, 212, 215
Trouvères, xi, 67, 118, 195

Uinniau, 166, 171, 173
Ulrich von Zatzikhoven, 48, 49, 53, 84
Ulster, 2, 53, 63, 69, 72, 188, 195
Urien, 14, 29, 33, 34, 53, 63, 64, 91, 188, 211, 214

Victricius, 169
Villémarque, Viscount Hersart de la, 36
Virgil, 24
Vita Gildae, 34, 35, 46, 49, 51, 72, 123
Vita Merlini, 144, 149
Vita Sancti Ambrosii, 169

Volsungasaga, 8, 42
Vulgate, 9, 41, 80, 86, 133, 146, 148, 149, 159, 196

Wace, 23, 24, 25, 27, 100, 149
Weddynge of Sir Gawen, 185, 219
Weston, Jessie, ix, 2, 70, 108, 112, 113, 114, 115, 122, 125, 127, 138, 159
Wife of Bath's Tale, 185, 219
Wigalois, 84
Willehelm, 158
Wolfram von Eschenbach, ix, 130, 135, 144, 145, 158, 187, 220

Y Gododdin, xii, xv, xvi, 29, 63, 75, 91, 135, 139, 201, 211, 212, 214
Ymddiddan, 34, 35, 46, 51, 72, 77, 187, 215
York, 133, 134, 135, 139, 208
Yspaddaden, 153
Yvain, xiii, 11, 14, 20, 22, 24, 25, 32, 43, 47, 50, 63, 64, 70, 90, 116, 120, 157